Nietzsche's Search for Philosophy

Also available from Bloomsbury

Nietzsche and Political Thought, edited by Keith Ansell-Pearson
Henri Bergson: Key Writings, edited by Keith Ansell-Pearson
Bergson: Thinking Beyond the Human Condition, by Keith Ansell-Pearson
Nietzsche's 'Beyond Good and Evil', Christa Davis Acampora,
Keith Ansell-Pearson

Nietzsche's Search for Philosophy

On the Middle Writings

By Keith Ansell-Pearson

Bloomsbury Academic
An imprint of Bloomsbury Publishing Plc

B L O O M S B U R Y
LONDON · OXFORD · NEW YORK · NEW DELHI · SYDNEY

Bloomsbury Academic
An imprint of Bloomsbury Publishing Plc

50 Bedford Square	1385 Broadway
London	New York
WC1B 3DP	NY 10018
UK	USA

www.bloomsbury.com

BLOOMSBURY and the Diana logo are trademarks of Bloomsbury Publishing Plc

First published 2018

British Library Cataloguing-in-Publication Data
A catalogue record for this book is available from the British Library.

ISBN: HB: 978-1-4742-5469-4
PB: 978-1-4742-5470-0
ePDF: 978-1-4742-5471-7
ePub: 978-1-4742-5472-4

Library of Congress Cataloging-in-Publication Data
A catalog record for this book is available from the Library of Congress.

Typeset by Deanta Global Publishing Services, Chennai, India
Printed and bound in Great Britain

For my friends, who keep me inspired,
and for Nicky,
who keeps me joyfully alive.

Contents

Acknowledgements

Versions of the chapters of this book were given as papers at various conferences, workshops and colloquia held at the following universities: Auckland, Birmingham, Concordia, Leiden, Liverpool, Monash (and the Monash Centre in Prato), Rice, Sydney, Texas A&M, University of North Texas at Denton, Warwick and the Royal Institute of Philosophy, London, and I am grateful for the invitations I received and to the audiences at these events for their questions and contributions. A shorter version of Chapter 1 will appear in Celine Denat & Patrick Wotling (eds.), Humain, trop humain *et les débuts de la réforme de la philosophie* (Reims: Éditions et presses de l'université de Reims, 2017). A version of Chapter 2 will be published in Paul Katsafanas (ed.), *The Nietzschean Mind* (Routledge, 2017). Chapter 3 draws on material I first published as 'Nietzsche, the Sublime, and the Sublimities of Philosophy', *Nietzsche-Studien*, volume 39, 2010 and also for the Afterword to the Stanford University Press edition and translation of *Dawn* (2011). Chapter 4 utilizes material that was first published as 'Beyond Compassion: On Nietzsche's Moral Therapy in Dawn', *Continental Philosophy Review*, 44: 2, 2011. Chapter 5 draws on material first published in Paul Bishop, *A Companion to Friedrich Nietzsche: Life and Works* (Camden House, 2012). Chapter 6 is a modified version of an essay first published in a special issue of *The Agonist*, the online journal of the New York Nietzsche Circle, volume X: II, Spring 2017. It also utilizes material that was first published as 'Heroic-Idyllic Philosophizing: Nietzsche and the Epicurean Tradition', published in Anthony O' Hear (ed.), *Philosophical Traditions* (Cambridge University Press: Royal Institute of Philosophy Supplement, 74, 2014). I am grateful to the editors and publishers of these publications for allowing me to republish material here.

I am indebted for support, advice and encouragement, as well as the sharing of ideas and of work, to the following people: Christa Davis Acampora, Dorian Astor, Babette Babich, Charles Bambach, Rebecca Bamford, Christine Battersby, Paul Bishop, Nandita Biswas Mellamphy, Frank Chouraqui, Daniel W. Conway, Christine Daigle, Carol Diethe, Christian Emden, Ken Gemes, Robert Guay, Beatrice Han-Pile, Rainer J. Hanshe, Lawrence Hatab, Kathleen Higgins, Horst Hutter, Christopher Janaway, Duncan Large, Vanessa Lemm, Paul S. Loeb,

John Mandalios, Mark Migotti, Katrina Mitcheson, Simon O' Sullivan, Paul Patton, James I. Porter, Martine Prange, John Richardson, Alan D. Schrift, Herman Siemens, Brittain Smith, Andreas Sommer, Werner Stegmaier, Tracy B. Strong, Patrick Wotling, Dale Wilkerson and James Williams. I owe a special debt of gratitude to Michael Ure whose work has served as a constant source of inspiration and instruction in the course of researching and writing this book. I am also grateful to the four readers of the manuscript who provided me with valuable advice that helped shape the final design of the book. The sound advice of Bob Guay and Paul Loeb is especially appreciated. I was fortunate enough to have a year's study leave in 2017, and I am grateful to the University of Warwick for its support of my research. Thanks to Liza Thompson and Frankie Mace, my editors at Bloomsbury Press, for their patience and unwavering support. Finally, thanks are due to my colleagues at Warwick for their support and friendship, especially Miguel Beistegui and Stephen Houlgate, to my Warwick students past and present, and last, but not least, to my family for their tremendous love.

Editions of Nietzsche's Writings
Used with Abbreviations

AC   *The Anti-Christ*, trans. Judith Norman (Cambridge: Cambridge University Press, 2005).

BGE   *Beyond Good and Evil*, trans. Marion Faber (Oxford: Oxford University Press, 1998).

BT   *The Birth of Tragedy*, trans. Ronald Speirs (Cambridge: Cambridge University Press, 1999).

D   *Dawn: Thoughts on the Presumptions of Morality*, trans. Brittain Smith (Stanford: Stanford University Press, 2011).

EH   *Ecce Homo*, trans. Duncan Large (Oxford: Oxford University Press, 2007).

GM   *On the Genealogy of Morality,* trans. Carol Diethe (Cambridge: Cambridge University Press, 2006).

GS   *The Gay Science*, trans. Walter Kaufmann (New York: Random House, 1974).

HAH   *Human, all too Human*, volume one, trans. Gary Handwerk (Stanford: Stanford University Press, 1995).

HAH II *Human, all too Human: volume two*, trans. Gary Handwerk (Stanford: Stanford University Press, 2013).

KGB   *Nietzsche Briefwechsel: Kritische Gesamtausabe*, ed. G. Colli and M. Montinari (Berlin and New York: Walter de Gruyter, 1981).

KGW   *Werke. Kritische Gesamtausgabe,* ed. G. Colli and M. Montinari (Berlin and New York: Walter de Gruyter, 1967).

KSA   *Friedrich Nietzsche: Sämtliche Werke. Kritische Studienausgabe*, ed. G. Colliand M. Montinari (Berlin, New York and Munich: dtv and Walter de Gruyter, 1967–77 and 1998).

KSB   *Sämtliche Briefe. Kritische Studienausgabe*, ed. G. Colli and M. Montinari (in 8 volumes) (Berlin, New York and Munich: dtv and Walter de Gruyter, 1975–84).

MOM   *Mixed Opinions and Maxims* in HH II.

PT   *Philosophy and Truth. Selections from Nietzsche's Notebooks of the Early 1870s*, ed. and trans. Daniel Breazeale (New York: Humanities Press, 1979).

PTAG   *Philosophy in the Tragic Age of the Greeks*, trans. Marianne Cowan (Washington DC: Regnery Press, 1962).

PP   *The Pre-Platonic Philosophers*, trans. and ed. Greg Whitlock (Urbana: University of Illinois Press, 1999).

TI   *Twilight of the Idols*, trans. Duncan Large (Oxford: Oxford University Press, 1998).

TSZ   *Thus Spoke Zarathustra*, trans. R. J. Hollingdale (Middlesex: Penguin: 1969).

UO II   *Unfashionable Observations. On the Utility and Liability of History for Life*, trans. Richard T. Gray (Stanford: Stanford University Press, 1995).

UO III   *Unfashionable Observations. Schopenhauer as Educator*, trans. Richard T. Gray (Stanford: Stanford University Press, 1995).

UO IV   *Unfashionable Observations. Richard Wagner in Bayreuth*, trans. Richard T. Gray (Stanford: Stanford University Press, 1995).

WP   *The Will to Power*, trans. Walter Kaufmann and R. J. Hollingdale (New York: Random House, 1968).

WS   *The Wanderer and His Shadow* in HH II

Note: References in the text to Nietzsche's writings are to section and aphorism numbers, unless stated otherwise.

Introduction

Nietzsche sometimes says in his writings that Schopenhauer lacked development and history – he has a single conception of life and perception of the world from first to last (see, for example, D 481). The same cannot be said of Nietzsche whose thinking undergoes an extraordinary and striking development in the course of just two decades of writing and thinking. This book traces some of the most important moments in this development as they concern the tasks and projects of his middle writings. These are the texts *Human, all too Human* (volume one published in 1878), *Dawn* (1881) and *The Gay Science* (1882). In recent years a great deal of attention has been lavished on the late texts, the so-called classic Nietzschean texts such as *Beyond Good and Evil* (1886) and *On the Genealogy of Morality* (1887). This is often referred to as the 'hard' Nietzsche, in which the philosopher assumes the guise of a polemicist and takes to task all things modern and decadent, and in the process celebrates the will to power as a principle of life, including its dominating and exploitative aspects. This book pursues a different course, looking at materials and texts that until quite recently have largely been overlooked and neglected.[1]

Ruth Abbey has written that, 'Our intuitions about who Nietzsche is and what he stands for have often been formed in neglect of ignorance of the works of the middle period.'[2] She rightly considers the texts that make up this period to be rich and fruitful ones that merit close attention in their own right and not simply as a prelude to Nietzsche's so-called mature works.[3] I agree with Abbey when she says that in his middle writings Nietzsche's intellectual curiosity roams and inquires more freely: in these texts he is genuinely exploratory and less dogmatic and essentialist than in his late writings.[4] Still, having noted these points it is something of a myth to contrast the middle and late periods in terms of 'soft' and 'hard' Nietzsches: the middle Nietzsche can be hard in his own way, as when he argues against Christ and the warmest heart in *Human, all too Human* (HAH 235), and also when he categorically states that in order to promote free-minded ways of thinking and living we need to get beyond our compassion (D 146).

Along with recent scholarship, then, I am keen to propose we reassess the place occupied by the middle writings in Nietzsche's corpus and grant them a genuine importance (it should be noted that I am not assuming that there is a single project at work in these middle writings, and they are not to be treated as a homogeneous set).

It is customary to divide Nietzsche's corpus into three distinct phases, early, middle and late. The early, youthful phase is represented by *The Birth of Tragedy* and the four untimely meditations, the second 'positivist' phase by the books of aphorisms, *Human, all too Human, Dawn* and *The Gay Science*, and the final phase by the polemical texts such as *On the Genealogy of Morality* and *The Anti-Christ*. What this overlooks are the continuities between Nietzsche's early, unpublished philosophical reflections – on Democritus, on teleology since Kant and on the pre-Platonic philosophers – and the philosophy of the free spirit. As Paolo D'Iorio also points out, the attempt is often made, through this tripartite division, to minimize the importance of the free-spirit period texts, sometimes to privilege a largely bogus continuity between *The Birth of Tragedy* and *Thus Spoke Zarathustra*. As he further notes, the only truly distinct phase in the evolution of his philosophy is the Wagnerian period of *The Birth of Tragedy*.[5] Nietzsche himself came to think that texts such as *Dawn* and *The Gay Science* could serve as an introduction to and preparation for *Thus Spoke Zarathustra*. He liked to say to friends of the relation between the middle writings and *Zarathustra* that he had written the commentary before the text.[6] It is clear that the middle writings have been sorely neglected in the reception of Nietzsche, and key questions concerning their character and the role they occupy in Nietzsche's thinking as a whole are often marginalized.

Nietzsche's middle writings are important because they afford an excellent set of glimpses into the workings of one of modernity's most original and independent minds: we see at work in these texts the application of naturalistic modes of demystification and an intellectual laboratory of quite novel philosophical experimentation. Michel Foucault had a particular penchant for these texts and wrote instructively of the challenge the 'Nietzsche' contained within them presented for thought. After one has been trained in the great, time-honoured university traditions, Foucault wrote, one comes across these texts that can only strike one as strange, witty and graceful. The task, as he saw it, was to resist the temptation to dismiss them and instead subject them to the maximum of philosophical intensity and identify their philosophical effects.[7] Foucault's attitude is laudable. Nietzsche prided himself on his philosophical heterodoxy and indeed by contemporary standards of what counts as philosophy he is an anomalous case: we find little in the way of conventional arguments in his writings, and yet we do find a remarkable commitment to new modes of self-knowledge and a rare dedication to philosophy's original vocation: the discovery of possibilities of life.

I am interested in this book, then, in what happens to one's appreciation of Nietzsche's thought, including its relation to philosophy and the history of philosophy, when one focuses on these middle writings. We know some of the possibilities if our focus is on the late Nietzsche. Martin Heidegger gives us Nietzsche as the philosopher of the will to power and the last metaphysician of the West; Gilles Deleuze gives us Nietzsche as the critical and clinical genealogist and in the guise of a superior empiricist; Gianni Vattimo gives us a Nietzsche who does not complete and exhaust the tradition but seeks a twisting free of metaphysics and heralds the inauguration of post-metaphysical 'weak' thinking. Most attention has been focused on the late Nietzsche and many key commentators, such as Heidegger and Deleuze, have very little to say on the middle period Nietzsche.[8] Foucault was personally inspired in his own research programmes by these 'witty and graceful' texts, as he called them, but he did not subject them to any elaborate reading or interpretation, and by the time of his late work and turn to questions of self-cultivation he seems to have forgotten the texts and fails to mention them, even though they are highly pertinent to his concerns.

It is my contention that an ethos of Epicurean enlightenment pervades Nietzsche's middle writings with Epicurus celebrated for his teachings on mortality and the cultivation of modest pleasures. Although the late Nietzsche has problems with Epicurus, in his middle writings he writes in praise of him and draws upon his philosophy as a way of promoting what we can call an Epicurean care of self and world. We need to discover this Nietzsche for ourselves and in part as a way of contesting Heidegger's reading of Nietzsche that focuses on the late writings, mostly the *Nachlass*, and construes all the major concepts of the late period, notably the will to power and the overman, as indicating that Nietzsche is the 'technological' thinker of our age and whose major concept is the will to power and its desire for mastery of the earth through the will to will. My view is that we need a much more subtle and nuanced appreciation of Nietzsche than the Heideggerian reading permits, and one way to develop this is to focus on the neglected middle writings. Within the so-called continental philosophy Heidegger's 'Nietzsche' has perhaps been the dominant influence.

It has at least two main contentions: first, that the real Nietzsche is to be found in the *Nachlass* of the mid to late 1880s, and second that Nietzsche does not overcome metaphysics, as he claims to do, but merely inverts it.[9] For all the impressive brilliance of his reading, Heidegger's confrontation with Nietzsche carries real dangers: the thesis that Nietzsche is the last metaphysician of the West has arguably led to sterility in continental receptions of Nietzsche and, more pressingly perhaps, we lose sight of the practical-therapeutic dimension of Nietzsche's philosophy and its attempt to overcome metaphysics, and we stop reading the published texts. In my view the costs have been high and it is now time to focus our attention on the published texts and the actual and, in many instances, neglected details of Nietzsche's search for philosophy.

The appeal of Epicurean teaching to Nietzsche lies in the fact that it offers to humankind a heroic-idyllic mode of philosophizing (WS 295). Aspects of it have been captured well by John Cottingham in his summary of the ancient doctrine of Epicurus. He sees it as a model of the good or flourishing life that deploys the tools of reason to understand how human beings can cultivate worthwhile lives and 'delivered from false hope and superstition'.[10] We need, in Cottingham's words, 'the courage necessary to resist false comfort by facing the real nature of the world in which we find ourselves,'[11] understanding the limits of human life and then experimenting to find out what might be possible within these limits. Although an attempt at a synoptic ethics that aims to understand the workings of the universe as a whole, Epicurean doctrine places the study of nature in the service of our ethical formation and reformation. Karl Jaspers notes that one enters the garden of Epicurus, overcoming oneself, in order to abandon it once again, and this neatly captures something of the character of Nietzsche's attachment to Epicurus in the course of his intellectual development.[12]

II

The focus of the book is what I am calling Nietzsche's search for philosophy. As Karl Jaspers notes in his appreciation of Nietzsche's philosophical activity, Nietzsche's life was a 'philosophical life', one that was 'energized to communicate itself by the awareness of a task, an experiencing of thoughts as creative forces'.[13] Nietzsche's attempt to unify thought and life means that the task is not one of simply presenting mental processes; rather, the task is to speak of things that one has experienced.[14] We need to bear in mind though that for Nietzsche experience is not a substance that is certain of itself and neither is cognition ever a permanent and unchanging knowledge.[15] As he puts it in his remarkable 1886 preface to the second edition of *The Gay Science*, as human beings we are not 'thinking frogs' and neither are we 'objectifying and registering mechanisms with their innards removed' (GS Preface 3). As questioners we know that the 'trust in life has gone' and 'life itself has become a *problem*' (GS Preface 3). The task is not to become gloomy and despondent, but to learn how to love life differently and to discover 'a new happiness' (GS Preface 3). For Nietzsche this requires a highly spiritualized or refined mode of thinking and of being in the world, in which we are attracted to things problematic and are able to take 'delight in an *x*' (GS Preface 3).

Nietzsche's philosophical project is not reducible to a single practice. He proposed that as a writer he enjoyed the 'multifarious art of style', and one might add to this that he practises a multifarious art of philosophizing. Of course, there are certain traits of the philosophical life that Nietzsche champions and that need to inform any conception of philosophical practice, including a commitment to historically informed reason, to coolness, to sobriety and to keeping one's enthusiasm in bounds. However, he certainly does not think that we are single persons and the same goes for the philosopher who, he says, must constantly lose and re-find his identity. He writes of the thinker traversing many kinds of health and with it passing through an equal number of philosophies (GS Preface 3). As I read Nietzsche, he is suggesting that through practices of observation and self-observation we human beings, largely unknown to ourselves, can become our own experiments. We are to become strangers to our ordinary and habitual selves, viewing ourselves afresh as experiments of living and feeling and of knowledge. For Nietzsche 'the human being' is a bloodless fiction and 'society' is a general concept (D 105). We are to resist, then, the conforming demands of society and attempt to deconstruct and reconstruct ourselves as unique individuals. Nietzsche stresses that we *are* experiments; the task is to *want* to be such (D 543).

My practice in the book is to read with Nietzsche, to attempt to comprehend and illuminate his aphorisms and show the context of his concerns in which he pursues his philosophical questioning.[16] I seek to demonstrate the nature of his philosophical search for knowledge and wisdom, including the emphasis on the human, all too human, the compensations and promises of a philosophy of the morning (new dawns) and the cultivation of philosophical cheerfulness through the practice of the gay science. For Karl Jaspers, Nietzsche makes possible 'the elevation of human existence'.[17] I am convinced Nietzsche was right when he claimed in *Ecce Homo* that in his work we find *ecstasies* of learning. I have set myself the task of seeking to convey something of these ecstasies in the book that follows, mindful of Lawrence Hatab's warning that when we '"translate" Nietzsche into our professional philosophical agenda, we do what must be done, but in so doing we bring to ruin something special and vital. … It seems we must "murder to dissect"'.[18]

Nietzsche wants his readers to share in the adventure of knowledge undertaken in his middle writings. Above all, he wants a new *vita contemplativa* to be cultivated in the midst of the speed and rapidity of modern life; we need to slow down and to create the time needed to work through our experiences. In *Human, all too Human* Nietzsche makes an appeal to the *vita contemplativa*, noting that the modern age is poor in great moralists with the likes of Pascal, Epictetus, Seneca and Plutarch being little read today (HAH 282). The free spirit exists as a 'genius of meditation' and in an age where time for thinking, and tranquillity while thinking, are lacking: 'With the tremendous acceleration of life, the spirit and the eye have grown accustomed to seeing and judging partially or falsely, and everyone resembles the traveller who get to know a land and its people from the train' (HAH 282).

The book is made up of six chapters. There is a chapter devoted to each of the main texts that constitute Nietzsche's middle writings, and followed by what might be called a subsidiary chapter on a prominent theme, or set of themes, that appear in each text. The first chapter is on *Human, all too Human* and focuses on what philosophy means for Nietzsche in his turn of 1878–9 to a scientifically informed philosophical practice. Here I am largely interested in Nietzsche's attachment to philosophical sobriety and coolness in which a chief aim of philosophy is to temper mental and emotional excess. The subsidiary chapter here is on a neglected, but important, topic in Nietzsche, which is his critical concern with fanaticism. The third chapter is on *Dawn*, in which Nietzsche now practises the passion of knowledge and approaches life, as well as the tasks of philosophy, in an experimental mood, acutely aware, and affirmative of the fact, that with the attachment to his passion humanity will make sacrifices of itself – of its sense of who and what it is, and what it might become – to the cause of knowledge. Although his thinking is highly suggestive and elliptical with respect to this question of sacrifice, I try to make some sense of his conception of the 'sublimities of philosophy' that are to be attained through this passionate practice of knowledge. I also show that he is mindful of the need to place this practice in the context of a proper appreciation of the economy of life as a whole, and so as to ensure that we do not become boring to ourselves and in the process bored with life. The subsidiary chapter here is on what I call Nietzsche's attachment to a philosophy of modesty: this modesty refers to his conception of 'morality' where he thinks we are in need of more modest words. Nietzsche, I show, wishes to replace the exaggerated claims made on behalf of 'morality' with an ethics centred on self-care. In the fifth chapter I turn my attention to *The Gay Science* and focus on the theme of philosophical cheerfulness, seeking to demonstrate the different senses Nietzsche gives to this cheerfulness and to illuminate something of its main characteristics. The subsidiary chapter here is on how he stages conceptions of pleasure and especially joy in the middle writings, including *The Gay Science*. I conclude with some reflections on Nietzsche's Epicurean inspirations and attachments, and I negotiate a position with respect to the late Nietzsche's critique of Epicureanism.

Let me say something in a little more detail about each one of the texts that make up Nietzsche's middle writings. There is some truth in Paul Franco's view that it is during the middle period 'that Nietzsche truly becomes Nietzsche'.[19] With the publication of *Human, all too Human* however, which commences the free-spirit period of his output and development, Nietzsche thought he had, in fact, taken repossession of himself, liberating himself from what in his nature did not truly belong to him, such as 'idealism'. Where humanity wishes to see 'ideal' things, in this text Nietzsche will see the 'human, all too human'. Nietzsche says he tracks down with a 'merciless spirit' all the hiding places where the ideal takes its home, illuminating the whole 'underworld' of this ideal, including locating its sources in human projection and fantasy. Errors, he says, are placed on ice and the ideal is made to die through exposure, including such ideals as the genius, the saint, and the hero, as well our investment in such ideals as the morality of compassion and the ontological ideal of the thing in itself. The text amounts to a remarkable, and yet complex, break with Nietzsche's first intellectual incarnation as a disciple of Schopenhauer and Wagner, and that had characterized his early writings (1872–6). In *Ecce Homo*, however, Nietzsche writes that his break with his former self, as well as with his former loyalties and commitments, was part of a greater need on his part to reflect on himself. When set against his 'task' in life – including carrying out the philosophy of the revaluation of values – his whole existence as a trained and practising philologist appeared as quite 'useless' and 'arbitrary'. As he says, 'realities' were completely lacking in his knowledge and the 'idealities' he had committed himself to were worth 'damn all' (EH 'HAH,' section 3). He felt the need then to pursue 'real' knowledge, consisting in physiology, medicine and natural science, with a return to historical studies made only when he felt compelled by the need to assume the responsibility of his task.

Human, all too Human is, however, and as I endeavour to show, a complex set of texts if one takes into account, which is not often done, its subsequent volumes, *Mixed Opinions and Maxims* and *The Wanderer and His Shadow.* Nietzsche is clearly at his most positivistic in volume one of the text, *Human, all too Human.* Here he favours a hard-nosed scientific practice that deflates the ideals, and the pretensions to truth and knowledge, of religion, of morality and of art. The text espouses, however, its own ideal of the free spirit, to be conceived as a spirit that hovers over human life without any real attachment, hovering over human customs, conventions and traditions, and that seeks to communicate the 'joy' it experiences from this supposed emancipation from the affects or emotions. It is a curiously passionless joy, one that divorces scientific practice and knowledge from the ends of eudaemonia or human flourishing. Indeed, Nietzsche sees the primary effects of genuine knowledge to be one of disappointment, even despair (see HAH 34 in particular). I seek to show that Nietzsche's thinking on this set of issues undergoes a subtle but significant development with the subsequent texts that make up the project of the 'human, all too human'. My reading is, I believe, the first in the commentaries produced on the texts to identify this shift and take cognizance of it. Whereas in volume one of HAH Nietzsche negotiates the competing claims of the positivist goal of science and eudaemonistic philosophy by aligning himself with the former, in MOM and WS he seeks to marry the project of naturalistic demystification with a project of seeking 'spiritual-physical health and maturity' (MOM 184). Having noted this, though, a definite philosophical search is underway in these texts in which Nietzsche favours a project of sobriety that supposes philosophical moderation in an effort to combat both human neurosis and a sentimental, self-intoxicating world view.

In the final part of my opening chapter I seek to illuminate the nature of Nietzsche's interest in Epicurus and his discovery of the 'heroic-idyllic', including the heroic-idyllic mode of philosophizing. What appeals to Nietzsche about Epicurus is the teaching on mortality and the general attempt to liberate the mind from unjustified fears and anxieties. He was inspired by Epicurus's conception of friendship and the ideal of withdrawing from society and cultivating one's own garden. If, as Pierre Hadot has suggested, philosophical therapeutics is centred on a concern with the healing of our own lives so as to return us to the joy of existing,[20] then in the texts of his so-called middle period, Nietzsche can be seen to be an heir to this ancient tradition. Indeed, if there is one crucial component to Nietzsche's philosophical therapeutics in the middle writings that he keeps returning to again and again, it is the need for spiritual joyfulness and the task of cultivating in ourselves, after centuries of training by morality and religion, the joy in existing.

The difference from Epicurus is that he is developing a therapy for the sicknesses of the soul under modern conditions of social control and discipline. Nevertheless, it is the case that Nietzsche at this time is seeking to restore something of the concerns of an ancient conception of philosophy. Nietzsche recognizes in Epicurus what he calls in one note a 'refined heroism', and here the thought seems to centre on conquering the fear of death, of which Nietzsche says he has little (KSA 8, 28 [15]). For Epicurus the study of nature should make human beings modest and self-sufficient, taking pride in the good that lies in themselves, not in their estate, and as opposed to the display of learning coveted by the rabble.[21]

In the middle writings, as I have contended, Nietzsche is committed to a philosophical therapeutics in which the chief aim is to temper emotional and mental excess. One might contend that there is an Epicurean inspiration informing Nietzsche's actual philosophical practice at this time. According to one commentator, Epicurean arguments 'have a clear therapeutic intent: by removing false beliefs concerning the universe and the ways in which the gods might be involved in its workings, they eliminate a major source of mental trouble and lead us towards a correct and beneficial conception of these matters'.[22] In part, Nietzsche conceived the art of the maxim in therapeutic terms. In the middle writings, then, Epicurus is one of Nietzsche's chief inspirations in his effort to liberate himself from the metaphysical need, to find serenity within his own existence and to aid humanity in its need to now cure its neuroses. Epicureanism, along with science in general, serves to make us 'colder and more sceptical', helping to cool down 'the fiery stream of belief in ultimate definitive truths', a stream that has grown so turbulent through Christianity (HAH 244). The task, Nietzsche says, is to live in terms of 'a constant spiritual joyfulness (*Freudigkeit*)' (HAH 292) and to prize 'the three good things': greatness, repose and sunlight, in which these things answer to thoughts that elevate, thoughts that quieten, thoughts that enlighten and, finally, 'to thoughts which participate in all three qualities, in which everything earthly comes to transfiguration: it is the kingdom where there reigns the great *trinity of joy* (*Freude*)' (WS 332).

Dawn (1881) is a quite remarkable text containing many hidden riches. It also happens to be the most neglected text in Nietzsche's corpus and in spite of the efforts of commentators, including myself, to draw readers' attention to its singular brilliance and importance. *Dawn* is a path-breaking work and an exercise in modern emancipation – from fear, superstition, hatred of the self and the body, the short cuts of religion and the presumptions of morality. In *Dawn* Nietzsche is less of the disappointed idealist he was in his previous text, *Human, all too Human,* more assertive about the emerging rights of new individuals who have hitherto been decried as freethinkers, criminals and immoralists, more metaphorically exuberant, and with glimpses of new dawns on the horizon about to break. Nietzsche offers his readers wise counsel, outlining in the book a therapy made up of slow cures (D 462) and small doses (D 534). Although there is no master concept at work in *Dawn,* and no overarching method (but a plurality of methods that add up to an experimental philosophy), the text may be better for their absence, helping to constitute one of Nietzsche's most subtle and delicate experiments at writing and thinking.

According to Rüdiger Safranski, Nietzsche was a master of shading the particular tinge, colour and mood of experience and someone who used their own solitude and suffering as a springboard to construct a new philosophy, often providing exquisite depictions of the world while racked with pain. We see this informing the work of *Dawn.* Moreover, Nietzsche is not content with mere expression and self-expression, but rather uses the example of his own experience to probe new and challenging questions. As Safranski astutely notes, Nietzsche is 'a passionate singularist' in the sense that for him the world is composed of nothing but details; even the self can be approached in such terms, that is, as a detail that is composed of further details. In the analysis of the detail there is no point of completion or termination: 'There are only details, and although they are everything, they do not constitute a whole. No whole could encompass the plethora of details.'[23] By paying attention to the details of existence we may discover ourselves in ways that surprise and enlighten us. As Nietzsche likes to point out, the journey of self-discovery has consequences that are frightful and fearful at one and the same time. Nietzsche's opening up of himself to great currents, oceanic expanses and departures for new shores, is metaphorical imagery by which he intends to explore the vast unknown territory of human consciousness and existence.

In *Dawn* Nietzsche is tracing a history of human fear and self-torment in an effort to liberate us from the past and its inheritance. However, his evaluations of our inheritance – of the origins and sources of human identity in fear; of the cruel practices employed by the ancient discipline of customary morality; and of Christianity – are not simply negative but subtle and nuanced (which does not prevent him from making certain key decisions about the future direction of humanity). Nietzsche notes that cultural institutions and mores instil in the passions, and contrary to their nature, a belief in their duration and responsibility for this duration, and gives the example of the institution of marriage which has this effect on the passion of love. While such transformations introduce much hypocrisy and lying into the world, they also bring with them 'a *suprahuman*, human-exalting concept' (D 27). On the one hand, and on a wider scale, an 'obscure fear and awe' has directed humanity in its consideration of 'higher and weightier affairs', and in the process a fearful humanity has prejudged and paralysed thinking, choosing instead to enslave itself to self-abasement, self-torture and much torment of body and soul (D 107; see also 142). On the other hand, however, it is possible to locate in the history of human rituals, including rituals of sacrifice, a 'prodigious training ground of the intellect' (D 40). As Nietzsche notes, it is not only religions that have been hatched and nurtured on this soil but also the 'prehistoric world of science' as well as the poet, the thinker, the physician and the lawgiver: 'The fear of the incomprehensible, which, in ambiguous fashion, demanded ceremonies from us, metamorphosed gradually into a fascination with the hardly-comprehensible, and where one knew not how to explicate, one learned to create' (ibid.). He goes so far as to claim that it is fear and not love that has furthered the universal knowledge of humanity – where love is deceptive and blind (it harbours a secret impulse to elevate the other as high as possible), fear has a capacity for genuine discernment, for example, discerning the powers and desires of a person or an object (D 309). For Nietzsche we are both heirs to, and continuers of, a history of sacrifice and of the sublime; the difference is that now for us the promise of happiness – which centres on a strengthening and elevation of the general feeling of human power – seeks to remain true to our mortal dwelling on the earth. Our task is now to take our time in our search; we are no longer looking for a single answer to our questions or some ultimate solution to the riddles of existence.

I regard these proposals for how we are to practice philosophy as among the most instructive and fertile in Nietzsche's corpus. *Dawn* is a text that has yet to have its moment and an encounter with its search for philosophy is largely unknown to its readers. I make only a modest and provisional contribution to the task of staging or preparing the groundwork for such an encounter.

Nietzsche clearly saw *The Gay Science* as the final instalment of his free-spirit 'trilogy' for he had written on the back cover, 'With this book we arrive at the conclusion of a series of writings by FRIEDRICH NIETZSCHE whose common goal is to erect a new image and ideal of the free spirit,' and then listed the two volumes *Human, all too Human, Dawn* and the new text. The title of the book is a rich and fertile one, suggesting the idea of a science – as well as a practice of knowledge and scholarship and an intelligence – that is gay, cheerful and joyous. Like its predecessor *Dawn*, *The Gay Science* covers myriad topics, but it differs in that it contains some of Nietzsche's grandest ideas such as the death of God and the eternal recurrence. Indeed, Richard Schacht has argued that *The Gay Science* goes beyond the other volumes that make up the so-called free-spirit trilogy 'in both coherence and content'.[24] He is surely right in his suggestion that in the book we ultimately encounter something more than the disjointed collection of aphorisms and meditations that it appears to be at first glance. 'In this work,' Schacht writes, 'the philosopher emerges with greater clarity than in any of his previous works,'[25] a debatable point I think given the brilliance of the neglected text, *Dawn*. The book is a sustained effort to sketch the outlines of a reinterpretation of nature and humanity, one that brings Nietzsche into rapport with Spinoza. Indeed, Nietzsche claimed to have discovered in the early 1880s a precursor in Spinoza. In a letter to Franz Overbeck from the end of July 1881 – close to the time when he began work on materials that would eventually find their way in *The Gay Science* – Nietzsche enumerates the points of doctrine he shares with Spinoza, such as the denial of free will, of a moral world order and of evil, and also mentions the task of 'making knowledge the most *powerful affect*' (die Erkenntniß zum *mächtigsten Affekt* zu machen; KSB 6, 111).[26]

As Pierre Klossowski notes, the gay science is the fruit of 'the greatest imaginable solitude',[27] and seeks to address those rare and few solitary spirits who have seceded from society. Indeed, in the book Nietzsche invites his imagined free spirits to practise a specific 'morality':

> Live in seclusion so that you *can* live for yourself. Live in *ignorance* about what
> seems most important to your age. … And the clamor of today, the noise of

wars and revolutions should be a mere murmur for you. You will also wish to help – but only those who distress you *understand* entirely because they share with you on suffering and one hope – your friends – and only in the manner in which you help yourself. I want to make them bolder, more persevering, simpler, gayer. I want to teach them what is understood by so few today, least all by these preachers of pity: *to share not suffering but joy.* (GS 338)

It seems clear that Nietzsche sought to found a philosophical school modelled on Epicurus's garden.[28] For some commentators, Nietzsche's ultimate goal is the shaping of the future of European humanity and society, and on this conception of his philosophy the retreat into an Epicurean-inspired community of friends is merely a temporary expedient in which free spirits work on themselves so as to become philosophical legislators of a future culture. As Horst Hutter has written, 'Such fraternities of free spirits would be necessary to traverse the period of nihilism until a future point in time, when direct political action would again become possible.'[29] Although I am not convinced Nietzsche ever arrived at an adequate or satisfactory conception of politics – here I dissent from Hutter's view – it is in his middle writings that he is most attentive to the needs of a specifically modern humanity: he has a keen sense of justice, a concern with the democracy to come free of vested interests and he has much to offer an evolving free-minded culture.

In my reading of *The Gay Science* I seek to illuminate the meaning of Nietzsche's cheerfulness (*Heiterkeit*) – with respect to the death of God and with respect to the project of the gay science as a whole. Let me make some comments on this in the introduction in an effort to illuminate what is a highly complex mode of cheerfulness that Nietzsche puts into play. In the preface to the second edition of *The Gay Science*, which Nietzsche composed in the autumn of 1886, he speaks as a convalescent for whom the gay science signifies the 'saturnalia of a spirit' who has patiently resisted a terrible, long pressure, without submitting and without hope, but who suddenly finds himself attacked by hope, including the hope for health (GS Preface 1). He states that a philosopher who has traversed many different kinds of health has gone through an equal number of philosophies and philosophy is nothing other than this 'art of transfiguration' (*Kunst der Transfiguration*) by which the thinker transposes his states into a spiritual form and distance (GS Preface 3). It is certain that our trust in life has gone, and gone forever, simply because life has become a problem for us. Nietzsche counsels us, however, that we should not jump to the conclusion that this problem necessarily makes us gloomy. Love of life is still possible, only it is now like the love of a beloved object that causes doubts in us. Taking delight in the problem of life entails a highly spiritualized thinking that has overcome fear and gloominess. Nietzsche's cheerfulness stems from his experiences of knowledge, including the experience of disillusionment and despair that can result from the practice of the love of knowledge – this is the 'long pressure' that needs to be resisted. Nietzsche's love of knowledge embraces the demands of this love and represents, then, a victory, something that one has won. He will, in fact, frequently speak of gay or joyful science as a reward, for example, 'a reward for a long, brave, diligent, subterranean seriousness' (GM Preface 7). Knowledge is thus to be conceived in terms of a 'world of dangers and victories in which heroic feelings ... find places to dance and play' (GS 324).

III

With this study I seek to make a contribution to the growing appreciation of Nietzsche's middle writings, to aid both pedagogy and research with respect to an appreciation of these highly fertile and path-breaking texts. After reading Nietzsche for several decades I find there is some truth in the observation of Havelock Ellis that the works Nietzsche produced between 1878 and 1882 represent the maturity of his genius.[30] My aim, however, is not to unduly privilege these middle writings over the early and late writings since there are valuable resources in the early writings, such as the untimely meditations (or 'unfashionable observations', as the most recent translation has it), especially for a critique of the present; the late writings have a brilliance all of their own and in spite of an 'indulgence in dangerous political fantasies',[31] they contain tremendous resources for carrying out all kinds of vitally important philosophical projects. Although the academic world is now littered with books on Nietzsche, including many excellent ones, my hope is that as a probing of his neglected, formative middle writings this work will serve to educate and inspire old and new readers alike.

Nietzsche's search for philosophy attains some of its richest moments and insights in his middle writings. In these writings Nietzsche embarks on a genuinely exploratory search for knowledge and wisdom and sets us, his modern readers, tasks that we can still aspire to be equal to today. In the middle writings we encounter a Nietzsche quite different to the legend that circulates in popular culture and even academic culture. This is a Nietzsche committed to human emancipation through individual and social enlightenment and experimentation. He writes of the need to constitute ourselves as small, experimental states in which we aim to fashion out of ourselves a way of being that others will behold with pleasure, providing 'a lovely, peaceful self-enclosed garden' and with a gate of hospitality (D 174). Furthermore, Nietzsche stresses that his 'campaign' against morality is *not* a gunpowder campaign; rather, and provided we have the necessary subtlety in our nostrils, we are to smell in it much sweeter scents. Nietzsche sees social change coming about through small-scale individual experimentation and a free-spirited avant-garde who aim to provide a new ploughshare of potential universal benefit (D 146).

Nietzsche is undoubtedly new and idiosyncratically so, but he is not so idiosyncratic as to be philosophically unrecognizable and indigestible. We are still living and thinking in the wake of his event and there is much to assimilate, including the attachment to a philosophy of modesty (especially when it comes to 'morality') and the tasks of 'the passion of knowledge' and 'the incorporation of truth'. In his lifetime Nietzsche saw himself as intellectually isolated and something of a philosophical outsider. However, much of the philosophical revolution he sought to bring into being is now widely practised in philosophy: I like to believe we have assimilated the passion of knowledge as a mode of philosophical askesis and that we have become the experimenters of knowledge he hoped we would. For this is Nietzsche's great insight: we *are* experiments, and the task is to *want* to be such (D 453). It is this event of science and of philosophy that we are still seeking to be equal to, and as both human and superhuman.

Cooling Down the Human Mind: Nietzsche On Philosophy and the Philosopher in *Human, all too Human*

Introduction

Human, all too Human (HAH), published in 1878, is typically construed as the beginning of a new phase in Nietzsche's intellectual development and as being his most positivistic text in which the scientific interpretation of the world is privileged and guides the inquiry into religion, metaphysics, art and culture. Nietzsche conceives philosophy as a practice of a sober mind that cools down a human mind prone to neurosis. Philosophy, in concert with science, has the task of tempering emotional and mental excess. Indeed, Nietzsche defines the philosopher as a human being who speaks 'from a cool, invigorating resting place' (WS 171). Nietzsche goes so far as to hold that the Socratic schools of philosophy, in their concern with human happiness (eudemonia), have retarded the progress of science (HAH 7). Although aspects of this project, including a commitment to science, continue in the subsequent volumes of *Human, all too Human*, there is a fundamental reorientation with Nietzsche now positively reappraising Socrates and the antique philosophers such as Epicurus and Epictetus. In the case of Socrates, Nietzsche holds that 'all the roads of the most varied philosophical ways of life lead back to him', and in which there is revealed a capacity to rejoice in life and in one's own self (WS 86). With respect to Epicurus and Epictetus, these, for Nietzsche, are thinkers in whom wisdom assumes bodily form (MOM 224). This reappraisal suggests that in the subsequent volumes of HAH, notably *Mixed Opinions and Maxims* (1879) and *The Wanderer and His Shadow* (1880), Nietzsche has altered his conception of philosophical practice in quite a fundamental way. The major claim I wish to make in this chapter is the following: whereas in volume one of

HAH Nietzsche negotiates the competing claims of the positivist goal of science and eudemonistic philosophy by aligning himself with the former, in MOM and WS he seeks to marry the project of naturalistic demystification with an ethical project of seeking 'spiritual-physical health and maturity' (MOM 184). It is this development on Nietzsche's part I wish to trace and illuminate in this chapter. Such transitions and transformations in Nietzsche's free-spirited thinking in HAH have gone unnoticed in the literature to date on these texts.

In the volumes of HAH – and in the subsequent text, *Dawn* – Nietzsche favours a project of sobriety that supposes philosophical moderation in an effort to combat both human neurosis and a sentimental, self-intoxicating world view (which he associates with Rousseau). In his middle writings Nietzsche is committed to a philosophical therapeutics in which the chief aim is to cool down the human mind. In part, he conceives the art of the maxim in therapeutic terms. The modern age has forgotten the art of reflection or observation, in which it is possible to gather maxims 'from the thorniest and least gratifying stretches of our lives' so as to make ourselves feel better, to give ourselves a lift and a tonic. We can return to life revivified rather than depressed from our encounter with thorny problems, and with 'presence of mind in difficult situations and amusement in tedious surroundings'. There is a need, therefore, for modern spirits to learn how to derive pleasure from the art of the maxim, from its construction to its tasting. Nietzsche notes that it is virtually impossible to say whether the inquiry into the 'human, all too human' will work more as a blessing than a curse to the welfare of humanity; at any rate, and for the time being, the issue is undecided (HAH 38). He further notes that because science, like nature, does not aim at final ends, any fruitfulness in the way or promoting the welfare of humanity will be the result of science's attaining something purposeful without having willed it. But where science is needed now, as part of general therapeutic practice of reflection and observation, is in cooling down the human mind: 'Shouldn't we, the *more spiritual* human beings of an age that is visibly catching fire in more and more places, have to grasp all available means for quenching and cooling, so that we will remain at least as steady … and moderate as we are now' (HAH 38). The illnesses and neuroses we encounter in humanity require that ice packs be placed on them.

Nietzsche sees the present age as moving in the direction of a temperate zone of culture (HAH 236). Here he contests Schopenhauer's suprahistorical standpoint, the standpoint of a metaphysical philosophy, which perceives no progress taking place in the last four millennia with regard to philosophy and religion. The zone of the past can be compared to a tropical zone in which violent contrasts, abrupt changes between day and night, and a reverence for everything sudden, mysterious and terrible predominate. In this zone 'we see how the most raging passions are overpowered and shattered by the uncanny force of metaphysical conception' and 'feel as if savage tropical tigers were being crushed before our eyes in the coils of colossal serpents'. Today, Nietzsche speculates, in this time of transition to a different zone, and which we label 'progress', we inhabit a spiritual climate with no such events, 'our imagination has been tempered, even in dreams we scarcely come close to what earlier periods beheld when awake'. Nietzsche alerts us to the danger of an overstimulation of the nervous and intellectual powers such is, as a result of the sum of sensations, knowledge and experiences, the whole burden of culture: 'Indeed, the cultivated classes in European countries are thoroughly neurotic' (HAH 244). Our concern is to maintain our health in every possible way and live in hope of a new Renaissance. To keep at bay and from overgrowing us the deeply moving sensations instilled in us by centuries of Christianity, as well as the work of metaphysically inspired philosophers, poets and musicians, we have recourse to a scientific spirit which makes us colder and more sceptical, cooling down 'the scorching stream of a faith in final, definitive truths' (HAH 244). It is to the Italian Renaissance that we owe all the positive forces of modern culture: the liberation of thought, disdain for arbitrary authorities, the triumph of cultivation over the arrogance of lineage, the unfettering of the individual, an ardour for veracity and against appearance and mere effect, and an enthusiasm or passion for science (HAH 237). Nietzsche thus pins his hope for the future on these developments in culture without reliance on metaphysics and the errors of religion, as well as forsaking the harshness and violence that have hitherto been the means for binding one person or one people powerfully to another. It is the task of a new humanity to 'take in hand the earthly governance of all humanity', and its '"omniscience"' must watch over the future destiny of culture with a sharp eye' (HAH 245). This requires at the same time that we do justice to the past and tradition, for example, by recognizing that the activity of the fiercest forces was 'necessary so that a milder cultural dispensation could later establish itself'. This means recognizing that those fearsome energies we now call 'evil' have been in history 'the cyclopean architects and builders of humanity' (HAH 246).

Of course, we can acknowledge that the whole of humanity is merely a developmental phase of a certain species of animal of quite limited duration. If human beings descended from apes, as the new science of evolution teaches us, it is quite possible that we will becomes apes again without anybody taking an interest in this comic ending. This is to say that the decline of universal world culture might one day lead to a heightened repulsiveness and bestialization of humanity – but it is 'because we can envision this perspective' that 'we are perhaps in a position to prevent the future from reaching such an end' (HAH 247). Nietzsche insists that it is impossible to go backwards, to 'go back to the old' since 'we *have* burned our boats; all that remains is to be bold, regardless of what may result' (HAH 248). It may appear that the world is becoming more chaotic every passing day or year, with the old being lost and the new seeming feebler, but we have no option but to '*step forward*' and move on (ibid.). Nietzsche even admits that 'every better future that we wish upon humanity is also in many respects necessarily a worse future' (HAH 239). This is because we can no longer rely on the forces that united previous cultures, forces of consolation provided by religion and metaphysics: 'What grew out of religion and in proximity to it cannot grow again if religion has been destroyed' (ibid.).

Nietzsche holds that all the important truths of science need to gradually become everyday, ordinary things. However, because it lacks the intense pleasure of what has been conquered – for example, the pleasures afforded by religion and metaphysics – and has taken away the consolations they offered, there arises the need in a higher culture for the dual brain. Nietzsche envisages a higher culture in which human beings have a dual brain made up of two compartments, one with which to experience science and one to experience non-science (HAH 251). He stipulates this as a requirement of health in which the realm of science and the realm of metaphysics, religion and art will be closed off from one another with one unable to confuse the other. One region will be the source of power (*Kraft*) and of pleasure, the other will serve as a regulator. One will allow for illusions, partiality and the passions that stimulate heat in us, while the other will avert the dangers of overheating stemming from these operations. In short, there is need of a culture that can do justice to our liking of illusion, error and fantasy – because it gives us so much pleasure and a confidence in life – and the need for the true. (This is now a new need in us that demands satisfaction.) This is not to say that there is no pleasure to be had from knowing (*Erkennen*), only that it is of a peculiar and more refined kind. In knowing we become conscious of our own strength, we become victors over older conceptions and their advocates, and we feel we are distinguishing ourselves from everyone else. The origin of the scholar, the artist, the philosopher and the moral genius lies, in fact, in a confused tangle of impulses and stimuli. This leads Nietzsche to the view that it is necessary to view everything human ironically with regard to its origin or coming into being (*Entstehung*). Indeed, this insight enables us to understand why there is such an excess of irony in the world (HAH 252). Nietzsche is not oblivious to the fact that there are dangers facing the development of the human intellect and spirit under modern conditions of life. Ours is an age of quickness that is fast becoming an enemy of slowness. A tremendous acceleration of life is taking place in which people more and more resemble the traveller who gets to know a land and its people only from looking out of the train window. This means we will increasingly deprecate an independent and careful attitude towards knowledge (*Erkenntniss*). Nietzsche thinks that the discrediting of the free spirit – the genuinely independent thinker – is already taking place with the rise of the scholar (HAH 282).

Introduction to the text

When *Human, all too Human* was published in 1878, Nietzsche was spending his last year as professor of classical philology at Basel University. The book was originally to be titled *The Ploughshare*, which was also to be used as the working title of *Dawn*, and it began life as an unfashionable observation titled *The Free Spirit*. According to Nietzsche work on the project was begun in August 1876 on his flight from the opening of the Bayreuth festival in the forests of Klingenbrunn. According to Peter Gast, however, Nietzsche began dictating drafts of the book to him between May and July, and then in September, of that year, so largely before Wagner's festival. Whatever the facts are, *Human, all too Human* signals a radical departure from Nietzsche's previous writings, both in content and in style. Nietzsche had been granted a year's sabbatical leave from Basel in October 1876. He spent the first six months in Sorrento, with Malwida von Meysenburg and Paul Rée, and the next six at various spas in Switzerland.[1] As with almost every book he now wrote, Nietzsche considered this one his most important book to date. He wanted the book published in May to coincide with the centennial celebration of Voltaire's birthday on 30 May. He also wanted the printing of the book to be a secret matter and even considered publishing it under a pseudonym, Bernard Cron, and about whom he devised a short biography.[2] Nietzsche was very much concerned with how the book would be received by Wagner and his old friends. Wagner sent Nietzsche a copy of Parsifal in January. Nietzsche had lost his faith in the Wagner cause and abandoned his belief that a cultural regeneration could take place through his music. Wagner's art was not a sign of a healthy German culture but rather, 'a baroque art of overexcitement and glorified extravagance'.[3] According to William Schaberg, Schmeitzner, Nietzsche's publisher and who talked Nietzsche out of his plans for using a pseudonym, was well aware that the book would trigger a confrontation between Nietzsche and Wagner, but looked forward to the sales that the scandal and publicity from it would generate. The printing and corrections to it took place between January and early April and complimentary copies of the book were shipped at the end of April. Two copies were sent to the Wagner's, and it is this exchange with Wagner that Nietzsche dramatizes in *Ecce Homo* by spiriting away four months, claiming erroneously that the two works arrived at their respective addresses at the same time through a miracle of meaning and accident (EH 'HAH,' section 5).

The book shocked many of its readers, including close friends such as Erwin Rodhe. Coming to the book from Nietzsche's earlier writings, Rohde compared the experience to like being chased from the *calidarium,* the steamy waters, into an ice-cold *frigidarium.* As the translator Gary Handwerk notes, *Human, all too Human* has a plain, straightforward style and a coldness of tone that alienated Nietzsche's readers to date: 'A curious exercise in self-control, it can scarcely be made to fit into the image that most readers have of Nietzsche as a writer.'[4] Such a style of writing is conducive to Nietzsche's overriding aim in the texts of the middle period: to temper emotional excess and cool down a human mind prone to neurosis.

At the start of section two of the book, which was originally conceived as the opening three aphorisms, Nietzsche argues that maxims about the human condition can aid the overcoming of life in its hardest moments. The book is composed of nine parts or chapters: one to four are concerned, respectively, with metaphysics, morality, religion and art. Marion Faber has noted that Nietzsche's main aim 'is not so much to construct new systems of values or beliefs as to shatter – with some regret for their loss – the old, erroneous ways of thinking'.[5] Sections five to nine provide an exposition of the free spirit, with the free-spirit being the philosopher who hovers 'above the human fray, coolly testing the culture for its truths and errors'.[6] Two sections of this second half of the book, sections six and seven, deal with the traditional domain of the aphorism, 'Man in Society' and on 'Woman and Child.' In section eight Nietzsche advances his views about politics. In the final section of the book, 'Man alone with Himself,' Nietzsche presents himself as a solitary wanderer who enjoys his own counsel and appeals to the goddess Justice he has sought to serve in the work. In 1879

Mixed Opinions and Maxims was published as an appendix to the work, and a further volume appeared in 1880 as *The Wanderer and His Shadow*. In 1886 the two were joined together and published as the second volume of HAH. Nietzsche also took the opportunity to add a concluding poem that serves as a postlude to the first volume and wrote prefaces for the two volumes. He revised the first three aphorisms and removed the dedication to Voltaire from the original title page, as well as the quotation from Descartes on method (on the method of 'Rightly Conducting Reason').

Human, all too Human is made up of 638 aphorisms that range from a few lines to a few pages, the majority of them taking the form of short paragraphs. Nietzsche's stylistic influences ranged from his German predecessors in the art form, such as Lichtenberg and Schopenhauer, to the French aphorists and moralists such as La Rochefoucauld and Chamfort. Nietzsche made the aphoristic form very much his own, as he did with the moralists' ideas and methodology. As Handwerk notes, 'The greater part of *Human, all too Human* does not really present maxims in the French style, each honed to ironic sharpness, each largely self-contained or connected only in loose thematic ways to others, but presents extended prose passages that often read more like mini-essays.'[7] Moreover, although certain sections or chapters do approximate his French models, such as six, seven and nine, Nietzsche's aphorisms typically carry a continuous line of thought from one section to the next, pursuing some particular idea through various perspectives in a logically coherent and rigorous way.[8] Handwerk is surely correct in his judgement that a principal influence comes from Schopenhauer's *Parerga and Paralipomena* in which Schopenhauer, especially in the second volume subtitled 'Stray yet systematically arranged thoughts on a variety of subjects,' blends the philosophical wit of the French moralists with his own more sustained and systematic analysis, making use of an aphoristic mode ranging from a single sentence to more than ten pages in length.[9] Equally important for Nietzsche is that the aphorism form allows analysis, 'to proceed in a distinctively interruptive mode, turning back on itself from section to section and abruptly shifting direction as Nietzsche moves to incorporate new considerations into his analysis.'[10] As Handwerk rightly points out, 'The sequence of individual aphorisms and the shaping of those turns were matters of major importance for Nietzsche.'[11] Thus, the 'aphorism enacts at the level of form a quite specific reflective procedure; it presents concentrated bursts of thought set one against the other by the space for reflection that exists between them.'[12]

In the text Nietzsche lets it be known that he maintains that there has not yet been any philosopher who has not eventually looked down upon the philosophy he invented in his youth with disdain, or at least with suspicion (HH 253), but he does not spell out the nature of his break with his younger incarnation or the nature of his shift of concerns and foci. In *Ecce Homo* Nietzsche looks back on *Human, all too Human* as the 'monument of a crisis' (EH 'HAH'). As Richard Schacht has noted, this has more than one sense: there was the crisis of multiple dimensions of his own life, notably severely crippling health problems, and a crisis in his own intellectual development.[13] Although the crisis was his own, it presaged, says Schacht, 'the larger crisis toward which he came to see our entire culture and civilization moving, and subsequently came to call "the death of God"'.[14] In the text we encounter a mind in transition, 'moving in many different directions and in many different ways, heedless of disciplinary boundaries and norms, with only Nietzsche's interests and intellectual conscience as his map and compass'.[15] In its construction and wide-ranging interests it is an affront to academic philosophy as practised at the time and subsequently. Again, Nietzsche was writing a book that was not what was expected by a professor of classical philology and his resignation from his post has something of the air of inevitability about it.

On display in the text is, as Schacht has noted, a much more sober and analytical, colder and wiser thinker that in his previous incarnations. He puts it accurately, I think, when he characterizes the new orientation in Nietzsche's thinking as a shift from romanticism to severely analytical naturalism. In this naturalistic world picture there is no benevolent deity and no beneficent rationality at work. The task is to take the sublime inventions of human nature – our view of our moral sensations, the souls of artists and writers, the phenomena of the religious life – and show them to be strictly 'human, all too human', 'shifting the presumption from their sublimity to the suspicion that their appearance of sublimity may well be deceiving'.[16] Schacht deftly captures the nature of this sort of inquiry as follows:

> The spirit of the investigation is profoundly and pervasively affirmative; for the passion that drives it is not only that of an honesty that will tolerate no nonsense or groundless wishful thinking, but also of a desperate search for enough to work with and ways of doing so to sustain ourselves despite all. To call this 'secular humanism' would be to sell it short; for while Nietzsche's outlook is radically secular, he is far from taking humanity either in general or as embodied in each and every one of us to be the locus of meaning and value. But it is a kind of

tough-minded and yet doggedly affirmative naturalism, the upshot of which is that our all-too-human humanity leaves a good deal to be desired, and yet gives us something to work with that it not to be despised.[17]

What remains constant in Nietzsche's development from the early to the middle writings is his concern with the fate of philosophy and the prospect of possibilities of life. However, his attention is now focused not on antiquity but on the present and its possible future developments. His aim is to encourage human beings to live without superstition and fear, especially generated by our attachment to religious concepts (angels, original sin and salvation). But there is still the need to overcome metaphysics and the metaphysical need. This need expresses itself in a longing to resolve 'the first and last things' and to deal with the outermost theoretical regions.[18] A twofold task involved: to relinquish the need of metaphysics and to appreciate that the greatest advancements of humanity have emanated from metaphysics (however illusory metaphysical notions have provided our existence with a sense of purpose, even destiny). In short, it is a question of doing justice to all things. It is also a question of administering doses and effecting change through measure, of recognizing that transitional zones of thought are necessary in the spiritual economy.

In an unpublished note of 1877 Nietzsche wanted to make clear to his readers that he had abandoned 'the metaphysical-artistic views' of his early writings (1872–6) (KSA 8, 23 [159]). In particular, he wanted to overcome what he calls his 'deliberate holding on to illusion' as the foundation of culture (KSA 10, 16 [23]).[19] Nietzsche was seeking to overcome what he called Jesuitism, which he located in his predecessors in German philosophy and himself. In the words of one commentator, this means not allowing the uncovering of the limits of human knowledge to be conducted in such a way that the task also gives free rein to metaphysics and the metaphysical need.[20]

Nietzsche's embracing of the scientific spirit now means that Schopenhauer can no longer be upheld as a philosophical role model. In his early writings Schopenhauer is held up as a philosophical exemplar on account of his efforts to reinvent philosophy of a way of life: he reawakens the need for wisdom and not just knowledge (see UO III). Schopenhauer, for Nietzsche, is not a mere scholar. He knows how to unlearn pure science, and he does not allow himself to get entangled in a web of conceptual scholasticisms. He is said to be 'simple, honest, and crude': 'Schopenhauer is valuable because he calls to mind the memory of *naïve, universal* truths' (KSA 7, 19 [26]). In his middle-period writings, however,

Nietzsche detects a major flaw in Schopenhauer's philosophy. In spite of the fact that there is a strong ring of science in his teaching, the scientific spirit is not strong enough in it and, as a result, the entire medieval Christian world view could celebrate its resurrection. Schopenhauer does not master the scientific spirit; rather the metaphysical need does (HAH 26). However, Nietzsche's assessment of Schopenhauer's achievement aspires to be a judicious one. He further notes that what we gain from him is the ability to place ourselves, and our sensations, back into older, powerful ways of viewing the world. He enables us to do justice to Christianity and to Asian religions too. 'The gain for history and justice', Nietzsche writes, 'is very great' (HAH 110). Where Schopenhauer makes a blunder is over the value of religion with respect to knowledge, which he does by according it (Christianity for example) an allegorical sense and significance.

One important move that now takes place in Nietzsche's thinking concerns the antique philosophers and their discovery of possibilities of life. He returns to this theme of the discovery of possibilities of life in *Human all too Human* in an aphorism entitled 'The tyrants of the spirit' (HAH 261). At first appearance it might seem that the Greek philosophers who deprive themselves of the illuminating warmth of myth wanted only to live in the gloom. Nietzsche argues, however, that they were seeking a brighter sun since the myth was not clear to them and they needed and wanted the clarity that only knowledge can provide. At this time knowledge was still young and each philosopher who felt its lustre became a spiritual tyrant. The early philosophers had no intimation in fact of the difficulties and dangers of the paths of knowledge, so that each one had the expectation of reaching through knowledge the centre of all being with a single leap and that would enable them to solve the riddle of the world. In this respect they were absolute beginners and, as such, fundamentally naïve. They had a robust faith in themselves and in their 'truth', a truth they used to overthrow their predecessors and each other. Never has the possession of truth been as happy as it was at this time. But never has there been more arrogance as well. Perhaps, Nietzsche speculates, the lawgiver Solon is an exception who, as a legislator, practised a more sublimated form of tyranny. Plato was also a lawgiver, along with the likes of Parmenides, Pythagoras and Empedocles, but it is Plato who most acutely felt he had failed in this desire and at the end his soul is filled, Nietzsche says, with the blackest bile. Eventually Greek philosophy is overtaken by the rise of sectarianism and numerous petty tyrants. The extraordinary feature of Greek history from our modern perspective, where things seem to endure for longer, is how turbulent it was, how fast things happen and move on.

With the Greeks things move both quickly forward and quickly downward. Rich developments can be overthrown virtually overnight, Nietzsche thinks, and gives the example of Socrates. He wonders whether Plato might have discovered a still even higher type of philosophic being if he had not fallen under the spell of Socrates. The pre-Platonic philosophers promise and announce new modes of existence but ultimately the supreme possibility of the philosophical life is lost. It is now very difficult for us to perceive this promise and to re-create these philosophical figures (Aristotle, Nietzsche notes, 'seems not to have any eyes in his head when he stands before depictions of them'). For Nietzsche we have here an example of the highest and the best emerging as a possible event and then falling into ruin. There have been echoes of this event since, but today it is impossible for anyone to have the naïve and clear conscience of the earliest philosophers. Nietzsche now proclaims that the time of these tyrants of the spirit is over. What remains is the need for some form of mastery (*Herrschaft*), but now this will take place in the hands of oligarchs of the spirit. There is a need for free spirits appropriate to the modern age.

Nietzsche's relation in his middle writings to his first intellectual incarnation as a young, classical philologist at Basel is quite complex. On the one hand he continues to uphold the idea of the philosopher as a figure who discovers these 'possibilities of life'. On the other hand, he is in search of new models of the philosophical life and holds that Schopenhauer, his great early educator, can no longer serve the role of a model. In the case of the great first philosophers, such as Heraclitus and Empedocles, we encounter a rare and impressive resourcefulness, a daring that is both desperate and hopeful, it is life pushing itself further and further, upwards and ever higher or more encompassing, as if the thinker possessed the spirit of one of the globe's great circumnavigators. This for the early Nietzsche is what the great thinker is, a circumnavigator of 'life's most remote and dangerous regions' (KSA 8, 6 [48]). As one commentator has put it, Nietzsche's account allows us to see the earliest philosophers as creative thinkers who give us new images of the world and establish new modes of life: there is not the one and only correct or proper way of living and it is not a question of discovering the objectively given essence of nature: 'They polyphonically and pluralistically represent opportunities of thinking and living, and role models for philosophers.'[21] However, we have seen that in HAH he now holds the time of these philosophers to be over and tasks appropriate to the modern age are now to be pursued. There is a need not only to elevate the human by 'holding onto the sublime', which is how the early Nietzsche defines philosophy and in contrast to science (*Wissenschaft*) (KSA 7, 19 [33]);[22] there is now the need to deflate and critique the 'ideals' of humankind and to highlight the 'human, all too human' origins and sources of our ideas and values. In *Human, all too Human* Nietzsche argues in favour of a historical approach for intellectual inquiry that, in conjunction with natural sciences, will lay out a new evolutionary approach to the faculty of human cognition and to questions of truth and knowledge. This is what he calls 'historical philosophizing', which is accompanied by 'the virtue of modesty' – modesty because there are no 'eternal facts' and no 'absolute truths' (HAH 2). Everything we can think about, Nietzsche appears to be saying, is perspectival and humanly conditioned. The fundamental task that he now outlines for philosophy is that of undertaking a history of the genesis of thought (HAH 17-18). The scientific spirit is now to be cultivated and at the expense of our inherited metaphysical need. The human animal is the product of a prehistoric labour going back thousands of years. What the human is now is not what it has been destined to be from time immemorial.

Nietzsche thinks that the impulse to want certainties in the domain of first and last things is best regarded as a '*religious after-shoot*'. It is a hidden and only apparently sceptical species of the metaphysical need. The first and last things refer to those questions of knowledge that concern themselves with the 'outermost regions' (how did the universe begin? What is its purpose? and so on). It is only under the influence of ethical and religious sensations that these questions have acquired for us such a dreadful weightiness. They compel the eye to strain itself, and where it encounters darkness it makes things even darker. Where it has not been possible to establish certainties of any kind in our efforts to penetrate this dark region, an entire moral–metaphysical world has been displaced into it, the fantasies of which posterity is then asked to take seriously and for truth.

This is why carrying out an inquiry into the sources and origins of our ethical and religious sensations are such important tasks. The main objective is a deflationary one. We do not require certainties with regard to the 'first and last things' – what Nietzsche calls 'the furthest horizon' – in order to live a 'full and excellent human life' (WS 16). He proposes that a fundamental rupture be affected with regard to customary habits of thinking. In the face of questions such as what is the purpose of man? What is his fate after death? How can man be reconciled with God?, it should not be felt necessary to develop knowledge against faith; rather we should practise an indifference towards faith and supposed knowledge in the domains of metaphysics, morality and religion.

Beyond the consolations of philosophy

Let me now focus on Nietzsche's conception of philosophy in the first volume of HAH. In all philosophies, Nietzsche states, we encounter 'so much high-flying metaphysics' and a corresponding dread for the seemingly insignificant solutions of physics: 'for the significance of knowledge (*Erkenntniss*) *ought* to seem as great as possible'. Philosophy has the same want as art – to give to life and action as much depth and meaning as possible; science, by contrast, seeks knowledge and nothing further 'whatever may come of it' (HAH 6). As an apology for knowledge, philosophers are optimists since they think that the highest usefulness can be assigned to knowledge. Nietzsche even thinks that philosophy, by fixing on the question of what knowledge can do for the happiness or well-being of human beings (for example, the Socratic schools), has retarded the advance of scientific inquiry. Philosophy, therefore, needs to reform itself and dedicate itself to working closely with the new sciences and in an effort to develop a new passion for knowledge and ensure that the rational pursuit of truth and knowledge are not made subservient to ethical considerations, such as a concern with happiness or flourishing. Nietzsche writes: 'Philosophy divided itself from science when it posed the question: what is that knowledge of the world and of life by which human beings will live most happily? This occurred in the Socratic schools: by keeping their eye upon *happiness*, they tied up the veins of scientific inquiry – and do so to this day (HAH 7).'

It is on this basis that Nietzsche thinks a new training in thinking is necessary as there is a real danger that we will become gloomy, despondent and perhaps nihilistic in the wake of the dissolution of the metaphysical need, that is, the need that expresses itself in a longing to resolve 'the first and last things' and to deal with the outermost theoretical regions. With the rise of positivistic science humanity is in danger of reaching a disabling point of disillusionment and despair. Is everything in human history an error, a piece of folly? Is all human knowledge implicated in error and ignorance? Is all human existence characterized by senseless suffering and vengeance against life? What will be our new consoling thoughts? Do we still need consolations? If we do, will this not stand in the way of our acquisition of truth, the object of which is not to offer consolation? If human beings exist as truthful beings but employ philosophy as therapy in the sense of seeking a cure for themselves, does this not suggest that they are not, in fact, seeking truth at all? But if the character of truth as a whole is one that makes us ill should we not abolish it in the same way the Greeks abolished gods once they were unable to offer consolation?

At this point in his development Nietzsche seems most keen to raise these kinds of questions; his overriding concern is not necessarily with resolving all the issues that existence now throws up for us moderns. Certainly, we can longer commit ourselves to the dogmas of religion and metaphysics once we have in our hearts and heads the 'strict method of truth'; and yet, on the other hand, the development of humanity has made us so delicate and sickly that we need remedies and consolations of the highest kind. As a consequence, will humanity not bleed to death from its recognition of truth? We would, Nietzsche surmises, readily exchange the false assertions regarding God as the watcher and witness of every action and thought, along with other dogmas of religion, for truths that would be just as salutary and soothing, and just as beneficial to us as the errors. The difficulty is that such truths do not exist: truth does not exist to console and at best philosophy can set probabilities against the inherited errors. Nietzsche's solution to this predicament is to argue that a degree of levity and even melancholy is better than any romantic return to the past and accommodation with metaphysical dogmas and reassurances. There may be suffering, 'but one cannot become a leader and teacher of humanity without suffering' (HAH 109). In HAH Nietzsche does acknowledge, however, that science has its promises, including as little pain as possible and as long a life as possible: 'a sort of eternal bliss, admittedly a very modest one in comparison with the promises of religions' (HAH 128).

Nietzsche holds that a new habit of comprehending, a habit that does not wish to love or hate but only to know, is gradually implanting itself in us that will in the future that is distant (it is not our time) be powerful enough to give humanity the strength and wisdom to bring forth into existence a new kind of human being: wise, just and innocent (HAH 107). But why do we need to be just and in what does the affirmation consist in being so? For Nietzsche, it resides in the recognition that humanity has been constituted on the basis of a set of errors that have educated it. These are errors of the intellect and of morality. They include errors concerning human descent, uniqueness and destiny. We say 'yes' to these errors since we wish to be just towards the past and our evolution; we recognize that they have played a formative role in the education of humanity, but also because we have an intimation that we are involved in a process of overcoming and conquering them. To achieve this goal it is necessary to revalue values and to challenge the faith of the metaphysicians in the opposition of values. Nietzsche begins this task in an essential way in HAH. The aim is to show that truth arises out of error, self-illumination out of errancy, altruism out of egoism and vanity, good inclinations out of evil ones and so on (HAH 107). The new truth we need to cultivate is simply the truth of becoming: everything, including the whole field of morality and the intellect itself, 'has come to be, is changeable, unsteady, everything is in flux' (HAH 107.). Our hope, however – the hope of free spirits at least – and without which we may not have the confidence in life and its future that is necessary to execute new tasks, is that although everything is indeed changeable and in flux it is also leading towards a single goal and a new goal. This goal is that of a new mature humanity.

Nietzsche's model of the free spirit at this time is a specific and a curious one. He posits a 'free' and 'fearless hovering' above all things, including human beings and their customs, laws and traditional evaluations as the most desirable condition (HAH 34). In addition, the free spirit has purified itself of the affects and communicates the 'joy' of this elevated condition of passionless contemplation. Although free spirits are to take joy in this view from above, the joyful science at work in HAH is, as Michael Ure has noted, a curiously joyless one: it exists without great passion or enthusiasm.[23]

Nietzsche's dilemma in *Human, all too Human*

The central dilemma at the heart of the book and the project of 'human, all too human' has been ably recognized by Jürgen Habermas: it centres on the tensions generated by Nietzsche's commitment to the scientific pretensions of positivism on the one hand and the attention he pays to the claims of the eudemonistic goals of classical philosophy on the other.[24] Building on Habermas's insight, Michael Ure has recently and instructively expounded these tensions in some detail, and I wish to comment on his account.

On Ure's account Nietzsche is seeking 'to renovate the ancient model of philosophy in light of the new naturalisms'.[25] In short, Nietzsche retains the Hellenistic notion of a global evaluation of life – the view from above – that follows from physics or a systematic view of nature. The new naturalisms Nietzsche is wedded to are primarily the evolutionary naturalisms of the nineteenth century, and the attempt is being made to refract the new naturalistic theories through the ancient model of philosophy and its 'spiritual exercises'. [26] However, as Ure recognizes, Nietzsche is clearly ambivalent about the ancient project and for this reason: If philosophy is construed primarily as an art of living, will it not sacrifice truth for the sake of flourishing or happiness? This has long been the concern over Epicurean teaching, for example, in which physics is subordinated to ethics and in which, as Ure puts it, serenity is secured at the price of disturbing scientific inquiry. On the other hand, however, as he notes, Nietzsche seems unable to rest content with a strictly conceived positivist programme: 'He is just as concerned with addressing or ameliorating the potentially "tragic" consequences of pursuing knowledge of science at any cost.'[27] These consequences include those that Nietzsche brings to the fore in HAH 34: disillusionment and despair. Nietzsche's dilemma, therefore, 'turns on the idea that truth and flourishing might be incompatible.'[28] It is clear that for him there is no pre-established harmony between the advancement of truth and the well-being of humanity (see HAH 517). Indeed, Nietzsche recognizes that the psychological dissection of the human, all too human has consequences that are at one and the same time frightful and fruitful. So, whereas the ancient model of philosophy brings with it certain epistemic hazards, such as the possible sacrifice of truth, positivism brings with it dangers of a uniquely existential kind, such as the endangering of the needs of the flourishing life.

How does Nietzsche come to resolve the tensions generated by his commitment to positivism (science) and his concern with the prospects of our leading new flourishing lives? In the subsequent texts of his free-spirit period, Nietzsche is less the disappointed idealist and becomes increasingly committed to an experimental project of philosophy in which the overriding goal is to usher in new dawns involving new ways of thinking, living and feeling. He retains his commitment to science – knowledge in its broadest sense – but raises questions about the role of truth and knowledge within the whole economy of life and asks after their incorporation (GS 110). In addition, science needs to be brought into contact with the needs of life and its growth; for example, we can pose the question: To what extent can science help to create new values? Can science join forces with artistic energies, practical wisdom and the art of living so as to give rise to a new higher organic system? (GS 113) We are implicated in a process of historical becoming and are seekers of a new great health: the task is to grow and to flourish but in the new-found post-metaphysical and post-moral conditions we find ourselves in.

By the time of the second instalment of HAH, Nietzsche appears less wedded to a positivist programme and is now keen to relate the story of a natural history of humankind in a way that fulfils the aims of therapeutic emancipation. For example, in *Mixed Opinions and Maxims* (MOM), he writes:

> Natural history, as the history of the wars and victories of moral-spiritual force in opposition to fear, imagination, indolence, superstition, folly, should be narrated in such a way that everyone who hears it would be irresistibly impelled to strive for spiritual-physical health and maturity, to feel gladness at being the heir and continuer of humanity, to sense his need for ever nobler undertakings (Nietzsche, MOM 184).

This citation is a significant one since it brings into relief in a highly instructive manner Nietzsche's two main concerns once his thought has started to mature circa 1879–80 and take on its enlightened shape, namely, on the one hand, his commitment to naturalism – to be pursued through the study of natural history – and, on the other hand, the concern with an emancipatory philosophical therapeutics. It is interesting to reflect on the fact that Nietzsche conceives natural history 'as the history of the wars and victories of moral-spiritual force', and he is clearly stating his naturalist-minded agenda when he refers to the need to combat 'fear, imagination, indolence, superstition, and folly'. Nietzsche is practising the philosophy of the morning and in search of the mysteries of the dawning day; what is required is a free mind, that is, one suspicious of reaching final, definitive truths and willing to revise its thoughts in the bright morning light of fresh experiences and new experiments: an artful philosophical practice. Nietzsche's thinking aims for a new sobriety: it seeks to approach the world beyond both theology and the struggle against it. The world is neither good nor evil, neither the best nor the worst. Good and evil, he argues following in the footsteps of Spinoza, only make sense with reference to human beings, and even then they are not justified in the typical ways they get deployed. He invites us to renounce both the view that curses the world and the view that extols it. In this way we will do away with the tediously overused words optimism and pessimism (HAH 28). In this search for philosophical sobriety, Epicurus comes to play an important role in Nietzsche's thinking, and evident in volume two of HAH: in an era of moralism and fanaticism, the teachings of the soul-soother of later antiquity remain for Nietzsche as relevant as ever.

Philosophy in *Mixed Opinions and Maxims* and *The Wanderer and His Shadow*

Before I look at the figuration of Epicurus in volume two of HAH, let me highlight some interesting aspects of Nietzsche's conception of philosophy in this second volume.

Nietzsche continues to position himself in opposition to 'the fogs of a metaphysical-mystical philosophy' (MOM 28). He also rejects the 'gleaming mirage' of a philosophical system (MOM 31). However, he is now in search of a *blending together* of knowledge and wisdom (MOM 180), as well as a philosophy of spiritual health (MOM 356). He is convinced that the walls that separate nature and spirit, human and animal, ethics and physics are breaking down (MOM 185), and this offers prospects for a novel synthesis of philosophy and science, or knowledge and wisdom. He holds up Epictetus as a teacher of wisdom in which wisdom 'is the whispering of the solitary with himself in the crowded marketplace' (MOM 386). Perhaps most surprising of all is the recognition Nietzsche accords Socrates as a philosophical exemplar of first-rate importance: against priests and idealists of every kind he teaches a care of self and does not unduly concern himself with human beings in the abstract and with an equally abstract conception of science (WS 6). Indeed, Nietzsche looks forward to a time when humanity will advance morally and rationally by taking in its hands the memorabilia of Socrates rather than the Bible, 'and when Montaigne and Horace will be utilized as the forerunners and signposts for understanding the simplest and most imperishable mediator-sage' (WS 86). All the roads of the most varied ways of living philosophically lead back to Socrates and in these different ways we can identify the most important task of a life: to rejoice in life and also rejoice in one's own self. Nietzsche goes so far to esteem Socrates over Christ because he is cheerful in his seriousness and his wisdom is of a playful kind: this, he says, 'constitutes the best spiritual condition for humans' (WS 86).[29]

It is with the aid of such teachings derived from Socrates and the antique schools that Nietzsche will endeavour to refashion the tasks of morality. He writes, for example, of transforming the passions of humanity into 'delights' (WS 37), of a morality of continual self-mastery and self-overcoming in both large and the smallest of things (WS 45), of an ethics of moderation based on the individual virtues such as justice and peace of mind (WS 212). In all of this the task is to become 'spiritually joyful, bright, and sincere' (WS 88). More than this free spirits are willing to '*look directly at* the great task of *preparing* the earth for a growth in the greatest and happiest fertility' (WS 189). If we call upon the thinker for assistance, we do so not simply as an educator but rather 'as someone self-educated', one who has experience (WS 267). Nietzsche reserves his strongest criticism for Plato with his simple-minded understanding of ethical realities and his deficient understanding of human beings. Plato is said to lack a history of moral sensations, adequate insights into the origin of the good and useful qualities of the human soul (WS 285).

Nietzsche and Epicurus

Nietzsche is inspired in his middle writings by the Epicurean garden practice of philosophy. We know he had plans to create his own garden in the style of Epicurus and it deeply influences his conception of philosophical practice.[30] If, as Pierre Hadot has suggested, philosophical therapeutics is centred on a concern with the healing of our own lives so as to return us to the joy of existing,[31] then in the texts of his middle period Nietzsche can be seen to be an heir to this ancient tradition. If there is one crucial component to Nietzsche's philosophical therapeutics in the texts of his middle period that he keeps returning to again and again, it is the need for spiritual joyfulness and the task of cultivating in ourselves, after centuries of training by morality and religion, the joy in existing. In the final aphorism of *The Wanderer and His Shadow*, he writes, for example:

> Only the *ennobled human being may be given freedom of spirit;* to him alone does *alleviation of life* draw near and salve his wounds; only he may say that he lives for the sake of *joy* (*Freudigkeit*) and for the sake of no further goal. (WS 350)

Epicurus famously writes that the arguments of a philosopher that do not touch on the therapeutic treatment of human suffering are empty. The analogy is made with the art of medicine: just as the use of this art is to cast out sicknesses of the body, so the use of philosophy is to throw out suffering from the soul. It is in the texts of his middle period that Nietzsche's writing comes closest to being an exercise in philosophical therapeutics. It endeavours to revitalize for a modern age ancient philosophical concerns, notably a teaching for mortal souls who wish to be liberated from the fear and anguish of existence, as well as from God, the 'metaphysical need',[32] and are able to affirm their mortal conditions of existence. As a general point of inspiration one might adopt Hadot's insight into the therapeutic ambitions of ancient philosophy that was, he claims, 'intended to cure mankind's anguish' (for example, anguish over our mortality).[33] This is evident in the teaching of Epicurus which sought to demonstrate the mortality of the soul and whose aim was, 'to free humans from "the fears of the mind"'.[34] Similarly, Nietzsche's teaching in *Dawn* is for mortal souls (D 501). In the middle period, then, Epicurus is an attractive figure for Nietzsche because of the emphasis on a modest lifestyle and the attention given to the care of self. Nietzsche wants free spirits to take pleasure in existence, involving taking pleasure in themselves and in friendship. The difference from Epicurus is that he is developing a therapy for the sicknesses of the soul under modern conditions of social control and discipline. *Dawn* 174 makes this clear when, in response to what he sees as the tyrannical encroachments of sympathetic morality within commercial society, Nietzsche writes of cultivating a self that others can behold with pleasure within a self-enclosed garden and that also provides a gate of hospitality (D 174).

Nietzsche claimed to have understood the character of Epicurus differently from everybody else (GS 45). However, he was not alone in the nineteenth century in employing the name of Epicurus to signal the need for a reformation of philosophy in accordance with Epicurean principles of living. For Marx, writing in the 1840s, and in defiance of Hegel's negative assessment, Epicurus is the 'greatest representative of the Greek enlightenment',[35] while for Jean-Marie Guyau, writing in the 1870s, Epicurus is the original free spirit. 'Still today it is the spirit of old Epicurus who, combined with new doctrines, works away at and undermines Christianity.'[36] Like these other nineteenth-century interpreters, Nietzsche is acutely aware that Epicurean doctrine has been greatly maligned and misunderstood in the history of thought. One commentator on Epicurus's philosophy speaks of the 'slanders and fallacies of a long and unfriendly tradition' and invites us to reflect on Epicurus as at one and the same time the most revered and most reviled of all founders of philosophy in the Greco-Roman world.[37] Since the time of the negative assessment by Cicero and the early Church Fathers, 'Epicureanism has been used as a smear word – a rather general label indicating atheism, selfishness, and debauchery.'[38] As Nietzsche observes in *The Wanderer and His Shadow:*

> Epicurus has been alive in all ages and lives now, unknown to those who have called and call themselves Epicureans, and enjoying no reputation among philosophers. He has, moreover, himself forgotten his own name: it was the heaviest burden he ever cast off. (WS 227)

Epicurus assumes a prominent role as a philosophical figure in the second volume of HAH. Two aphorisms from MOM reveal the importance Epicurus holds for Nietzsche in his middle period. In the first Nietzsche confesses to having dwelt like Odysseus in the underworld and says that he will often be found there again. As someone who sacrifices so as to talk to the dead, he states that there are four pairs of thinkers from whom he will accept judgement, and Epicurus and Montaigne make up the first pair he mentions (MOM 408).[39] In the second aphorism Epicurus, along with the Stoic Epictetus, is revered as a thinker in whom wisdom assumes bodily (*leibhaft*) form (MOM 224). The point is perhaps obvious: philosophy is not simply sophistry or *paideia* but an incorporated practice that enables the individual to negotiate and affirm the most demanding and challenging questions of existence, including, notably, such tests of the self as the fact of our mortality and the question of how to live. An ethos of Epicurean enlightenment pervades Nietzsche's middle-period texts with Epicurus celebrated for his teachings on mortality and the cultivation of modest pleasures. Although Epicurus is first and foremost an ethical teacher, he also embodies Nietzsche's ideal of the philosopher: he is sober, rational and cool, and his teaching serves to make us 'colder and more sceptical' (HAH 244).

The teaching of Epicurus is centred on the study of nature, and this is its first and most fundamental principle. But Epicurus does not restrict himself to being a philosopher-scientist simply producing a doctrine of physics. Rather, he wishes to be a teacher, and to this end he produces a summary of his system so as 'to facilitate the firm memorization of the most general doctrines, in order that at each and every opportunity [his readers] may be able to help themselves on the most important issues, to the degree that they retain their grasp on the study of nature'. [40] According to one commentator, Epicurean arguments, 'have a clear therapeutic intent: by removing false beliefs concerning the universe and the ways in which the gods might be involved in its workings, they eliminate a major source of mental trouble and lead us towards a correct and beneficial conception of these matters'.[41] Moreover, as Foucault shows, Epicurus has an 'ethopoetic' appreciation of knowledge, which is a mode of knowledge that provides an *ethos*. In the Epicurean texts knowledge of nature is called *phusiologia*, which is a 'modality of knowledge (*savoir*) of nature insofar as it is philosophically relevant for the practice of the self' (see Epicurus, *Vatican Sayings* 45).[42] Epicurus opposes knowledge as *paideia*, which is a cultural learning that aims at glory and is little more than a kind of boastful knowledge. Foucault notes that Epicurus rejects this mode of knowledge as a culture of boasters, one mainly developed by concocters of words that seek admiration from the masses. The knowledge Epicurus promotes is one that prepares the self for the events of a life. Foucault explains:

> What does *phusiologia* do instead of producing people who are only pompous and inconsistent boasters? It *paraskeue*, that is to say it prepares ... *Paraskeue* is the equipping, the preparation of the subject and the soul so that they will be properly, necessarily, and sufficiently armed for whatever circumstance of life may arise. ... It is the exact opposite of *paideia*.[43]

The knowledge that is *phusiologia* serves to provide the individual with boldness and courage, what Foucault calls a kind of intrepidity, a preparedness that enables the individual to stand firm not only against the (many) beliefs that others seek to impose on him, but also against the hazards of life and the authority of those who wish to lay down the law: 'absence of fear, a sort of recalcitrance and spiritedness if you like: this is what *phusiologia* gives to the individuals who learn it'.[44] This means that, strictly speaking, *phusiologia* is not a branch of knowledge (*savoir*), but rather a knowledge (*connaissance*) of nature, of *phusis*, to the extent that this knowledge serves as a principle of human conduct and as the criterion for setting individuals free.[45] The aim of this knowledge of nature is to transform the subject, one that is originally filled with fear and terror before nature to one that is a free subject able to find within itself, 'the possibility and means of his permanent and perfectly tranquil delight'.[46]

For Epicurus, then, the mind has a tendency to live in fear of nature, to be overly and unduly anxious about existence and is easily led astray by religious teachings that tempt the person to embrace metaphysical-moral doctrines, that is, doctrines that fail to appreciate that there is a natural causal order and that we, as human beings, are fully implicated in it. On Epicurean teaching the natural world is an order of things devoid of design, agency, intention and revelatory signs. For Epicurus, what is needed for the popularization of philosophy are 'simple principles and maxims', ones that can aid the mind to readily assimilate, when occasions necessitate, the core doctrines derived from the study of nature: 'It is not possible', he writes, 'to know the concentrated result of our continuous overview of the universe unless one can have in oneself a comprehensive grasp by means of brief maxims of all that might also be worked out in detail with precision'.[47] Epicurus states clearly the aim of the exercise: it is to bring calm to one's life, in which one has a mind that is all too quickly agitated by our being in the world and by the things that afflict us. We need, then, to observe things in accordance with our sense perceptions and in accordance with our actual feelings, and 'so that we can have some sign by which we make inferences both about what awaits confirmation and about the non-evident'.[48]

From these basic philosophical principles Epicurus builds up a philosophy of nature that is highly novel and far-reaching, anticipating much modern scientific thought, as well as ecological thought.[49] For example, he wants us to appreciate the following key insights and to then adopt them as part of a practice of wisdom: (1) first, nothing comes into being from what is not for if it did 'everything would come into being from everything, with no need of seeds'; (2) second, when something disappears it is not destroyed into nothing since if it was all things would have been destroyed, 'since that into which they were dissolved does not exist'; (3) third, the totality of what exists has always been just like it is now at present and like it will always be simply because there is nothing else than what there is, that is, nothing for it to change into: 'There exists nothing in addition to the totality, which could enter into it and produce the change'.[50] The 'totality' of which he speaks is made up of bodies and void. Our sense perception, he argues, testifies to the former, and it is through sense perception that we infer by reasoning what is not evident, namely, the void: if this did not exist (space and intangible nature), then bodies would be devoid of a place to be in and to move through, and it is obvious that they do move. The principles of bodies are atomic in nature, and here we refer to the composition of bodies, in which some exist as compounds and some as things from which the compounds are made. The elements out of which things are made are 'atomic and unchangeable' in that they are not destroyed into non-being but remain 'firmly during the dissolution of compounds, being full by nature and not being subject to dissolution in any way or fashion'.[51]

Even when he is outlining the details of his physics, as in the letters to Herodotus and Pythocles, Epicurus never tires of drawing attention to the blessedness that comes from knowledge, by which he means knowledge of nature, including meteorological phenomena. The task is to strip the workings of the natural world of the activity of the gods and to free it of agency and teleology. This is an aspect of the teaching that impresses itself upon Nietzsche as when he calls for the de-deification of nature and the naturalization of humanity (GS 109), as well as, on a more practical and mundane level, the need to avoid the danger of 'spiritual unfreedom' in the face of the 'beautiful chaos of existence': this takes place when we allow in through the back door, and in our interpretation of the things that happen to us in a life, providential design and goodness. In interpreting the fortunes that strike one in life, and bestowing a significance on them, the danger is that we will allow back into our lives the intentions or designs of the gods, be it some kind of petty deity who has our best interests at heart or even, says Nietzsche, the gods of Epicurus (the ones that are most indifferent to our existence). The solution Nietzsche proposes to our predicament is in accordance with the teaching of Epicurus: to leave the gods in peace and 'rest content with the supposition that our own practical and theoretical skill in interpreting and arranging events has now reached a high point' (GS 277). In addition, we can acknowledge that good old chance sometimes plays with us: 'Now and then chance guides our hand, and the wisest providence could not think up a more beautiful music than that which our foolish hand produces then' (ibid.).

In the Epicurean teaching natural phenomena admit of a plurality of explanations, but in spite of this plurality – say with respect to explaining lightning, thunder, the formation of clouds, the waning and waxing of the moon, the variations of the length of nights and days and so on – the task is to ascertain natural causes, and in this respect knowledge of celestial phenomena has no other end 'than peace of mind and firm conviction' (see letter to Pythocles). Epicurus states clearly and emphatically:

> For in the study of nature we must not conform to empty assumptions and arbitrary laws, but follow the promptings of the facts; for our life has no need now of unreason and false opinion; our one need is untroubled existence.[52]

The enjoyment of life assumes a distinctive character in Epicurus. In the letter to Menoeceus, Epicurus seeks to identify what the study of philosophy can do for the health of the soul and on the premise that, 'Pleasure is the starting-point and goal of living blessedly.'[53] Epicurus stresses that he does not mean the pleasures of the profligate or of consumption; rather, the task is to become accustomed to simple, non-extravagant ways of living. Although Epicurus regards *voluptas* as the highest good, in which we can take delight in all that nature has provided to stimulate pleasure, it is an error to suppose that for him happiness is to be found 'simply in eating, drinking, gambling, wenching, and other such pastimes'.[54] Nietzsche seems to have fully appreciated this point. The key goal for Epicurus is to liberate the body from pain and remove disturbances from the soul. Central to his counsel is the thought that we need to accustom ourselves to believing that death is nothing to us; our longing for immortality needs to be removed: 'There is nothing fearful in life for one who has grasped that there is nothing fearful in the absence of life.'[55] What appears to be the most frightening of bad things should be nothing to us, 'Since when we exist, death is not yet present, and when death is present, then we do not exist.'[56] The wise human being 'neither rejects life nor fears death. For living does not offend him, nor does he believe not living to be something bad.'[57] If, as Epicurus supposes, everything good and bad consists in sense-experience, then death is simply the privation of sense-experience. The goal of philosophical training, then, is freedom from disturbance and anxiety in which we reach a state of psychic tranquillity (*ataraxia*): the body is free from pain and the soul is liberated from distress. Several commentators note that the Greek word *hedone* could just as well be translated as delight or joy, denoting the sweetness of life and not simple-minded sensualist gratification.[58]

As I have noted, it is in the second volume of HAH that important references to, and portraits of, Epicurus are to be found. For Nietzsche, Epicurus's teaching can show us how to quieten our being and so help to temper a human mind that is prone to neurosis. Nietzsche is attracted to the Epicurean emphasis on the modesty of a particular type of human existence. He admires Epicurus for cultivating a modest existence and in two respects: first, in having 'spiritual-emotional joyfulness (*Freudigkeit*) in place of frequent individual pleasures', as well as 'equilibrium of all movements and pleasure in this harmony in place of excitement and intoxication' (HAH II, p. 400; see also KSA 8, 41 [48]), and, second, in withdrawing from social ambition and living in a garden as opposed to living publicly in the marketplace.[59] As Nietzsche stresses, 'A tiny garden, figs, a bit of cheese, and three or four friends besides – this was luxuriance for Epicurus' (WS 192).[60] Nietzsche is appreciative of what one commentator has called the 'refined asceticism' we find in Epicurus, which consists in the enjoyment of the smallest pleasures and the disposal of a diverse and delicate range of sensations.[61]

We can note something of the character of Nietzsche's particular appreciation of Epicurus: it is not Epicurus the atomist that he focuses attention on, but Epicurus the ethicist, that is, the philosopher who teaches a new way of life by remaining true to the earth, embracing the fact of human mortality and denying any cosmic exceptionalism on the part of the human. In WS Nietzsche describes Epicurus as 'the soul-soother (*Seelen-Beschwichtiger*) of later antiquity' who had the wonderful insight that to quieten our being it is not necessary to have resolved the ultimate and outermost theoretical questions (WS 7). To those who are tormented by the fear of the gods, for example, one may point out that if the gods exist they do not concern themselves with us and that it is unnecessary to engage in 'fruitless disputation' over the ultimate question as to whether they exist or not. Furthermore, in response to the consideration of a given hypothesis, half belonging to physics and half to ethics, and that may cast gloom over our spirits, it is wise to refrain from refuting the hypothesis; instead one may offer a rival hypothesis, even a multiplicity of hypotheses. To someone who wishes to offer consolation – for example, to the unfortunate, to ill-doers, to hypochondriacs and so on – one can call to mind two pacifying formulae of Epicurus that are capable of being applied to many questions: 'Firstly, if that is how things are they do not concern us; secondly, things may be thus but they may also be otherwise' (WS 7).

In interpreting Epicureanism as a science that tempers emotional and mental excess, Nietzsche is, in fact, following a well-established tradition in nineteenth-century thought that appreciates this point. As Friedrich Albert Lange notes in his *History of Materialism* (1866), a text that deeply impressed the young Nietzsche: 'The mere historical knowledge of natural events, without a knowledge of causes, is valueless; for it does not free us from fear nor lift us upon superstition. The more causes of change we have discovered, the more we shall attain the calmness of contemplation; and it cannot be supposed that this inquiry can be without result upon our happiness.'[62] If we can come to regard change in things as necessarily inherent in their existence, we free ourselves from our natural terror at this order of change and evolution. If we believe in the old myths, we live in fear of the eternal torments to come; if we are too sensible to believe in these torments, we may still apprehend the loss of all feeling which comes with death as an evil, as if the soul could continue to feel this deprivation. As every student of philosophy knows, the event of death for Epicurus is an affair of indifference precisely because it deprives us of all feeling. As Lange glosses Epicurus: 'So long as we are, there is as yet no death; but as soon as death comes, then we exist no more.'[63] If events can be explained in accordance with universal laws, with effects attributable to natural causes, an important goal of philosophy can be attained and secured, chiefly liberation from fear and anxiety.

Nietzsche finds in Epicurus a victory over pessimism in which death becomes the last celebration of a life that is constantly embellished.[64] This last of the Greek philosophers teaches the joy of living in the midst of a world in decay and where all moral doctrines preach suffering. As Richard Roos puts it, 'The example of Epicurus teaches that a life filled with pain and renunciation prepares one to savour the little joys of the everyday better. Relinquishing Dionysian intoxication, Nietzsche becomes a student of this master of moderate pleasures and careful dosages.'[65] In Epicurus Nietzsche discovers what Roos calls aptly an 'irresistible power' and a rare strength of spirit, and quotes Nietzsche from 1880: 'I found strength in the very places one does not look for it, in simple, gentle and helpful men. … Powerful natures dominate, that is a necessity, even if those men do not move one finger. And they bury themselves, in their lifetime, in a pavilion in their garden' (KSA 9, 6 [206]).[66]

The Epicureanism we can find in Nietzsche in his middle writings indicates his preference for individual therapy and self-cultivation over large-scale social transformation and political revolution. For Nietzsche the garden of Epicurus does not represent, as might be supposed, a retreat from existence. Rather, it is for him a place where one can find the time necessary to undertake the labours of the free spirit. The Epicurean attachment of life entails a specific mode of being in the world, a new attunement to nature as a source of pleasure, removing oneself from the false infinite and stripping away various disabling phantasms such as the idea of immortality with its regime of infinite pleasures and eternal punishments. There remains a strong and firm desire for life but, as Nietzsche points out, this voluptuous appreciation and enjoyment of life is of a modest kind (see especially GS 45): it is modest in terms of the kinds of pleasure it wants from existence and cultivates, and in terms of its acknowledgement of the realities of a human existence. This is a happiness that Nietzsche appreciates and admires, seeing it as the essential component of the heroic-idyllic mode of philosophizing in which the mind's illusions about the world are stripped away and one is left with a way of being in the world that brings true pleasure since the mind has been liberated from the terrors, superstitions and phantoms that disturb it. This, then, is a philosophy as a project of demystification, with the human being living a modest life. This Epicurean way of life and of being the world is based on a free-spirited search for knowledge, and this might be the reason why even the late Nietzsche, who is critical of Epicurus, can continue to write of an Epicurean 'bent for knowledge' that does not easily let go of the questionable character of things (GS 375).

Conclusion

Epicureanism is but one component guiding his middle-period search for philosophical sobriety and serenity. I do not wish to unduly overstate its importance, and I do not deny that there are other important intellectual resources informing his quest for free-minded modes of inquiry, such as he finds in the examples of figures like Montaigne and Voltaire.[67] It might be asked: Is not Epicureanism a non-political philosophy that advocates withdrawal from the world and from humankind so as to foster personal serenity in the comfort of one's garden? In fact, Nietzsche attacks the idea, which he associates with the interest in Montaigne, that the task of philosophy is to achieve personal serenity (UO IV: 10). His preference is for slow and diligent intellectual work, involving a careful working through of problems that are both individual and social, and he envisages transformations taking place over a long *durée*. Nietzsche embraces the need for experimentation with respect to both individual and social levels of existence: only in this way can we develop genuine knowledge about who we are, what we may become and what we might be capable of. We have to be able to put to the test our aspirations and ideas. For the greater part of its history the human being has lived in a condition of fear and as a herd-conforming animal. Nietzsche's philosophy of the morning looks ahead to a new dawn in human existence in which individuals will have conquered this fear and cultivate their lives in a way that is conducive to themselves and beneficent to others. Nietzsche is not, I think, recommending self-withdrawal and isolation as the ultimate cure to one's predicament; rather, these are means or steps on the way to working on oneself so that one can become genuinely beneficent towards others. Nietzsche is committed to an ethics of self-cultivation, in which one endeavours to fashion out of oneself something the other can behold with pleasure, 'a peaceful, self-enclosed garden … with high walls to protect against the dangers and dust of the roadway, but with a hospitable gate as well' (D 174).

In conclusion to this chapter let me pose the following question: How representative are Nietzsche's middle-period Epicurean commitments of his stance towards politics and the need for social transformation as a whole? Horst Hutter has argued that Nietzsche's ultimate goal is the shaping of the future of European humanity and society, and on this conception of his philosophy the retreat into an Epicurean-inspired community of friends is merely a temporary expedient in which free spirits work on themselves so as to become philosophical legislators of a future culture. He writes: 'Such fraternities of free spirits would be necessary to traverse the period of nihilism until a future point in time, when direct political action would again become possible.'[68] One thinks in this regard of what Nietzsche says in *The Wanderer and His Shadow*:

> We withdraw into concealment: but not out of any kind of personal ill-humour, as though the political and social situation of the present day were not good

enough for us, but because through our withdrawal we want to economize and assemble forces of which culture will *later* have great need, and more so if this present remains *this* present and as such fulfils *its* task. We are accumulating capital and seeking to make it secure: but, as in times of great peril, to do that we have to *bury* it. (WS 229)

Nietzsche on Enlightenment and Fanaticism

Introduction

The topic of fanaticism has been almost wholly neglected in the literature on Nietzsche and yet it is crucial to understanding the intellectual stance of the middle writings.[1] Focusing on the problem of fanaticism in Nietzsche can do two things: first, it can illuminate the nature of his attack on morality and its immodest claims; and, second, it can shed light on the specific mode of philosophizing that Nietzsche is keen to unfold and stage in his middle writings. Nietzsche has a definite project in these texts that centres on cooling down a human mind prone to neurosis, and he appeals to various philosophical sources to mount a programme of mental reform from the ancient likes of Epicurus (WS 7 & 295) and Epictetus (D 131 & 546) to modern figures such as Voltaire (HAH 221). In this chapter I seek to illuminate Nietzsche's stance on fanaticism, which, I endeavour to show, is best seen in the context of his reception of the Enlightenment and his search for a new enlightenment.[2] It is often said that Nietzsche is a thinker with a revolutionary agenda. It is important to appreciate, however, that he is decidedly anti-revolution, which he associates with the cultivation of fanaticism. What he prizes is what he finds in Voltaire: the highest freedom of spirit with an absolutely unrevolutionary disposition (HAH 221).

Nietzsche and the enlightenment

As one commentator has noted, in the eyes of many of his adherents as well as opponents, Nietzsche is an anti-Enlightenment irrationalist.[3] In his well-known construction of the philosophical discourse of modernity, Jürgen Habermas depicts Nietzsche as the modern enemy of reason par excellence.[4] One of the reasons why a study of the middle-period Nietzsche is important, and proves so fruitful, is that it can show this viewpoint to be a caricature, if not an outright distortion. Nietzsche is hostile to the French Revolution, but seeks in his writings to sever the link between enlightenment and revolution because he suspects that revolution breeds fanaticism and is a throwback to a lower stage of culture. As Nicholas Martin notes, Nietzsche takes the Enlightenment very seriously and as a cultural critic of the late nineteenth century he cannot afford to escape its legacy.[5] He is an admirer of the critical and rationalist spirit of the Enlightenment, of both the eighteenth-century version, as we find it in the likes of Voltaire and Lessing, and earlier incarnations, such as we find it in the likes of Epicurus, Petrarch and Erasmus. Nietzsche shares many of the ideas and commitments of the modern Enlightenment, including the attack on superstition, religious dogmatism, rigid class structures, outmoded forms of governance and rule, and so on. Its fundamental spirit is one of demystification, of liberation of the human from its chains (see WS 350), seeking 'to provide the individual with the critical tools to achieve autonomy, to liberate himself from his own unexamined assumptions as well as the dictates of others'.[6] Nietzsche is an enlightenment thinker, then, in this critical sense: his overriding aim is to foster autonomy and maturity in his readers. In this respect Nietzsche is an inheritor of Kant, as he acknowledges in *Dawn*.[7] In fact, he presents himself as being even more faithful to the rational spirit of enlightenment than Kant was with his incomprehensible residues, such as the thing in itself and the categorical imperative (D 207).

Nietzsche is keen to expose what he takes to be a delusion in the theory or doctrine of revolution. The error, he contends, belongs to Rousseau, namely, that buried within the accrued habits and vices of civilization there lays concealed an original or primordial but stifled human goodness:

> There are political and social visionaries who ardently and eloquently demand the overthrow of all social order in the belief that the most splendid temple of a beautified humanity would immediately be raised, as if by itself. In these dangerous dreams, we can still hear an echo of Rousseau's superstition. (HAH 463)

On the Rousseauian-inspired picture, as Nietzsche conceives it, not only is there a stifled human goodness buried underneath the weight of civilization, but the blame for such stifling is to be levelled squarely at the institutions of culture, such as embodied in state, society and education. However, Nietzsche holds that historical experience teaches us an important lesson, namely, that revolutions bring with them, 'a new resurrection of the most savage energies in the form of the long-buried horrors and excesses of the most distant ages'

(HAH 463). He does not deny that revolutions can be a source of vital energy for a humanity that has grown feeble, but he contests the idea that it can work as an organizer and perfecter of human nature. He thus appeals to Voltaire over Rousseau, that is, in his eyes to a nature that knows how to organize, purify and reconstruct, as opposed to a nature that is full of passionate follies and half-lies. Against the optimism of the spirit of revolution, Nietzsche wishes to cry with Voltaire, "*Écrasez l'infâme!*" It is the spirit of revolution that frightens off the spirit of enlightenment and 'of *progressive development*' – and it is this spirit of enlightenment that Nietzsche calls upon his readers to cultivate and nurture.[8] '*Écrasez l'infâme!*' is, of course, Voltaire's rallying cry against fanaticism, and as the motto of the French Enlightenment, it stands for 'the rejection of authority and obscurantism, the ground clearing sparked by the intellectual audacity that is the mark of the *Siècle des lumières*, the *Sapere aude*'.[9] It is precisely obscurantism that Nietzsche pits his philosophical wits against in the middle writings.

Nietzsche locates in the French Revolution's histrionicism, a 'bestial cruelty', as well as a 'sentimentality' and 'self-intoxication', and holds Rousseau responsible for being its intellectual inspiration and for setting the Enlightenment on 'its fanatical head'. He sees the Enlightenment as being, in fact, alien to the Revolution, which if it had been left to itself would have 'passed through the clouds as quietly along like as a gleam of light, satisfied for a long time simply with transforming individuals: so that it would only very slowly have transformed the customs and institutions of people as well' (WS 221). The task, he says, is to continue the work of the Enlightenment, in each and every individual, but also 'to strangle the Revolution at birth' and ensure it does not happen. In *Dawn* Nietzsche argues contra Rousseau that it is our 'weak, unmanly' societal notions of good and evil, and the way they dominate over body and soul today, that are making all bodies and souls weak, shattering the 'pillars of a *strong* civilization', which for Nietzsche can reside only in unfettered individuals who are self-reliant and independent (D 163).

The extent to which Nietzsche is an astute or serious reader of Rousseau is debatable. He ignores the role played by Rousseau in the struggle against intolerance and fanaticism, evident in the fact that Voltaire reprinted excerpts from Rousseau's writings in the collected volumes he published as part of his campaign against these phenomena.[10] As Nicholas Martin notes, Nietzsche's critical perspectives on intellectual figures such as Rousseau are more palatable if one sees his use of proper names as signifying psychological states and ideological positions rather than historical individuals.[11] What is clear is that

Nietzsche strongly allies himself with progressive forces but insists that social transformation, which is desirable, ought to be pursued gradually and patiently: there is no miraculous solution to human ills. Moreover, though, in his middle writings Nietzsche wishes humanity to go beyond religion altogether – see especially *Dawn* 96[12] – and so he necessarily positions Rousseau as an anti-Enlightenment enemy. For Rousseau fanaticism has its uses and philosophy its abuses. This is a position he makes clear in a long footnote in book four of *Emile*. Here he notes that while he agrees with Pierre Bayle that fanaticism is more pernicious then atheism, and acknowledges its cruel character, it is nevertheless 'a grand and strong passion which elevates the heart of man, making him despise death, and gives him a prodigious energy that need only be better directed to produce the most sublime virtues'.[13] Rousseau writes in praise of religion against philosophy, and as Hume noted, the *philosophes* rejected Rousseau because he was seen to 'overbound' in religion.[14]

Nietzsche positions himself against morality and religion, as Rousseau construes them, in his middle writings, especially *Dawn*. In particular, he is suspicious of morality's exalted language and the claim that morality puts us in contact with the sublime. Against such claims Nietzsche appeals to a philosophy of modesty and to the need for more modest words (see D Preface), and he even makes an appeal to a more modest conception of the sublime (D 449). Furthermore, against the tyrannical encroachments of modern morality, with its cult of the sympathetic affects, especially compassion and pity, he favours the cultivation of peaceful, self-enclosed gardens that feature gates of hospitality (D 174).

I want to now focus attention on a particular aphorism in *Dawn* so as to illuminate further Nietzsche's construal of his relation to enlightenment thinking. The aphorism is entitled 'The German's hostility to the Enlightenment'. In it Nietzsche wishes to take note of the intellectual contribution that Germany, including German philosophers, has made to culture at large. He sees German philosophy of the first half of the nineteenth century as a retrogressive force: 'They retreated to the first and oldest level of speculation, for, like the thinkers of dreamy ages, they found satisfaction in concepts rather than in explanations – they resuscitated a pre-scientific type of philosophy' (D 197). Nietzsche sees similar retarding forces operating in German history and German science. In the former a general concern was to accord honour upon primitive sensibilities, especially Christianity, but also folklore and folk language, oriental asceticism and the world of India.[15] In natural science German scientists have struggled against the spirit of Newton and Voltaire and, following Goethe and Schopenhauer, 'sought to erect once again the idea of a divine or a daemonic nature suffused with ethical (*ethischen*) and symbolic significance' (ibid.). Thus, Nietzsche infers, the proclivity of the Germans runs contrary to the Enlightenment as well as contrary to the revolution in society. The German spirit is antiquarian: 'Piety towards everything then in existence sought to metamorphose into piety towards everything that once had existed in order that heart and spirit might once again grow *full* and no longer have any room for future, innovative goals' (ibid.). German culture has erected a cult of feeling at the expense of a cult of reason with German composers – Nietzsche surely has in mind Wagner among others – being artists of the invisible, of raptures and of the fairy tale. Nietzsche objects to this cultural development, it is important to note, for one main reason: it serves to retard knowledge as in Kant's famous words to the second edition of the *Critique of Pure Reason* (1787) that he has found it necessary to deny knowledge in order to make room for faith and thus to draw up the limits of knowledge. Nietzsche makes it clear that he champions genuine enlightenment against all the forces of obscurantism (see also MOM 27):

> And strange to say: the very spirits that the Germans had so eloquently invoked became, in the long run, the most injurious for their invokers – history, understanding of origin and evolution, sympathy with the past, the newly aroused passion for feeling and knowledge, after having for a time appeared to be beneficial companions of the spirit of rapturous obscurantism and reaction, assumed one day by a different nature and now fly on the widest wings above and beyond their earlier invokers as new and stronger geniuses of *that very Enlightenment* against which they had been invoked. This Enlightenment we must now carry on – unperturbed that there has a existed a 'great Revolution' and then again a 'great reaction' against it, that indeed both still exist: they are, after all, the mere ripple of waves in comparison to the truly great tide in which *we* surge and want to surge! (D 197)

As Mazzino Montinari notes, a note from the spring of 1881 – that is, just prior to the publication of *Dawn* – provides additional clues for deciphering *Dawn* 197.[16] In it Nietzsche portrays the nineteenth century as one of reaction in which a conservative and preservative frame of mind predominates. The note runs as follows:

> 19th century, Reaction: people sought the *basic principles* of everything that had *lasted*, and sought to prove it was *true*. Permanence, fruitfulness and good conscience were seen as indices of truth! This was the conservative mentality:

they called everything that had not yet been shaken; they had the egoism of the possessors as their strongest objection to the philosophy of the 18th century: for the non-possessors and malcontents there was *still* the church and even the arts (for some highly talented individuals there was also the worship of genius by way of gratitude if they worked for the conservative interests). With *history* (*Geschichte*) (new!!!) people *proved* things, they became *enthusiastic* for the great fruitful complexes called cultures (*nations*!!!). A huge part of the *zeal for research* and of the *sense of worship* was thrown at the past: modern philosophy and natural science *forfeited* this part! – Now a **backlash**! History (*Historie*) *ultimately* proved something other than what was wanted: it turned out to be the most certain means of destroying those principles. Darwin. On the other hand sceptical historicism as aftereffect, empathy. People became *better* acquainted with the *motivating* forces in history (*Geschichte*), not our 'beautiful' ideas! Socialism has a *historical* foundation, similarly national wars for historical reasons! (KSA 9, 10 [D88])[17]

For Nietzsche, then, it is history that serves as the means of destroying the conservative principle, and this history includes Darwin's theory of evolution. What we need to learn and take cognisance of are the real forces operating in history and not our beautiful ideas. Everything that comes into existence – for example socialism – plants its own foundations in history. As Nietzsche presents it in *Dawn* 197, the basic idea is that the enlightenment project we are to further is to make its claim, 'not *against* but rather beyond a great revolution (socialism) and a great reaction, *beyond* the conservative frame of mind.'[18] It is thus an error in Nietzsche's account of the story to conceive the Enlightenment as the cause of the Revolution, a misunderstanding that is the 'reaction' itself and it would be equally an error to conceive the continuing enlightenment as the cause of socialism. As Montinari notes, the new great reaction in the form of the conservative mentality consists in this error. As he further notes, from 1878 onwards, Nietzsche considers a new enlightenment as the noble task for the free spirit of his own times. There have been to date two great historical periods in which an enlightenment has sought to flourish but has been halted by a paired revolution and reaction: first, the enlightenment of Italian and European humanism, or the Renaissance (Petrarch and Erasmus), but followed by the German Reformation and the Counter-Reformation; the Enlightenment of France, notably Voltaire, with the French Revolution and German romanticism as the corresponding revolution and reaction. In progress now is a third enlightenment, conceived by Nietzsche as a new enlightenment and which contrasts itself to both the great revolution and great reaction of modern times, socialism and conservatism (see HAH 26).[19] Nietzsche notes in HAH 26, entitled 'Reaction as progress', that in the previous two enlightenments the new free-spirited tendencies were not powerful enough to withstand the appearance of impassioned but backward spirits who conjured up once again a bygone phase of humanity. This is the case with Luther's Reformation in which 'all stirrings of the freedom of spirit were still uncertain, delicate, youthful' and 'science could not yet raise its head'. It is the case in the nineteenth century where Schopenhauer's metaphysics showed 'that even now the scientific spirit is not yet strong enough': in spite of the achieved destruction of Christian dogmas in Schopenhauer's doctrine, the whole medieval Christian world view once again celebrated its resurrection. Although there is in Schopenhauer 'a strong ring of science', this does not master his thinking; rather, it is the metaphysical need that does. But even in this reaction there is progress to be had thinks Nietzsche:

> It is surely one of the greatest and inestimable advantages we gain from Schopenhauer that he sometimes forces our sensations back into older, powerful ways of viewing the world and people to which no path would otherwise so easily lead us. The gain for history and justice is very great: I believe that without Schopenhauer's assistance, nobody now could easily manage to do justice to Christianity and its Asiatic relatives: to do so on the basis of present-day Christianity is impossible. Only after this great *success of justice*, only after we have corrected in so essential a point the way of viewing history that the Age of Enlightenment brought with it, can we once more bear the flag of the Enlightenment farther. (HAH 26)

As Martin notes, Nietzsche wants an 'enlightenment of the Enlightenment'.[20] Nietzsche sees the task as a never-ending critical process; the problem with revolutions is that they often aim at the achievement of an imagined end, and this longing for finality and resolution is ultimately seen by Nietzsche as a symptom and defining characteristic of nihilism.[21] What is clear is that Nietzsche construes the French Revolution as a counter-enlightenment development, 'a violent expression of repressed Christian *ressentiment* that overwhelmed and destroyed the last flowering of the noble, sceptical culture in Europe in seventeenth and eighteenth-century France'.[22] This commentator is correct to infer that the event of the Revolution was for Nietzsche a secularization of Christianity's slave revolt in morality in spite of the 'deceptive anti-Christian mask that the Revolutionaries chose to wear'.[23]

Nietzsche and fanaticism

Let me now turn in this section to probing Nietzsche's position on fanaticism. It is important to Nietzsche that his words are not those of a 'fanatic', that there is no 'preaching', and with no 'faith' being demanded; rather, he is keen to write and philosophize in terms of what he calls a 'delicate slowness' (EH Foreword; see also D Preface 5). In *Ecce Homo* he prides himself on his non-fanatical nature: 'You will not find a trace of fanaticism in my being' (EH 'Why I am so clever,' 10). This 'non-fanatical' Nietzsche emerges, or comes to the fore, in the middle-period texts. We live in fanatical times for Nietzsche and fanaticism is to be understood as ranging across religion, morality and philosophy.[24] Our attachment to ideas that are in danger of being adhered to fanatically totals up to three: the idea that there is a single moral-making morality, the idea that true life is to be found in self-abandonment and the idea that there are definitive, final truths. Nietzsche is a critic of all three ideas.

Dawn (1881) is an avowedly anti-revolution work in which Nietzsche seeks to promote a philosophy of the morning based on 'slow cures' (D 462) and 'small doses' (D 534). In his middle writings he displays a preference for individual therapy and self-cultivation over political revolution. Nietzsche explicitly writes against impatient political invalids and argues instead in favour of these small doses as a way of bringing about change (D 534). He is of the view that the last attempt in Europe at a transformation of evaluations, and specifically with regard to political matters, namely, the Great Revolution, 'was nothing *more* than a pathetic and bloody *quackery*' (D 534). The task, he says, is to continue the work of the Enlightenment in each and every individual but also 'to strangle the Revolution at birth' and ensure it does not happen (see D 197).

When Nietzsche writes in favour of a new enlightenment and contra fanaticism, he is addressing what he calls 'our current, stressed, power-thirsty society (*machtdürstigen Gesellschaft*) in Europe and America' (D 271). He seeks to draw attention to the different ways in which the 'feeling of power' is gratified through both individual and collective forms of agency (see D 184). At this stage in his thinking this is what he means by 'grand politics' (*grossen Politik*), in which the 'mightiest tide' driving forward individuals, masses and nations is '*the need for the feeling of power*' (*Machtgefühls*) (D 189). Sometimes this assumes the form of the 'pathos-ridden language of virtue', and although Nietzsche has a concern over the fanatical elements of a politics of virtue, his main concern at this time is that such behaviour gives rise to the unleashing of 'a plethora of squandering, sacrificing, hoping ... over-audacious, fantastical instincts ...' that are then utilized by ambitious princes to start up wars. (D 179) As one commentator points out, Nietzsche first introduces the notion of power into his writings not as a metaphysical truth or as a normative principle, but as a hypothesis of psychology that seeks to explain the origins and development of the various cultural forms that human beings have fashioned in order to deal with their vulnerability or lack of power.[25] As Nietzsche points out in *Dawn*, in the development of human history the feeling of powerlessness has been extensive and is responsible for the creation of both superstitious rituals and cultural forms such as religion and metaphysics (D 23). The feeling of fear and powerlessness has been in a state of 'perpetual excitation' for so long a time that the actual feeling of power has developed to incredibly subtle degrees and levels and has, in fact, become our 'strongest inclination' (D 23). We can safely say, he thinks, that the methods discovered to create this feeling constitute the history of culture (*Cultur*).

Today, Nietzsche notes, although the means of the appetite for power have altered, the same volcano still burns: what was formerly done for the sake of God is now done for the sake of money, 'for the sake of that which *now* imparts to the highest degree the feeling of power and a good conscience' (D 204). Nietzsche, therefore, attacks the upper classes for giving themselves over to 'sanctioned fraud' and that has 'the stock exchange and all forms of speculation on its conscience' (D 204). What troubles him about this terrible craving for and love of accumulated money is that it once again gives rise, albeit in a new form, to 'that fanaticism (*Fanatismus*) of the *appetite for power* (*Machtgelüstes*) that formerly was ignited by the conviction of being in possession of the truth' (D 204).

Through his psychological probing of the 'fantastical instincts' and of the need for the feeling of power, Nietzsche is led to cultivate scepticism about politics in *Dawn* and favours instead a programme of therapeutic self-cultivation. He favours, for example, the cultivation of 'personal wisdom' over any allegiances one might have to party politics (D 183). Moreover, as he says at one point in the book, we need to be honest with ourselves and know ourselves extremely well if we are to practice towards others 'that philanthropic dissimulation that goes by the name of love and kindness' (D 335). Nietzsche ultimately favours a project of free-minded social transformation in which small groups of free spirits will practice experimental lives, sacrifice themselves for the superior health of future generations, endeavour to get beyond their compassion, promote 'universal interests' and seek to 'strengthen and elevate the general feeling of human *power*' (D 146).

That fanaticism is a major concern of Nietzsche's is made explicit in the 1886 preface to *Dawn*, where he also writes as a teacher of slow reading and a friend of *lento*. In it Nietzsche exposes the seductions of morality, claiming that it knows how to 'inspire' or 'enthuse' (*begeistern*); and with his attempt to render the ground for 'majestic moral edifices' level and suitable for construction Kant set himself a 'rapturous' or 'enthusiastic goal' (*schwärmerischen Absicht*), one that makes him a true son of his century – a century which more than any other, Nietzsche stresses, can fairly be called 'the century of "rapturous enthusiasm"' or, indeed, 'fanaticism' (*Schwärmerei*). Although Kant sought to keep enthusiasm (*Enthusiasmus*) and fanaticism (*Schwärmerei*) separate, Nietzsche is claiming that there is in his moral philosophy what Alberto Toscano has called a 'ruse of transcendence', or the return of universally binding abstract precepts and authorities that are beyond the domain of human and natural relations.[26] Nietzsche's critical point is that Kant betrayed the cause of reason by positing a 'moral realm' that cannot be assailed by reason. Indeed, Nietzsche holds that Kant was bitten by the 'tarantula of morality Rousseau' and so 'he too held in the very depths of his soul the idea of moral fanaticism (*moralischen Fanatismus*) whose executor yet another disciple of Rousseau's, namely, Robespierre, felt and confessed himself to be' (D Preface 3). Although he partakes of this 'Frenchified fanaticism' (*Franzosen-Fanatismus*), Kant remains decidedly German for Nietzsche – he is said to be 'thorough' and 'profound' – in his positing of a 'logical Beyond', a 'non-demonstrable world', so as to create a space for the 'moral realm'.[27] Nietzsche wants this space to be subject to sceptical and critical inquiry.

Let me probe more deeply into the conception of morality that Nietzsche is taking to task in texts such as *Dawn*. The morality that humanity has cultivated and dedicated itself to is one of 'enthusiastic devotion' and 'self-sacrifice' in which it looks down from sublime heights on the more sober morality of self-control (which is regarded as egotistical). Nietzsche suggests that the reason why morality has been developed in this way can be attributed to the enjoyment of the state of intoxication that has stemmed from the thought that the person is one with the powerful being to whom it consecrates itself; in this way the feeling of power is enjoyed and is confirmed by a sacrifice of the self. For Nietzsche, of course, such an overcoming of the human self is impossible: 'In truth you only *seem* to sacrifice yourselves; instead, in your thoughts you transform yourselves into gods and take pleasure in yourselves as such' (D 215). Activities of self-sacrifice serve to intensify the feeling of power as one of the key needs of human life and are not to be taken at face value; this means that the sacrifice of the self is an appearance in which the value of the act resides in the pleasure one derives from it. In his consideration of intoxication, visions, trance and so on, Nietzsche is, then, dealing with the problem of fanaticism that preoccupies him in his middle and late periods (D 57–8, 68, 204, 298; see also MOM 15; BGE 10; GS 347; AC 11, 32, 54). As he notes, such 'enthusiasts' or fanatics (*Schwärmer*) will seek to implant the faith in intoxication 'as being that which is actually living in life: a dreadful faith!' (D 50) Such is the extent of Nietzsche's anxiety that he wonders whether humanity as a whole will one day perish by its 'spiritual fire-waters' and those who keep alive the desire for them. The 'strange madness of moral judgements' is bound up with states of exaltation (*Erhebung*) and 'the most exalted language' (D 189). Nietzsche is advising us to be on our guard, to be vigilant as philosophers against, 'the half-mad, the fantastic, the fanatical (*fanatischer*)', including so-called human beings of genius who claim to have visions and to have seen things others do not see. We are to be cautious, not credulous, when confronted with the claims of visions, that is to say he adds, 'of a profound mental disturbance' (D 66).

In criticizing fanaticism Nietzsche largely has in mind the Christian religion (though one also suspects he has Wagner in mind when he critically addresses genius). Christianity has brought into the world 'a completely new and unlimited *imperilment*', creating new securities, enjoyments, recreations and evaluations. Although we moderns may be in the process of emancipating ourselves from such an imperilment, we keep dragging into our existence the old habits associated with these securities and evaluations, even into our noblest arts and philosophies (D 57). Nietzsche holds that in wanting to return to the affects 'in their utmost grandeur and strength' – for example, as *love* of God, *fear* of God, fanatical *faith* in God and so on – Christianity represents a popular protest against philosophy and he appeals to the ancient sages against it since they advocated the triumph of reason over the affects (D 58).

As we have seen, in the preface to *Dawn* Nietzsche accuses Kant of fanaticism and claims that Kant was bitten by Rousseau, that 'tarantula of morality' (D Preface 3).[28] However, although he criticizes the Kantian legacy in moral philosophy, he is, in fact, close to Kant on a number of points. We can note the following: for Kant, (1) the task of the Enlightenment is to be perpetual[29] and (2) revolution cannot produce a genuine reform in our modes of thinking but only results in new prejudices.[30] Where he thinks Kant is inconsistent is with respect to his ambition of imposing the demands of a universalist morality upon humanity. For Nietzsche we simply lack enough knowledge to morally legislate for individuals, let alone for humanity as a whole, and this insight forms a crucial part of his independent enlightenment project. Nietzsche contends, first, that the moral precepts directed at individuals are not, in fact, aimed at promoting their happiness; second, that such precepts are also not, in fact, concerned with the 'happiness and welfare of humanity'. Here his concern is that we simply have words to which it is virtually impossible to attach definite concepts, 'let alone to utilize them as a guiding star on the dark ocean of moral aspirations' (D 108). We cannot even appeal to evolution since 'evolution does not desire happiness; it wants evolution and nothing more' (D 108). Mankind lacks a universally recognized goal, so it is thus both irrational and frivolous to inflict upon humanity the demands of morality. Nietzsche does not rule out the possibility of *recommending* a goal that lies in humanity's discretion, but this is something that for him lies in the future. There is much critical working through and enlightenment-inspired undermining to be done first.

Nietzsche's stance contra revolution and on moral fanaticism – the objects he singles out for attack in the 1886 preface to *Dawn* – is part of an established tradition in German thought dating back to the 1780s and 1790s.[31]Although Nietzsche especially criticizes Kant in the preface to the text, he fails to consider in any serious or fair-minded way Kant's position on morality and revolution, and he has nothing to say on Kant's own critical position on the issue of fanaticism. The *Shorter Oxford Dictionary* defines fanaticism as 'excessive enthusiasm', especially in religious matters. Enthusiasm here is to be understood as 'rapturous intensity of a feeling on behalf of a cause or a person'.[32] This is part of Nietzsche's understanding of fanaticism and informs his critique of it. As such, he is perhaps closer to the likes of Locke and Hume than he is to Kant: where Locke and Hume critique enthusiasm, identifying it with what we would today call fanaticism, Kant is careful in some of his writings to distinguish between enthusiasm (*Enthusiasmus*) and fanaticism (*Schwärmerei*): where enthusiasm functions as a sign of a moral tendency in humanity, the pious fanatic has otherworldly intuitions.[33] Kant thus locates fanaticism (*Schwärmerei*) in the 'raving of reason' and 'the *delusion of wanting to SEE something beyond all bounds of sensibility*'.[34] Kant is looking for evidence of a 'historical sign', such as resides in an event (e.g. the French Revolution), that might indicate that man has the power of being the cause or author of his own improvement.[35] However, Kant is acutely aware of not being dogmatic here; that is, we cannot have too high an expectation of human beings in their progressive improvements, lest our aspirations turn into 'the fantasies of an overheated mind'.[36] Of course, this does not save Kant completely from the charge of moral fanaticism, but it does serve to indicate something of the complexity of his position.

Ultimately, Nietzsche and Kant diverge owing to the fact that they each have a different conception of what makes for signs of our moral maturity. For Kant this resides not simply in our being 'civilized' or 'cultivated' and other semblances of morality, but in our 'cosmopolitan' achievement and sense of moral purposiveness. For Nietzsche by contrast we stand in need of liberation from the fanatical presumptions of morality. There is a need to recognize our ethical complexity, for example, that it is naïve to posit a strict separation of egoistic and altruistic drives and actions, and that it is equally naïve to assume a unitary self that is completely transparent to itself. So what, in Nietzsche's eyes, makes for moral maturity? It is a question and task of *modesty* and for Nietzsche, as he makes clear in the preface to *Dawn*, the attack on 'morality' is based on a struggle for 'more modest words' (*bescheidenere Worte*) (D Preface 4). For Nietzsche we simply lack the knowledge into moral matters that morality presumes, and for him this necessitates experimentalism in the domain of ethical life. For example, it is necessary to contest the idea that there is a single moral-making morality since every code of ethics that affirms itself in an exclusive manner 'destroys too much valuable energy and costs humanity much too dearly' (D 164). In the future, he hopes, the inventive and fructifying person shall no longer be sacrificed and 'numerous novel experiments shall be made in ways of life and modes of society' (ibid.). When this takes place we will find that an enormous load of guilty conscience has been purged from the world. Humanity has suffered for too long from teachers of morality who wanted too much all at once and sought to lay down precepts for everyone (D 194). In the future, care will need to be given to the most personal questions and create time for them (D 196). Small individual questions and experiments are no longer to be viewed with contempt and impatience (D 547). Contra morality, then, he holds that we ourselves are experiments and our task should be to want to be such. We are to build anew the laws of life and of behaviour by taking from the sciences of physiology, medicine, sociology and solitude the foundation stones for new ideals, if not the new ideals themselves (D 453). As these sciences are not yet sure of themselves, we find ourselves living in either a preliminary or a posterior existence, depending on our taste and talent, and in this interregnum the best strategy is for us to become our own *reges* (sovereigns) and establish small experimental states.

In *Dawn* Nietzsche employs what we can call an 'antique care of the self' as a way of taking to task what he identifies as some troubling developments in modern society. Here the chief goal or end of the cultivation of self-sufficiency is freedom. He draws on the Stoic Epictetus to promote such a care of self, and what he admires in him is a non-fanatical (*nicht fanatisch*) mode of living. Although this ancient thinker was a slave, the exemplar he invokes is without class and is possible in every class. He serves as a counterweight to modern idealists who are greedy for expansion. Epictetus's ideal human being, lacking all fear of God and believing rigorously in reason, 'is not a preacher of penitence' (D 546). He has a pride in himself that does not wish to trouble and encroach on others: 'He admits a certain mild rapprochement and does not wish to spoil anyone's good mood – Yes, he can smile! There is a great deal of ancient humanity in this ideal!' (ibid.). The Epictetean is self-sufficient, 'defends himself against the outside world' and 'lives in a state of highest valor' (ibid.). Nietzsche offers this portrait of the Epictetean as a point of contrast to the Christian. The Christian lives in hope (and in the consolation of 'unspeakable glories' to come) and allows himself to be given gifts, expecting the best of life not to come from himself and his own resources but from divine love and grace. By contrast, Epictetus 'does not hope and does allow his best to be given him – he possesses it, he holds it valiantly in his hand, and he would take on the whole world if it tries to rob him of it' (ibid.).

This portrait of Epictetus contra the Christian provides us with a set of valuable insights into how Nietzsche conceives the difference between fanatical and non-fanatical modes of living: one way of life is self-sufficient and finds its pride in this, renouncing hope and living in the present; the other devotes itself to living through and for others, its attention is focused on the future (as that which is to come), and it lacks the quiet and calm dignity of self-sufficiency that is the Epictetean ideal (see also D 131). It is clear that with this usage of Epictetus Nietzsche is seeking a counter ideal to the ideal of morality. It conforms to his expectation of modesty and it works against the aspirations of morality.

Conclusion

At the outset of this chapter I claimed that a focus on the problem of fanaticism can help to illuminate two core aspects of Nietzsche's middle-period project:

the nature of his attack on the presumptions and prejudices of morality and the character of the mode of philosophizing he is keen to develop in the middle writings. Working through the problem of fanaticism not only influences Nietzsche in his thinking about an ethical reformation in his middle writings, it also defines significant aspects of his philosophical project as a whole at this time and centred on a therapeutic cooling down of the human mind. What is clear is that at this time in his intellectual development Nietzsche appeals to philosophical moderation over enthusiasm, sentimentality and self-intoxication. Nietzsche makes his standpoint clear in the various figurations we find in his middle writings of his position 'contra Rousseau'. Although Nietzsche makes clear that he is *gegen* Rousseau in *Dawn* 163 and then in the 1886 preface to that work, he first begins to position himself critically against Rousseau in the volumes of *Human, all too Human*. In *The Wanderer and His Shadow* Nietzsche warns against the moralism of Kant (and Schiller) that has its source in Rousseau and the reawakened Stoic Rome (WS 216). Although these intellectual positionings by Nietzsche may not do full justice to the thinkers in question, such as Rousseau and Kant, they do reveal something important about the character of his thinking and the nature of his fundamental project, such as the critique of morality and the appeal to modesty.

As part of his enlightenment commitments, Nietzsche positions himself in opposition to 'the fogs of a metaphysical-mystical philosophy' (MOM 28). He also rejects the 'gleaming mirage' of a philosophical system (MOM 31). However, he is in search of a blending together of knowledge and wisdom (MOM 180), as well as a philosophy of spiritual health (MOM 356). He is convinced that, thanks to the modern enlightenment project, the walls that separate nature and spirit, human and animal, ethics and physics are breaking down (MOM 185), and this offers prospects for a novel synthesis of science and philosophy, or knowledge and wisdom. In short, Nietzsche's philosophical commitment in the middle writings is informed by enlightenment sensibilities. Fanaticism for him is, in part, the stance of impatient political invalids. In seeking a quick fix to the ills of society revolution, and the fervour that drives it, is a poor vehicle for our education and maturation. It is for this core reason that Nietzsche rejects it and seeks to take it to task in his writings. Although there is much more to be said about Nietzsche's critique of fanaticism, I have sought here to open up some possible pathways by which the topic can be illuminated in his writings and shown to be of genuine importance for their proper appreciation.

Dawn and the Passion of Knowledge

Introduction

In a note from the end of 1880, Nietzsche writes that without the passions the world is reduced to being simply 'quantity and line and law and nonsense', presenting us with 'the most repulsive and presumptuous paradox' (KSA 9, 7 [226]). By the time of *Dawn* (1881) the pursuit of knowledge has become a passion for him, if not the overriding one. For Marco Brusotti this new emphasis represents a far-reaching break with the ideal of moderation and repose of soul espoused in *Human, all too Human*: 'The concept of the "passion of knowledge" … marks a clear turn in his interpretation of the free spirit. *Dawn* is the book in which this turn takes place.'[1] Although this may exaggerate the difference between the texts, according to Paul Franco in a recent appreciation of the texts of the middle period – is not the free spirit in *Dawn* characterized by detachment, moderation and mildness? – it does indicate an important change in Nietzsche's outlook.[2] Franco is surely right when he notes that while references to the moderating effect of knowledge are still to be found in *Dawn*, what catches our attention most is this appeal to the passion of knowledge. As he eloquently puts it: 'There is nothing utilitarian or bourgeois about the quest for knowledge for Nietzsche, and this gives his appropriation of the Enlightenment its peculiar, one might say romantic quality. He celebrates an Enlightenment that has been deepened by the experience of *Tristan and Isolde*.'[3] Knowledge is not simply an idle activity for Nietzsche but something to be pursued as a passion and requiring a cheerfulness or serenity in the face of its highs and lows, its ecstasies and disappointments. As he will express it in *The Gay Science*, life itself is to be treated as 'an experiment of the seeker for knowledge', and not as a duty, a calamity or a piece of trickery (GS 324). Knowledge for some can be a diversion or a form of leisure, but for the passionate seeker it offers 'a world of dangers and victories', one in which 'heroic feelings' can find places to dance and play. With the principle of 'life as a means to knowledge' lodged in one's heart, it is possible to live both boldly and gaily, and to laugh gaily too: 'Who knows how to laugh anyway and live well if he does not first know a good deal about war and victory?' (ibid.)

Nietzsche regards the drive for knowledge as young and raw, and compared to the older and more richly developed drives, it is ugly and offensive (which all drives have been at some point in their development). However, he confides that he wishes to treat it as a passion, 'as something with which the individual soul can work side by side, so that it can look back on the world in a helpful and conciliatory fashion: in the meantime, we need a non-ascetic renunciation of the world again!' (*KSA* 9, 7 [197]) Nietzsche places the passion of knowledge in the service of a philosophical project that aims at disabusing humanity of its consoling fictions – for example concerning the uniqueness of its origins and destiny – and encouraging it to pursue new truths and a new kind of philosophical wisdom. Through new and refined practices of observation and self-observation, we as human beings largely unknown to ourselves can become our own experiments: Nietzsche insists that we are experiments and the task is to *want* to be such. We are to become strangers to our ordinary and habitual selves, viewing ourselves afresh as experiments of living and feeling and of knowledge. For Nietzsche '*the* human being' is a bloodless fiction and 'society' is a general concept (D 105). As Foucault puts it in his reflections on the passion of knowledge, the critical task is to break with accustomed habits of knowing and perceiving, so that one has the chance to become something different than what one's history has conditioned one to be, to think and perceive differently. For Foucault this gives us, in fact, a definition of philosophical activity today, which consists in the critical work that thought brings to bear on itself. Instead, of legitimating what is already known, the task is to think differently, and this is an essential part of philosophical activity conceived as an *askēsis*.[4]

Foucault ultimately places this ascesis in the service of a care of self, a conception I examine in Chapter 4. Here I propose to focus my attention on the theme of experimentation and Nietzsche's conception of philosophy, especially his concern with the character of knowledge and what is involved in its practice as a passion.

The moment of *Dawn*

Nietzsche began research on what was to become *Dawn: Thoughts on the Presumptions of Morality* in January 1880. The manuscript was complete by 13

March 1881 and was published in June of that year. At this point in time Nietzsche has retired on a modest annual pension from his position at Basel University and is travelling in Europe, spending time in Riva, Venice, Marienbad, Stresa and Genoa, as well as his childhood home of Naumburg, seeking suitable conditions for his health and living on a highly restricted budget. In Genoa, where *Dawn* was completed, Nietzsche found a garret apartment in which he had to climb a hundred and sixty four steps to reach and which was itself located high up on a very steep street. Nietzsche was adjusting to a new lifestyle and the limitations imposed by his pension: the apartment in Genoa was without heating and the winter was extremely cold. His diet was often a simple one of risotto and calf meat with a frugal supper of porridge. Nietzsche was leading not only a frugal existence but a solitary one too. And yet it was under these harsh conditions that he wrote over the course of a year one of his 'sunniest' books. He would later reflect, in a letter to his admirer in Copenhagen, Georg Brandes, that his speciality was to 'endure extreme pain, *cru, vert*, with perfect clarity, for two or three consecutive days, accompanied by constant vomiting of bile'. Although the report had been disseminated that he was in a madhouse and had died there, nothing could have been further from the truth he confides: 'As a matter of fact my intellect only came to maturity during that terrible time: witness *Dawn*, which I wrote in 1881 during a winter of incredible suffering at Genoa, away from doctors, friends, or relations'. For himself, he adds, the book serves 'as a sort of dynamometer': 'I composed it with a minimum of strength' (10 April 1888; KGB III. 5, 290). Solitude was for Nietzsche a test of his independence. He wanted, he said, to be his own doctor, to be true to himself and not to listen to anyone else: 'I cannot tell you', he wrote on 24 November 1880 to his mother and sister Elisabeth, 'how much good *solitude* is doing me' (KGB III. I, 51).

The text grew out of notebooks Nietzsche kept during this time, including notes for a new book to be entitled *L'Ombra di Venezia* (KSA 9, 47–102): the title pays homage to the welcome shade he had discovered for himself in the city of four hundred bridges and numerous dark and narrow streets.[5] He had been intrigued by the prospect and promise of a new dawn since the time of his early reflections on the ancient, pre-Platonic philosophers. In one note from 1872 to 1873 Nietzsche writes of the Greek reformer in which the role of the philosophers was to prepare the way for him and precede him 'as the dawn precedes the rising sun'. Alas, the sun did not rise in this instance, and the reformer failed with the dawn remaining 'a ghostly apparition' (KSA 7, 23 [1]). *Dawn (Morgenröthe*, literally 'morning redness') is one of Nietzsche's 'yes-saying' books, a work of enlightenment which, he tells his readers, seeks to pour out 'its light, its love, and its delicacy over nothing but bad things', giving back to these things the 'lofty right and *prerogative* of existence' (*EH* III 'D', 1). The Indian motto from the Rig Veda's 'Hymn to Varuna', 'there are so many dawns that have not yet broken' lies inscribed on the door to the book (ibid.). Nietzsche's amanuensis Peter Gast (Heinrich Köselitz) had written the motto on the title page while making a fair copy of the manuscript and this, in fact, inspired Nietzsche to adopt the new title and replace its original title of 'The Ploughshare.'[6] In 1888 Nietzsche speaks of the book as amounting to a search for the new morning that ushers in a whole series of new days and he insists that not a single negative word is to be found in it, and no attack or malice either. In this book we encounter a thinker who lies in the sun, 'like a sea creature sunning itself among rocks' (ibid.) – and the book was largely conceived in the rocks near Genoa in solitude and where, so Nietzsche discloses, he 'had secrets to share with the sea.'[7] *Dawn* is a book that journeys into the future, and which for Nietzsche constitutes, in fact, its true destination: 'Even now,' he writes in a letter of 24 March 1881 to his old friend Erwin Rohde, 'there are moments when I walk about on the heights above Genoa having glimpses and feelings such as Columbus once, perhaps from the very same place, sent out across the sea and into the future' (KGB III: 1, 75). Nietzsche's appeal to Columbus is figurative; he is, in fact, critical of the real Columbus (D 37). But as a figure of thought Columbus the seafarer serves *Dawn* well; he denotes 'the true experimenter, who may have an idea of where he thinks he is heading but is always prepared to be surprised by the outcome of his experiments.'[8]

In fact, the book is more complex than Nietzsche admits to in 1888. Some of this complexity is revealed in the letters he wrote to Peter Gast advising him of the title, which he kept changing, sometimes in slight and subtle ways. In a letter to Gast of 9 February 1881 the work is now to carry the title '*A Dawn: Thoughts on Moral Presumptions.*' By way of explanation Nietzsche added in his letter to Gast, 'There are so many bright and indeed red colours in it' (KGB III: 1, 61). However, a few weeks later Nietzsche wrote to Gast again expressing anxiety over the new title, considering it 'too gushing, oriental and of less good taste' (22 February; ibid., 63). Nevertheless he persisted with it for the time being and largely on account of the advantage it enjoys over the original title of giving the book a more cheerful tone and placing the reader in a different frame of mind: 'It stands the book in good stead, which would be much too *gloomy* without the glimpse of the morning!' This reveals that the book is, in fact, a complex one: there are sufficient grounds for gloom, but Nietzsche does not wish to be gloomy or promote gloominess; a book needs to emit rays of hope, expectation and anticipation even if the seriousness cannot be concealed. In a letter to Gast of 30 March Nietzsche reveals that he is basically writing for himself and for Gast, his closest associate and dearest companion (his fellow free spirit). He writes of gathering 'a treasure out of things that are our own, for our old age!', and of the need to 'be *vain for ourselves* and as much as possible!' (ibid., 77). In a letter to Gast of 10 April Nietzsche discloses that he has modified the title by simplifying it to *Dawn* and not *A Dawn*. By way of justification he adds: 'A title must, above all, be *quotable*' (*citirbar*) and that there was something too precious about the 'A' in the title (ibid., 83). The title that Nietzsche settled on for the book is significant for several reasons and is clear in the meaning of the word 'dawn', notably the expectation of a new beginning, the first light of day or daybreak, the incipient appearance of something, a new reality which is beginning to become evident and understood, and so on. As we have seen, the colour 'red' was important to Nietzsche in his own understanding of the book, and here he was perhaps influenced by Homer's *Odyssey* and the various references to 'the rosy-fingered dawn' which, in the tale, provides a sharp contrast to the gruesome battle scenes going on below (see references to the *Odyssey* and Odysseus in D 306, 562; see also MOM 408; see Homer, *The Odyssey*, 2:1–2, 12: 3–7). The German title of the work, *Morgenröthe*, specifies the precise but fleeting moment at which the sky is aflame with colour and before the red yields to the customary blue or grey. It suggests a time of possibility, invention, inspiration and renewal, in which the freshness of the new day augurs a new way of life.[9]

Dawn is a significant, if overlooked and marginalized, text in Nietzsche's corpus. As Duncan Large has noted, in *Dawn* and the subsequent text (its ideal companion in which the journey continues), *The Gay Science*, Nietzsche consolidates the anti-metaphysical stance initiated in the turn in his thinking represented by *Human, all too Human* of 1878, completing his metamorphosis from the Schopenhauer- and Wagner-adulating camel to a combative and exploratory lion, and from the ship of the desert to the ship of high seas.[10] He is charting new land and new seas, unsure of his final destination, and has the confidence needed to take risks and conduct experiments, even to suffer shipwreck in search of new treasure. In the text we encounter the free spirit setting off on a new course and away from the old philosophical world of metaphysical and moral prejudices. However, it is no exaggeration to claim that for the greater part of Nietzsche-reception *Dawn* has been among the most neglected text in Nietzsche's corpus, little studied even today, and perhaps for the following reasons: it deploys no master concept, it does not seek an ultimate solution to the riddles of existence (indeed, it warns against such a strategy), its presentation of themes and problems is highly nonlinear and it states his case for the future subtly and delicately. The death of God is presaged and, in fact, announced, but not presented in any dramatic form as we find in the next text, *The Gay Science* (section 125). But it is a text that has hidden riches, a text that has to be read between the lines, as Nietzsche disclosed to his sister Elisabeth in the case of the final book of the text.[11]

Dawn is composed of 575 aphorisms or short thoughts, some of only a single line, others running to three pages and grouped together in five books (the original plan was for a work of four books). As Arthur Danto notes, while each component piece has a title of its own, none of the five books does, hence it is unclear 'what, if any, principle of organization may have applied'. Further, 'the "thoughts" of one book seldom relate more closely to other thoughts in it than they do to those in other books', and it is true to say that occasionally we read a suite of thoughts on the same topic, for example, *Mitleid* from 132 almost to the end of book two.[12] In aphorism 454, entitled Interpolation, Nietzsche confides that the book is not one for reading straight through but for 'cracking open' (*Aufschlagen*) in which he wants the reader to place his head into it and out again, finding nothing about him that he is accustomed to. From this Danto infers that the absence of headings from the individual books of the work, along with the abrupt shifts from topic to topic, '*could* be devices for slowing the reader down'.[13] Although this is conjectural, it accords well with what Nietzsche says in his 1886 preface the book: he wishes to be the teacher of 'slow reading'. But it is also the case that in *Dawn* Nietzsche conceives philosophy as a form of entertainment (D 427), one that takes over a role hitherto assumed by religion, and it may be that in conceiving the book in a nonlinear fashion Nietzsche hoped to keep his readers intrigued by and interested in the problems of self, world and knowledge that he was pursuing and staging. God is dead, the world is bereft of the consolations of religion and metaphysical philosophy and our minds need cultivating in new ways; we need new interests and new things to keep us occupied and interested in life.

Concerning Nietzsche's style of writing, Danto I think puts it well when he describes the prose style of the work as 'a kind of eroticism of writing', one that requires from its reader a partnership in pleasure and intelligence. The text is characterized by sudden shifts of tone and rhythm, 'at one moment lyrical and at the next moment earthy', with moments of 'mock distance and then of sudden intimacy', and its 'jeers, sneers, jokes and whispers', all contribute to this eroticism.[14] As Danto further notes, while Nietzsche's voice has lost the professorial authority of the early writing, it has yet to acquire the strident conviction of a prophet unheeded that characterizes the later writings. He is right to suggest that in none of the books do we get a more palpable sense of spiritual well-being as we do in *Dawn*.

One of the heroes of the book is Epicurus who sought to demonstrate the mortality of the soul and whose aim was, 'to free humans from "the fears of the mind"'.[15] *Dawn* can be read in part, and on an existential or therapeutic level, as an attempt to revitalize for a modern-age ancient philosophical concerns, notably a teaching for mortal souls who wish to be liberated from the fear and anguish of existence, as well as from God, the 'metaphysical need',[16] and romantic music,[17] and are able to affirm their mortal conditions of existence (see D 501). In the book Epicurus is portrayed as the enemy of the idea of punishments in Hell after death, which was developed by numerous secret cults in the Roman Empire and was taken up by Christianity.[18] For Nietzsche the triumph of Epicurus's teaching resounds most beautifully in the mouth of the sombre Roman Lucretius but comes too early. Christianity takes the belief in 'subterranean terrors' under its special protection and this foray into heathendom enables it to carry the day over the popularity of the Mithras and Isis cults, winning to its side the rank of the timorous as the most zealous adherents of the new faith. (Nietzsche notes that because of the extent of the Jews' attachment to life such an idea fell on barren ground.) However, the teaching of Epicurus triumphs anew in the guise of modern science, which has rejected 'any other representation of death and any life beyond it' (D 72; see also D 150). Nietzsche is keen to encourage human beings to cultivate an attitude towards existence in which they accept their mortality and attain a new serenity about their dwelling on the earth, to conquer unjustified fears and to reinstitute the role played by chance and chance events in the world and in human existence (see D 13, 33, 36).[19] Nietzsche is in search of a new kind of community or people, a free-minded one which has the 'passion of knowledge', the willingness to experiment and is united by a shared commitment to new ways of thinking, feeling and existing.

The passion of knowledge

Throughout his corpus Nietzsche presents his readers with various riddles of knowledge, such as the well-known opening to the *Genealogy of Morality*: we are knowers who are *unknown* to ourselves. Is the passion of knowledge also a riddle? That Nietzsche appears to be dealing with a riddle is evident from the following note:

> The passion for knowledge sees *itself* as the *purpose* of existence – if it denies purposes, it sees itself as the most *valuable result* of all accidents. Will it *deny* the value? It cannot claim to **be** the highest *pleasure*? But to *search* for **that**? To design the being *most capable of pleasure*, as means and task of this passion? To heighten the senses and the pride, and the thirst, etc. (Nietzsche, KSA 9, 11 [69])

In this deeply enigmatic passage Nietzsche acknowledges that although the passion of knowledge refutes the doctrine that existence has a purpose, it comes to see itself as the end of existence and identifies value in this in spite of it being a total accident in evolution. If this is the case, then it follows a most difficult task presents itself, namely, how to bring into existence the being that is most capable of pleasure with respect to this new passion and as both means and task. Is this not the very project of Nietzsche's free-spirit middle period outlined in essence?

In 1881 Nietzsche makes the important discovery that he has a precursor. He is not to feel completely isolated and alone in his great task as a teacher of humanity. This precursor is Spinoza. Indeed, a Spinozist inspiration hovers over the first sketch of the eternal recurrence of the same drafted in the summer of 1881 and which, like *The Ethics*, is a plan for a book in five parts, culminating in a meditation on beatitude (KSA 9, 11 [141]). In a letter to his friend Franz Overbeck postmarked 30 July 1881, on the eve of the experience of the eternal recurrence, Nietzsche enumerates the points of doctrine he shares with Spinoza, such as the denial of free will, of a moral world order and of evil, and also mentions the task of 'making knowledge the most *powerful affect*' (die Erkenntniß zum *mächtigsten Affekt* zu machen; KSB 6: 111).[20] In a note Nietzsche also writes on Spinoza and himself as follows: 'Spinoza: We are only determined in our actions by desires and affects. Knowledge must be an affect in order to be a motive. I say: it must be a *passion* to be a motive' (KSA 9, 11 [193]). Nietzsche first writes of the passion of knowledge (*Leidenschaft der Erkenntnis*) in his published writings in *Dawn*. In aphorism 429 of the text he notes that the drive to knowledge has become so strongly rooted in us that we cannot now want happiness without knowledge. Knowledge has become a deep-rooted passion that shrinks at no sacrifice. Indeed, such is now our passion for knowledge that even the prospect of humanity perishing of this passion does not exert any real influence on us.

Edwin Curley has argued that to speak of knowledge as affect (or passion) is probably inexact from Spinoza's point of view since it is not clear that Spinoza would count knowledge as an affect at all.[21] Certainly Spinoza ascribes to knowledge a great power over the things he would count as affects, while recognizing that human power over the affects is limited: the power of knowledge is not absolute. This raises the question: Why does Nietzsche want knowledge to be practised as a 'passion'? It seems that this passion is an intrinsic part of what it is for Nietzsche to practise the new science he outlines for his reader, 'the gay science' in which there is a fusion of the affective and the cognitive. More than this, we can say the 'passion' is bound up for Nietzsche with the new sacrifice we moderns are willing to make: 'Knowledge has been transformed into a passion in us that does not shrink from any sacrifice and, at bottom, fears nothing but its own extinction' (D 429). Even the thought that humanity may be destroyed by this passion does not deter us and instead we feel elevated by it: we attain a new sublime with the sacrifices we are now prepared to make on account of the passion of knowledge (ibid.). Indeed, in D 45, Nietzsche notes that it is human sacrifices that have hitherto exalted (*erhoben*) and elevated (*gehoben*) people most. He thus refers to a 'self-sacrificing humanity' that would now sacrifice itself to knowledge, especially knowledge of truth, as the sole goal 'prodigious enough to be worthy of such a sacrifice ...' and simply 'because for truth no sacrifice is too great' (D 45).

What is the character of Nietzsche's investment in the passion of knowledge, which is clearly a curious passion? What hopes and expectations did he have with respect to practices of knowledge? One thing can be said for sure: with his attachment to the passion of knowledge, Nietzsche wanted to become a different kind of philosopher to Schopenhauer, one less hemmed in by the fears and frailties of personality and genuinely open to the world and its enigmas. Unlike Schopenhauer, Nietzsche will not cling to the need of metaphysics and the need for a metaphysical system. Indeed, Nietzsche deliberately cultivates the passion of knowledge contra Schopenhauer whom he regards as superficial in psychological matters: 'He neither enjoyed himself much nor suffered much; a thinker should beware of *becoming harsh*: where would he get his material from then. His passion for knowledge was *not great* enough for him to suffer on its behalf: he barricaded himself in. His pride, too, was greater than his thirst for knowledge, in revoking, he feared for his reputation' (KSA 9, 6 [381]).

Franco has rightly argued that although Nietzsche rejects Schopenhauer's ideal of pure, will-less knowing, he is defending the life of knowledge and science, including their contemplative aspects. However, for Nietzsche, contemplation 'does not mean passive reception but active, passionate experimentation'.[22] This is why Nietzsche advises in his middle writings the prudent management of the passions: such management is necessary if they are to be employed for the sake of knowledge. Again, Franco puts it well: 'Knowledge does not involve eliminating the affects or passions – that would be to castrate the intellect – but it does require that one be able to control the affects or passions so that one can deploy them in a productive way.'[23]

According to Robert Hull, Nietzsche's love of knowledge is part of 'an ongoing therapeutic *praxis*' designed to work against the seductions of philosophical and epistemological rhetoric, and this resistance may explain 'why he also enlists a fresh vocabulary to express himself, one free of the hazardous emotional baggage of traditional philosophy'. [24] As part of this search, Nietzsche gives the impression of wishing to reduce all passions with their 'raptures and convulsions' (MOM 172) to their minimum articulation. Nietzsche speaks of their conquest, mastery and overcoming and at this time he adopts Christ as a model. In an imitation of Christ, for example, he admonishes us not to judge but to be just (MOM 33). In *The Wanderer and His Shadow* 88 he writes of the 'spiritually joyful, luminous and honest (*aufrichtigen*) human being' that has overcome its passions, while in aphorism 37 of the same text he invites his reader to 'work honestly (*redlich*) together' on the task of 'transforming the passions (*Leidenschaften*) of mankind one and all into joys' (*Freudenschaften*). In *The Wanderer and His Shadow* 53 Nietzsche makes it clear that he regards the overcoming of the passions as a means and not an end in itself: the aim is to overcome them so as to enter into possession of the most fertile ground.

Nietzsche's primary commitment is to experimentation in which the love of knowledge gives humanity the right to self-experimentation. He invites us to replace the dream of immortality with a new sobriety towards existence, as this aphorism makes clear: 'With regard to knowledge (*Erkenntniss*) the most useful accomplishment is perhaps: that the belief in the immortality of the soul has been abandoned. Now humanity is allowed to wait; now it no longer needs to rush headlong into things and choke down half-examined ideas as formerly it was forced to do. For in those days the salvation of poor "eternal souls" depended on the extent of their knowledge acquired during a short lifetime; they had to *make a decision* overnight – "knowledge" took on a dreadful importance' (D 501). Nietzsche argues that we are now in a new situation with regard to knowledge and as a result we can conquer anew our courage for making mistakes, for experimentation and for accepting things provisionally. Without the sanction of the old moralities and religions, individuals and entire generations 'can now fix their eyes on tasks of a vastness that would to earlier ages have seemed madness' (ibid.). What a strange and curious passion the passion of knowledge is! It operates like an unrequited love, it presents tasks that run ahead of humanity that then has to prove equal to it, and we may perish of it as experiments. In a note from 1880 Nietzsche seems sure that we shall meet our demise with this peculiar passion:

> Yes, we shall be destroyed by this passion! But that is not an argument against it. Otherwise, death would be an argument against the life of an individual. We *must* be destroyed, as humans and as humankind! Christianity showed the only way, through extinction and the denial of all coarse drives. Through the renunciation of action, of hatred of loving, we get to that point on the path of passion for knowledge. Contented *spectators* – until nothing more is to be seen! Despise us for that reason, you who act! We shall take a look at your contempt –: go *away* from us, from humankind, from thing-ness, from becoming – .(KSA 9, 7 [171])

I have noted the affinity that Nietzsche experienced with Spinoza. However, as Yirmiyahu Yovel points out, there are important differences between Spinoza and Nietzsche in their conceptions of knowledge. For Spinoza the immediate affective tone of knowledge is joy (a feeling of the enhanced power of life), whereas in Nietzsche the painful nature of knowledge is repeatedly stressed. (Indeed, Nietzsche measures the worth of a person by how much truth that person can bear and endure.) For Nietzsche, then, knowledge – in the sense of critical enlightenment and disillusionment – is a source of suffering and primarily a temptation to despair, and this means that the gay science, or joyful knowledge, is 'a task and goal', not the 'normal outcome'.[25] In a revealing note from 1880 Nietzsche writes:

> People have warbled on to me about the serene happiness of knowledge – but I have not found it, indeed, I despise it, now I know the bliss of unhappiness of knowledge. Am I ever bored? Always anxious, heart throbbing with expectation or disappointment! I bless this misery, it enriches the world thereby! In doing so, I take the slowest of strides and slurp down these bittersweet delicacies. (KSA 9, 7 [165])

For Nietzsche the pursuit of knowledge must have its hazards and dangers, and this sentiment deeply informs the project of the gay science in which life appears as an experiment for the seeker of knowledge and that rarely, if ever, disappoints. As he expresses it in a note from 1881: 'I no longer want any knowledge without danger: let there always be the treacherous sea or the merciless high mountains around the seeker of knowledge' (KSA 9, 7 [165]). He accepts that the passion for knowledge may come to a tragic end, but refuses to feel fear in the face of its pursuit, and as a passionate seeker he is keen to distinguish himself from the scholar: 'Are you scared? As much as with any passion! – Usually, however, you scholars are without passion, instead you have *got accustomed to your boredom!*' (Nietzsche, KSA 9, 7 [302])

Dawn and questions of knowledge

In *Dawn* Nietzsche has a great deal to say about knowledge: about what it is, about the challenges and difficulties it presents and about its future directions. The text advances a conception of plural modes and methods of knowledge. For Nietzsche it is no longer a question of the philosopher estranging him or herself from sensory perception and exalting the self to abstractions, in which we would then inhabit the palest images of words and things, playing with invisible, intangible and inaudible beings and out of disdain for the physically palpable. We can no longer have this Platonic admiration for the dialectic as our sole method and as practised by the good, desensualized person. Rather, we need to appeal to a multiplicity of faculties, methods and procedures, including the Platonic:

> The thinker needs fantasy, the leap upward, abstraction, desensualization, invention, presentiment, induction, dialectics, deduction, critique, compilation of material, impersonal mode of thought, contemplativeness and comprehensiveness, and not least of all, justice and love towards everything present. (D 43)

Nietzsche affirms what he calls 'the passion of knowledge' and speaks in glowing terms of those great philosophers, such as Plato and Aristotle from the ancients and Descartes and Spinoza from the early moderns, who found in knowledge, that is, 'in the activity of a well-trained, inquisitive, and inventive understanding the highest happiness: such thinkers actually enjoyed knowledge!' (D 550) He clearly wishes his readers to be inspired by these examples of philosophers who practised the rigours of knowledge. What Nietzsche is resisting in part is the appeal to an '"inner sense" or "intellectual intuition"', since such an appeal ends up wanting not philosophy but religion (D 544).

It is clear that in *Dawn* Nietzsche has a sublime commitment to a project of knowledge, but also a measured one. In aphorism 45, entitled 'A Tragic Ending for Knowledge', he notes that it is human sacrifice that has traditionally served as the means of producing exaltation; this sacrifice has elevated and exalted the human being. What if mankind were to now sacrifice itself: to whom would it make the sacrifice? Nietzsche suggests that it would be the knowledge of truth since only here could the goal be said to be commensurate with the sacrifice, 'because for this goal no sacrifice is too great'. But this goal remains too distant and lofty; much closer to home is the task of working out the extent to which humanity can take steps towards the advancement of knowledge and ascertaining what kind of knowledge-drive could impel it to the point of extinction 'with the light of an anticipatory wisdom in its eyes'. However, we may need the help of other species on other planets in order to pursue the practice of knowledge with enthusiasm:

> Perhaps one day, once an alliance for the purpose of knowledge has been established with inhabitants of other planets and one has communicated one's knowledge from star to star for a few millennia: perhaps then enthusiasm for knowledge will swell to such a high tide! (*D* 45)

For Nietzsche a chief task we godless moderns face is to purify ourselves of the origins and sources of our desire for the sublime, since the higher feelings associated with it are bound up with humanity's investment in an imaginary world: an exalted humanity is full of self-loathing and this needs to be conquered. However, he does not propose that we simply jettison the sublime, but that we go in search of new experiences of it. These will centre on knowledge and self-experimentation. Through knowledge a purified humanity can conquer the fear and anxiety that has captivated previous humanity and taught it to kneel down before the incomprehensible. In accordance with the tradition stretching from Longinus to Kant and Schiller, Nietzsche employs the sublime in connection with notions of elevation, exaltation, loftiness, ennoblement and the attainment of newly discovered heights of experience. At the same time, it is bound up for him with practices of purification and sublimation that involve the conquest and overcoming of traditional and conventional conceptions of reality and of what is possible in experience. In *Dawn* Nietzsche's concern is with a transitional humanity that is moving from a heritage of religions and moralities to something new, in fact, to uncharted conditions of existence. He is keen to militate against the sublime of dread and terror and to configure the sublime in a more modest and even humbling manner.[26] For Nietzsche the new sublimities of philosophy are bound up with a new comportment towards existence as it now concerns us as searchers of knowledge – and a new fearlessness is required as we embark on this search free of the prejudices of morality.[27] We are in the process of becoming creatures that exist largely to know and who seek to conquer the elevation offered by morality.

In a number of aphorisms in book five of *Dawn*, Nietzsche configures the operations of philosophy in relation to the sublime and reflects on its sublimities. Philosophy's love of knowledge – and to be a lover of knowledge is for Nietzsche to be an essentially unrequited lover – now develops as a form of passion that shrinks at no sacrifice. In aphorism 429 he notes that we moderns fear a possible return to barbarism and not because it would make us unhappier since in all ages barbarians have been happier peoples. Rather, he argues, our drive to knowledge has become so strong for us that we now cannot tolerate the idea of happiness without knowledge: 'The restlessness of discovery and divining has become just as appealing and indispensable to us as an unrequited love is to the lover; a love he would never trade at any price for a state of apathy; indeed, perhaps we too are *unhappy* lovers!' (D 429) We now honestly believe, Nietzsche writes, that 'under the pressure and suffering of *this* passion the whole of humanity must believe itself to be more sublime (*sich erhabener*) and more consoled than previously, when it had not yet overcome its envy of the cruder pleasure and contentment that result from barbarism' (ibid.). Nietzsche holds that we feel more consoled, I think, because of our growth in intellectual strength: we have the chance of knowledge and rendering things comprehensible, and with this there comes a new courage, fearlessness and cheerfulness (*Heiterkeit*). We even entertain the thought that humanity might perish of its new-found passion for knowledge, though clearly Nietzsche is not an advocate of this. As he notes, such a thought can hold no sway over us. Our evolution is now bound up with this passion, however, and the task is to allow ourselves to be ennobled and elevated by it: 'If humanity is not destroyed by a *passion* it will be destroyed by a *weakness*: which does one prefer? This is the main question. Do we desire for humanity an end in fire and light or in sand?' (ibid.)[28]

Nietzsche employs the sublime to address what philosophy now means and does in relation to the emerging science (*Wissenschaft*) of knowledge. He draws a comparison with rococo horticulture, which arose from the feeling that nature is ugly, savage and boring and thus the aim was to beautify it. This is now what philosophy does with science, beautifying what strikes us as ugly, dry, cheerless and laborious. Philosophy is a species of art and poetry and thus a form of entertainment: it wants to entertain (*unterhalten*) 'but, in accordance with its inherited pride, it wants to do this in a more sublime and elevated manner (*in einer erhabenen und höheren Art*) and before a select audience' (D 427). Nietzsche already has here, then, the conception of the project of the gay science with its mixture of poetry, song, the philosophical aphorism and dedication to science. In this aphorism from *Dawn* Nietzsche speaks of philosophy enabling us to wander in science as in wild nature and without effort or boredom. Such an ambition for philosophy is one that makes religion, hitherto the highest species of the art of entertainment, superfluous. Eventually a cry of dissent against philosophy may emerge, one voiced by pure scientism and naturalism: '"back to science," to the nature and naturalness of science!' At this point, Nietzsche notes, an age of humanity's history may then commence that discovers the mightiest beauty in precisely the wild and ugly sides of science, 'just as it was only from the time of Rousseau that one discovered a sense for the beauty of high mountains and the desert' (ibid.). In short, Nietzsche can see no good reason why humanity cannot grow in strength and insight with science even it entails shedding many illusions about ourselves and that have served to console us so far.

In book five of *Dawn* he is now envisaging how a new comportment towards life can exist for us modern free spirits who have renounced so much (God, religion, the first and last things, romantic music and so on). Nietzsche in fact raises the question whether the philosopher of the morning is really renouncing things or gaining a new cheerfulness or serenity:

> To relinquish the world without knowing it, like a *nun* – that leads to an infertile, perhaps melancholic solitude. This has nothing in common with the solitude of the thinker's *vita contemplativa*: when he elects *it,* he in no way wishes to renounce; on the contrary, it would amount to renunciation, melancholy, downfall of his self for him to have to endure the *vita practica*: he relinquishes the latter because he knows it, knows himself. Thus he leaps into *his* water, thus he attains *his* serenity. (D 440)

For the thinker who now has the new dedication to knowledge and can recognize the extent of its future-oriented character – it is such because the discoveries of knowledge always run ahead of a humanity that in time will seek to become equal to it – existence is lived magnanimously. In an aphorism entitled 'The thinker's magnanimity' Nietzsche writes:

Rousseau and Schopenhauer – both were proud enough to inscribe upon their existence the motto: *vitam impendere vero* ('to dedicate one's life to truth'). And again – how they both must have suffered in their pride that they could not succeed in making *verum impendere vitae*! ('to dedicate truth to life') – *verum*, as each of them understood it – in that their lives tagged along beside their knowledge like a temperamental bass that refuses to stay in tune with the melody! But knowledge would be in a sorry state if it was meted out to every thinker only as it suited his person! And thinkers would be in a sorry state if their vanity were so great that they could only endure this! The great thinker's most beautiful virtue radiates precisely from: the magnanimity with which he, as a person of knowledge (*Erkennender*), undauntedly, often shamed, often with sublime mockery (*mit erhabenem Spotte*) and smiling – offers himself and his life in sacrifice. (D 459)

Neither Rousseau nor Schopenhauer, Nietzsche is arguing, possessed the cognitive maturity that allows for knowledge and life to enter into a new marriage in which knowledge elevates and pulls life up with it: their emotional personalities interfered too much to permit this process to take place (D 497).[29]

We can contrast this with the depiction that Nietzsche provides of the likes of Plato, Spinoza and Goethe in the aphorism entitled 'The purifying eye.'[30] In the genius of these natures we find a spirit that is only loosely bound to character and temperament, 'like a winged essence that can separate itself from the latter and soar high above them (*sich dann weit über sie erheben kann*)' (D 497). Nietzsche then contrasts this genius with another kind, namely, those thinkers who boast of it but who in fact have never escaped from their temperament, and he gives as an example the case of Schopenhauer. Such geniuses are unable to fly above and beyond themselves but only ever encounter themselves wherever they fly. Nietzsche does not deny that such genius can amount to greatness, but he is keen to point out that what they lack is that which is to be truly prized – 'the *pure, purifying eye*'. Such an eye is not restricted in its vision by the partial sightedness created by character and temperament and can gaze at the world 'as if it were a god, a god it loves' (ibid.). Although these geniuses are teachers of 'pure seeing', Nietzsche is keen to stress that such seeing requires apprenticeship and long practice.

It is clear that for Nietzsche true genius is something extremely rare simply because so few can free themselves from their temperaments and character.[31] Most of us see existence through a veil or cloak. He challenges us to reflect on whether we are in fact suited for knowing what is true or not. Our mind may be too dull and our vision may be too crude to permit us access to such knowledge. He runs through the many subjective elements of our perception and vision of the world, how, for example, we are often on the lookout for something that affects us strongly and at other times for something that calms us because we are tired: 'Always full of secret predeterminations as to *how* the truth would have to be constituted if you, precisely you, were able to accept it!' (D 539) To attain objectivity of perception and vision is hard for human beings – to be just towards something requires from us warmth and enthusiasm, and the lovable and hateful ego appears to be always present – and may in fact be only attainable in degrees. We may, then, have good reasons for living in fear of our own ghost: 'In the cavern of every type of knowledge, are you not afraid once more of running into your own ghost, the ghost that is the cloak (*verkleidet*) in which truth has disguised itself from you?' (ibid.) For Nietzsche both Goethe and Schopenhauer are geniuses: the difference is that one is more capable than the other of pure seeing and hence more profound.

In the aphorism entitled 'Tyrants of the spirit,' Nietzsche suggests that we should no longer feel the need to rush knowledge along to some end point. There is no longer the need, he holds, to approach questions and experiments as if the solutions to them had to correspond to a typical human time span. We are now free to take our time and go slowly: 'To solve everything at one fell swoop, with one single word – that was the secret wish: this was the task one imagined in the image of the Gordian knot or of Columbus' egg; one did not doubt that in the realm of knowledge as well it was possible to reach one's goal after the manner of an Alexander or a Columbus and to solve all questions with *one* answer' (D 547). The idea evolved that there was a riddle to solve for the philosopher and that the task was to compress the problem of the world into the simplest riddle-form: 'The boundless ambition and jubilation of being the "unriddler of the world" were the stuff of thinker's dreams' (ibid.). Under such a schema of the task of thinking philosophy assumed the guise of being a supreme struggle for the tyrannical rule of spirit reserved for a single individual. (Nietzsche thinks that it is Schopenhauer who has most recently fancied himself as such an individual.) The lesson to be drawn from this inheritance is that the quest for knowledge has been retarded by the moral narrow-mindedness of its disciples; in the future, Nietzsche declares, 'It must be pursued with a higher and more magnanimous basic feeling: "What do I matter!" stands over the door of the future thinker' (ibid.).

Nietzsche directly addresses the question of the direction of this new philosophy of the morning: Where is it headed with all its detours? He himself raises the suspicion that it may be little more than the translation into reason of a concentrated drive, 'for mild sunshine, clearer and fresher air, southerly vegetation, sea air, transient digests of meat, eggs, and fruit, hot water to drink, daylong silent wanderings ... almost soldierly habits', and so on. In short, is it a philosophy 'that at bottom is the instinct for a personal diet' and hygiene, one that suits a particular idiosyncratic taste and for whom it alone is beneficial? He continues:

> An instinct that is searching for my own air, my own heights, my own weather, my own type of health, through the detour of my head? There are many other and certainly more loftier sublimities (*höhere Erhabenheiten*) of philosophy and not just those that are more gloomy and more ambitious than mine – perhaps they too are, each and every one, nothing other than intellectual detours for these kinds of personal drives? – In the meantime (*Inzwischen*) I observe with new eyes the secret and solitary swarming of a butterfly high on the rocky seashore where many good plants are growing; it flies about, untroubled that it only has one more day yet to live and that the night will be too cold for its winged fragility. One could certainly come up with a philosophy for it as well: although it is not likely to be mine. (D 553)

Although Nietzsche can observe and appreciate the butterfly in a new way, as he now can all things of nature, its mode of life is too simple and untroubled – it lives solely in the moment – in contrast to the philosophy of life his search is opening up, which is one of deep and troubled fascination and with ever-new peaks of elevation.[32] It is clear in the passage I have just cited that Nietzsche is not attaching himself to the sublimities of philosophy in what he calls their loftier and gloomy form, and this is because he not does wish to reach a point of transcendence or otherworldliness. He lacks the ambition for the sublime in this sense and instead seeks a sublime that involves and rests on a sublimation of the drives, such as the instinct for his own heights and his own health and as these take place through the detour of his head. He comes to know himself through his head, of course, but what is motivating his search are the instincts and drives of his body.

For Nietzsche the consolations of religion are rapidly disappearing from our consciousness (see MOM 169 & D 68). The new and modest sublimities of philosophy he is fashioning for himself can be understood as affording new consolations. What has gone for us free-spirited moderns are precisely those things Boethius sought as consolation from philosophy: belief in ultimate goodness, in an avenger and a final improver, belief in providence, resting in endless trust and so on (GS 285). While the passion of knowledge does not exist in order to console us or to satisfy the heart's desire – indeed, it challenges us to the very core of our being since truth and knowledge reveal that we are not what we take ourselves to be as self-originating agents or subjects – philosophy can entertain us (hold our attention) in new ways and free spirits console themselves in entertaining the thought that the personal sacrifices they make to knowledge may contribute to the greater health of a future humanity.

A parable about the sea and the city

Book five of *Dawn* begins with an aphorism entitled 'In the great silence,' which stages an encounter with the sea. The scene that Nietzsche depicts is one of stillness and solitude: 'Here is the sea, here we can forget the city' (D 423). After the noisy ringing of bells announcing the angelus,[33] which produce the sad and foolish yet sweet noise that divides night and day, all becomes still and the sea lies pale and shimmering but unable or unwilling to speak; similarly, the night sky plays its everlasting evening game with red and yellow and green but chooses not to speak. We are encompassed on all sides by a 'tremendous muteness' that is both lovely and dreadful and at which the heart swells. But is there not hypocrisy in this silent beauty? Nietzsche invites us to ask: Would it not speak well and evilly if it so wished? Would it not mock our feeling of sympathy (*Mitgefühl*) with it? A voice, Nietzsche's voice, then interrupts and declares, 'So be it! I am not ashamed of being mocked by such powers.' This voice pities nature for its silence and on account of the malice that ties its tongue. In this scene the heart, the regulating source of life's blood flow, continues to swell and is startled by 'a new truth': '*It too cannot speak*, it too mocks when the mouth calls something into this beauty, it too enjoys its sweet silent malice' (ibid.). The voice begins to hate speech and even thinking for behind every word it hears the error of laughter, of imagination and delusion. Should one not, then, mock at one's pity and at one's mockery? What riddle of existence are we caught up in? Has not all become dark for the philosophy of the morning? The aphorism concludes as follows: 'O sea! O evening! You are terrible mentors! You teach the human being to *cease* being human! Ought he to sacrifice himself to you? Ought he to become as you are now, pale, shimmering, mute, monstrous (*ungeheuer*), reposing above himself? Sublimely above himself? (*Über sich selber erhaben*)' (ibid.).

What kind of sublime state is it that the human being might attain here? How can the human being cease being itself? Is this what has really taken place in this experience? The reader has good reason to pause and reflect on what might be expressed in the aphorism. One response might be to suggest that the encounter with the sea challenges our human sense of scale and measure, confronting us with something immense and monstrous. But here we have to be careful because of the 'mockery' that greets us in the experience. All the names we might come up with to describe the mute sea will come back to us: profound, eternal and mysterious. Are we not endowing the sea with our own names and virtues?[34] Do we ever escape the net of language; do we ever escape the human?[35]

The basic contrast that Nietzsche is making in the aphorism is between stillness and noise (sea and city): in our encounter with the sea, it might be suggested, we quiet our being, become calm and contemplative, think about more than the here and now, the merely fleeting and transient. In *Dawn* 485 Nietzsche has 'B' state, 'It seems I need distant perspectives to think well of things.' If in the volumes of *Human, all too Human* Nietzsche had urged his readers to renounce the first and last things and devote instead their energy and attentiveness to the closest things (WS 16), the distant things, including distant times, return in *Dawn*, perhaps prompted by an encounter with the sea. *Dawn* 441 entitled 'Why what is closest becomes ever more distant' captures this new sense of perspective: 'The more we think about everything that we were and will be, the paler what we are right now becomes. ... We grow more solitary – and indeed *because* the whole flood of humanity resounds around us' (D 441). We have reason to pause because of the reference to the 'evening'.[36] For Nietzsche there are different ways of seeing, some more human than others and some that are superhuman (this is what he calls 'pure seeing'; see also *Dawn* 426 on the 'richer form of seeing'). The encounter with sea and evening serves to inspire us to think about these different ways of seeing; we no longer only inhabit the day with its ordinary, prosaic consciousness.

After the opening aphorism the next two consider truth and error and amplify what has been highlighted in the book's opening aphorism: the problem of the human is that it is an erring animal and dwells in the space of error. Nietzsche notes that errors have hitherto served as forces of consolation for humanity (errors of human judgement regarding freedom of the will and the unity of the world, for example).[37] If today we are seekers of truth, may we not, then, expect the same from truth? But can truths be capable of producing the effect of consolation? Is it not in the nature of truth precisely not to console? If human beings exist as truthful beings but employ philosophy as therapy in the sense of seeking a cure for themselves, does this not suggest that they are not, in fact, seeking truth at all? Nietzsche spells out the reason for our ambivalent stance towards errors. On the one hand it is on their basis that humanity has been elevated and has excelled itself again and again, for example, through errors as to its descent, uniqueness and destiny. On the other hand, it has to be noted that it is through the same errors that unspeakable amounts of suffering, persecution, suspicion and misery have come into the world.

Aphorism 507 of the text entitled 'Against the tyranny of the true' signals a warning concerning our devotion to knowledge through experimentation. Here Nietzsche stages an anxiety that takes on a more dramatic form in his later writings and their questioning of the will to truth. In this aphorism he asks why it should be considered desirable that truth alone should rule and be omnipotent. We can esteem it as a great power, but we should not allow it to rule over us in some tyrannical fashion. Much healthier is to allow truth to have opponents and for us to find relief from it from time to time, and be at liberty to reside knowingly in untruth. Failure to place truth within a rich economy of life will make it, and us in the process, 'boring, powerless, and tasteless' (D 507). In the next work, *The Gay Science*, the first three books of which Nietzsche initially conceived as a continuation of *Dawn*, Nietzsche focuses on the task of the 'incorporation' (*Einverleibung*) of truth and knowledge and holds this to be our new experiment (GS 110).

A number of questions and doubts might emerge from Nietzsche's outline of this new set of tasks for humanity. Let us accept that we wish to learn to know and become genuine knowers, but does this mean and must it mean always as human knowers? Would this not mean always playing a part in the same comedy and never being able to see into things except through the same pair of eyes? Might there not be beings with different eyes and better equipped for knowledge? Moreover, if we are condemned to see only with human eyes and to know with human minds, does this not signal in fact the impossibility of knowledge? As Nietzsche rhetorically puts it, do we come to know at the end of all our knowledge only our own organs? (D 483) Will this not lead to misery and disgust with ourselves? These are the questions Nietzsche considers in aphorism 483 and his answer to them provides one clue as to his conception of the image of the sea that the final book of the text starts with. He suggests that even when it proves to be the case that our search for knowledge returns us always to ourselves, this does not mean that new knowledge is not to be had, for even here we have a form of being that remains largely unknown and unexplored: 'This is a wicked attack – *reason* is attacking you! But tomorrow you will be right back in the midst of knowing (*Erkennen*) again and so also in the midst of unreason, by which I mean: in the *pleasure* (*Lust*) of being human. Let us go down to the sea!' (D 483; see also D 539) The question arises: Why would we from this experience go down to the sea? Would we encounter there only ourselves, or perhaps a challenge to ourselves that would lead us to discover ourselves – and the world – anew? For are we not fundamentally at the core unknown to ourselves? Contra the tendency towards self-loathing, then, Nietzsche is advising us that there are good reasons for taking pleasure or delight in our continuing human-ness. This occupies Nietzsche's attention in aphorism 551 entitled 'Of future virtues.'

In a study of the philosophy of fear, Lars Svendsen has argued, in a chapter that considers the sublime and that begins with a position attributed to Nietzsche, that fear is something that lends colour to the world and a world without it would be boring: 'In an otherwise secure world, fear can break the boredom. A feeling of fear can have an uplifting effect.'[38] While Nietzsche is not oblivious to the shock function that fright can sometimes play in human existence,[39] he does not hold in *Dawn* to the position Svendsen credits him with: 'Nietzsche complains that the world has lost much of its charm because we no longer fear it enough.'[40] In truth, in the passage on which this claim is based (*Dawn* 551), Nietzsche makes no such complaint and his position is subtler. Nietzsche is looking forward to new experiences and new possibilities of life, not backward to previous experiences and ancient reverences. He is taking cognizance of several facts as he judges them and noting that as the world becomes more comprehensible to us the more that solemnity of all kinds decreases. Hitherto, he notes, it was fear that informed humanity's attitude of reverence as it found itself overcome in the face of the unknown and the mysterious, forcing it to 'sink down before the incomprehensible'. He then asks whether the world will lose some its appeal once a new humanity comes into being that has grown less fearful in the face of the character of the world: Might it not also result in our own fearsomeness becoming slighter? His answer is negative and it is such because of the courage that he sees as among our new virtues. This is a species of courage so courageous that it feels itself to be '*above* people and things', it is a kind of 'excessive magnanimity' and, he notes, has hitherto been lacking in humanity (D 551).

Nietzsche concludes the aphorism by declaring the age of 'harmless counterfeiting' to be over and he looks ahead to the 'astronomers of the ideal' who will take over the role of the poets whose task was to be seers who could recount to us 'something of the *possible!*' (ibid.) In short, what Svendsen misses is the key point of book five of *Dawn* and around which its various insights hinge, namely, the promise of new dawns and an essential part of realizing this promise consists in conquering and purifying ourselves of the anciently established sublime.[41] If, as might be supposed, there are reasons for nihilism, there are also equally good reasons for its exact opposite: 'If only they wanted to let us experience in advance something of the *future virtues*! Or of virtues that will never exist on earth, although they could exist somewhere in the world – of purple-glowing galaxies and the whole Milky Ways of the beautiful! Where are you, you astronomers of the ideal?' (D 551)[42] Nietzsche does not, then, align his thinking with the cause of spreading fear or terror: 'The pessimist, who gives all things the blackest and gloomiest colours, makes use of only flames and bolts of lightning, celestial effulgence, and everything that has glaring brilliance and confuses the eye; brightness is only there for him to increase the horror (*Entsetzen*) and to make us sense that things are more terrifying (*Schreckliches*) than they really are' (D 561).

Nietzsche's encounter with the sea, then, seems to work as a metaphor for knowledge and its search: the search will inevitably take us in the direction of unfamiliar and even inhospitable lands and galaxies. On the one hand, Nietzsche recognizes that something as sublime as the monstrous sea is an alien world to the human when it is truly encountered and greets us, and our attempts to communicate with it, with a fundamental muteness. On the other hand, he does not wish us to experience terror in the face of this experience, say the terror of the sublime. Instead, we are to focus on coming up with a new set of vocabularies to describe our experiences and to go in search of new peaks and elevations of perception and insight, which we can call new sublimities.

Conclusion

Although knowledge has its origins in a contingent evolution and accidental birth, Nietzsche also wishes to place the passion of knowledge in the service of specific practical ends. These ends centre on a care of self and on the importance of individual and social experimentation. As we have seen, Nietzsche construes lovers of knowledge as unrequited lovers. According to Robert Pippin, there is no better image of philosophical eros than this: 'It dominates philosophy's self-image from Socrates on, rendering it useless and even comical in the eyes of nonphilosophers.' Indeed, he notes that for Nietzsche the philosophical type is precisely a person 'who can sustain an entire life of unrequited love'.[43] Although this is surely right, we should also not neglect the fact that Nietzsche places the passion of knowledge, including its adventure, in the service of specific practical and transformative ends. Nietzsche favours ethical and social experimentation that will endeavour to bring about human pluralization contra what he takes to be the fanatical claims and presumptions of morality. For Nietzsche it is necessary, for example, to contest the idea that there is a single moral-making morality since every code of ethics that affirms itself in an exclusive manner 'destroys too much valuable energy and costs humanity much too dearly' (D 164). In the future, he hopes, the inventive and fructifying person shall no longer be sacrificed and 'numerous novel experiments shall be made in ways of life and modes of society' (ibid). When this takes place we will find that an enormous load of guilty conscience has been purged from the world. Humanity has suffered for too long from teachers of morality who wanted too much all at once and sought to lay down precepts for everyone (D 194). In the future, care will need to be given to the most personal questions and create time for them (D 196). Small individual questions and experiments are no longer to be viewed with contempt and impatience (D 547). Contra 'morality', then, he holds that we ourselves are experiments and our task should be to want to be such.

A Philosophy of Modesty: Ethics and the Search for a Care of Self

Introduction

Two things of note ought to strike us about the Nietzsche of the middle writings. First, is the extent to which the philosophy is one of modesty: this is true of both the kind of work it sets out to do and the goals it sets for its readers as ethical subjects. Second, there is the peculiar character of Nietzsche's commitment to ethics. Nietzsche at times can appear as rationalist as Kant and yet he wants ethics, involving duties one has to oneself and to others, to be something pleasurable. Nietzsche has the hope that one day, after much long practice and daily work, each of us could say – as an ethical injunction since it cannot be anything else – 'We *want* to become those that we are,' (GS 335) not we need or we ought to become this, but that it is our desire, something we enjoy and take pleasure and pride in. The ethical aspiration is towards philosophy's traditional goals: rational mastery of the affects, autonomy or self-legislation, and with a more modern colouring, authenticity (see D 105). And yet, much of this, if not all, needs to be conceived according to Nietzsche in quite modest terms. Much of the work of the texts of the middle period is thus devoted to deflating the pretensions of the ego to claims of self-origination; this is what Nietzsche exposes as the Oedipal fantasy in which we exist, as it were, as our own mother and father (D 128). Although Nietzsche argues against Schopenhauer's doctrine on the immutability of character, arguing against him that we are not *fully* developed facts, it remains the case that for Nietzsche the liberty we have within our power is a modest and limited one: the liberty we have at our disposal is that of cultivating the drives, not some miraculous power of self-invention and self-creation ex nihilo (D 560).

Nietzsche's attacks on morality can mislead as if his aim was to remove us from the tasks of morality altogether. In fact, his goal is nothing other than a moral one, or perhaps it is best to say 'ethical', and for reasons that several later thinkers have argued, such as Deleuze and Foucault.[1] Nevertheless, I would maintain that we should not lose sight of the fact that Nietzsche's goal is a morality or, if we prefer, ethics of self-cultivation. He wants us to learn this skill or art as one that can be taken up by the self, as it works on itself, being as much as an aesthetic exercise as an ethical one. He describes this well in *The Gay Science* 290 where he writes of the importance of giving style to one's character. The task, says Nietzsche, is to cultivate the shoots of one's drives and affects, which one can do with the good or bad taste of a gardener, and in the French or English, or Dutch or Chinese style (D 560).

Perhaps the difficulty for some readers is that Nietzsche presents this becoming-ethical on our part in such seemingly uninviting terms: we are to remove ourselves from the mass of humanity, we need to endure long periods of solitude, we need to resist the temptation of the sympathetic affections and we need to get beyond our compassion. I want to show that Nietzsche has reasons, one's integral to his project, to support the mode of ethical practice he advocates. Nietzsche's campaign or polemic against morality begins in earnest in *Dawn* and it consists in (1) contesting and deflating the pretensions of the modern cult of the sympathetic affects, including compassion (*Mitleid*); (2) replacing this with a more modest conception of morality, namely, an ethics centred on the care of self. It is perhaps important to bear in mind what Nietzsche says about the book in *Ecce Homo*: although it mounts a 'campaign' against morality, the reader should not think it has about it 'the slightest whiff of gunpowder'; rather, the reader should 'make out quite different and more pleasing scents' (EH III 'D', 1).

A significant change takes place in Nietzsche's thinking with *Dawn*, which can be summarized as follows. In *Human, all too Human* Nietzsche had essentially been working under the influence of Paul Rée and his thinking about morality. The working assumption of Rée's approach is that we can give a strictly naturalistic account of morality in which morality is seen to be coextensive with the unegoistic instincts or drives. In short, Rée accepts the thesis of Kant and Schopenhauer that for morality to be possible the ego must not be present in actions judged to be of moral worth; the difference is that he pursues a naturalistic inquiry into this, in large part inspired by evolutionary theory, including Lamarckism and Darwinism.[2] In *Human, all too Human* (1878) Nietzsche is a psychological egoist and thinks 'morality' is simply an impossible demand humanity places upon itself. He borrows the key argument from Rée explicitly in the book: 'The moral person,' he writes, quoting from Rée's *On the Origin of Moral Sensations*, 'does not stand any nearer to the intelligible (metaphysical) world than the physical person,' and Nietzsche adds that this is an insight that needs to be hardened and sharpened 'by the hammerblows of historical knowledge' (HAH 37). By the time of *Dawn* (1881) Nietzsche is adopting a different approach and strategy: Why assume that morality is coextensive with the unegoistic? Perhaps there are many moralities and no single moral-making morality. This is indeed the position he adopts in the text and is what allows for his first proper revaluation of values. The significance of this change in his thinking largely explains the change in therapy that is evident in the text: it is no longer simply a question of psychological dissection, in which we are not sure whether such dissection will be of benefit to humanity or work to its detriment (HAH 38); rather, it is now that Nietzsche sees much more fruitful possibilities opening up – new dawns in effect – and he is much more cheerful about the task of exposing the prejudices and presumptions of morality.

Nietzsche's thinking aspires to be a practical philosophy. He writes in *The Gay Science* (1882): 'I favour any skepsis to which one can reply: "let us try it!" I do not wish to hear anything of all those things and questions that do not permit any experiment' (GS 51). In *Dawn* he states that we ourselves are experiments and our task should be to *want* to be such. We are to build anew the laws of life and of behaviour by taking from the sciences of physiology, medicine, sociology and solitude the foundation stones for new ideals, if not the new ideals themselves (D 453). As these sciences are not yet sure of themselves, we find ourselves living in either a preliminary or a posterior existence, depending on our taste and talent, and in this interregnum the best strategy is for us to become our own *reges* (sovereigns) and establish small experimental states. My claim is that we should read such a statement – the invocation to live experimentally – in terms of a series of modest proposals that Nietzsche is making about our ethical (re-) formation.

Nietzsche's thinking is best conceived, then, as a philosophy of modesty. In *Human, all too Human* he announced his project as one of 'historical philosophizing' and declared that its key virtue will be that of modesty (*Bescheidung*) – if everything that there is has come to be, then there are no eternal facts or absolute truths (HAH 2). Similarly, in the preface to *Dawn*, where he calls for the 'self-overcoming of morality' 'out of morality', Nietzsche takes morality to task because he says, our taste prefers 'more modest words' (*bescheidenere Worte*) (D Preface 4). This concern with cultivating modesty informs Nietzsche's critique of morality and what he proposes to replace morality with, namely, an ethics of self-cultivation. The problem, as we shall see, lies with the presumptions of morality that lead us to live in denial of our ethical complexity and the fact that we are *not* the authors of our being in the world (as morality supposes). Or, at the very least, we conceive this in very immodest terms as if we had fantastic powers of self-invention and, indeed, of freedom.

In this chapter I want to show in what ways Nietzsche fruitfully connects with Foucault's conception of philosophical practice as bound up with a care of self. When he is at his most positivistic – for example, in the opening chapter of volume one of *Human, all too Human* – Nietzsche casts suspicion on the motivations of the Socratic schools and their preoccupation with happiness and serenity. In subordinating knowledge to ethical practice (the care of self), these schools are said to have 'tied up the veins of scientific inquiry' (HAH 7). However, by the time of *Dawn*, if not earlier (e.g. aspects of volume two of HAH), Nietzsche is now writing in favour of such an ethical practice and even champions Socrates as a figure in whom philosophy becomes a search for an ethics of self-control and personal well-being (D 9). In seeking resources in ancient ethics – for example, reviving interest in figures such as Epicurus and Epictetus and their modes of life – Nietzsche is searching for an alternative to conceptions of moral life that prevail in his own time and that for him assume the form of a tyrannical encroachment on the needs of self-cultivation. Let me now bring this to light: my focus will largely be on the text, *Dawn* and subtitled 'thoughts on the presumptions of morality'.

The presumptions of morality

Throughout *Dawn*, Nietzsche operates with several critical conceptions of morality. With regard to the modern prejudice, which is one of the main foci of his polemic in the book, here there is the presumption that we know what actually constitutes morality: 'It seems *to do* every single person *good* these days to hear that society is on the road to *adapting* the individual to fit the needs of the throng and that the *individual's happiness as well as his sacrifice* consist in feeling himself to be a useful member of the whole' (D 132). As Nietzsche sees it, then, the modern emphasis is on defining the moral in terms of the sympathetic affects and compassion (*Mitleid*). We can, he thinks, explain the modern in terms of a movement towards managing more cheaply, safely and uniformly individuals in terms of '*large bodies and their limbs*'. This, he says, is the basic moral current of our age: 'Everything that in some way supports both this drive to form bodies and limbs and its abetting drives is felt to be *good*' (D 132).

He makes a number of objections to this tendency and drive and they run and recur throughout *Dawn*. Let me note some of them.

In the presumption that the essence of the moral is to be defined in terms of purely other-regarding actions, there is lacking appreciation of our ethical complexity and the fact that in any action multiple motives might be in play. For Nietzsche moral motives are epistemically opaque, and on this point he is close to Kant.[3] Kant acknowledges that we can never know with absolute certainty the nature of our motives: we may believe we have performed an action out of respect for the moral law, but in fact it may have been performed out of self-love or some other heteronomous inclination. Nietzsche adheres to this view because for him there are many motives informing any single action and these motives are hidden from the agent performing the action. As he indicates in his treatment of *Mitleid*, it may well be that honour, fear, self-defence or revenge are what moves us to help another, although we tell ourselves that it was an act performed solely for their well-being. As one commentator rightly notes, for Nietzsche human nature 'has depths and obscurities that make it extremely difficult, if not impossible to specify the drives and urges from which our actions stem'.[4] We are not transparent to ourselves in Nietzsche's view, and when we rely on introspection or self-consciousness to discover our motives and intentions, we are involved in processes of selection and interpretation; that is, we do not simply retrieve so-called 'mental facts' in such acts. Rather, we 'impose, form, organize, and categorize our inner experiences just as we do our outer experiences'.[5] Nietzsche insists that actions are never what they appear to be: 'We have expended so much labour on learning that external things are not as they appear to us to be – very well! The case is the same with the inner world!' (D 116).

In the book Nietzsche devotes a significant number of sections to the topic of *Mitleid*, largely concentrated in book two of the text. His aim is to outline some of the perspectives by which we can gain some genuinely reflective insight into the affect of compassion and to encourage us to pursue critical lines of inquiry, and so *Mitleid* will be shown to be not a pure other-regarding affection, to be an injurious affect, to have value for specific cultures and so on.[6] His criticism rests on a number of concerns. Let me mention three.

1. A concern that in extolling compassion as the panacea to our moral anxieties we are in danger of existing as fantasists. Nietzsche wonders

whether people speak with such idolatry about love – the 'food of the gods' – simply because they have had so little of it. But would not a utopia of universal love be something ludicrous? – 'Each person flocked around, pestered, longed for not by one love … but by thousands, indeed by each and everyone' (D 147). Instead, Nietzsche wants us to favour a future of solitude, quietude, and even being unpopular. The imperatives of philosophies of universal love and compassion will serve only to destroy us. If they tempt us we should put them to the test and stop all our fantasizing (D 137).

2. A concern that in its cult of the sympathetic affects modern society is in danger of providing the image of a single moral-making morality that amounts to a tyrannical encroachment on the requirements of individual self-cultivation. In an essay on pity and mercy in Nietzsche, Martha Nussbaum notes, correctly in my view, that Nietzsche's project is one that aims to bring about a revival of Stoic values – self-command and self-formation – within a post-Christian and post-Romantic context (she criticizes him for this Stoicism).[7] The picture frequently presented is one of Nietzsche advocating, in place of an ethics of sympathy or compassion, one of idiosyncratic self-assertion or the value of unbridled egoism. This is, clearly, a caricature, and fails to capture what we might call the Stoic demands that Nietzsche places on the self and its cultivation: harshness towards oneself, self-discipline, self-control, honesty and a profound love of fate.[8] An important aphorism in this regard is 139 which runs:

> You say that the morality of being compassionate is a higher morality (*Moral*) than that of Stoicism? Prove it! But remember that what is 'higher' and 'lower' in morality is not, in turn to be measured by a moral yardstick: for there is no absolute morality (*Moral*). So take your rule from somewhere else – and now beware! (D 139)

Here we see Nietzsche contesting the idea that there is a *single* moral-making morality – he does not contest the idea that morality is necessary, only that there is a single, absolute conception of it.

3. A concern that the metaphysical estimation of *Mitleid* by Schopenhauer – namely, that through *Mitleid* we pierce the veil of Maya and discover that all is One and 'this art thou' – is psychologically naïve and without penetration. In *Dawn* 142 Nietzsche refers to Schopenhauer's account of a 'mystical process' by which *Mitleid* makes two beings into one and describes it as 'rapturous and worthless poppycock' (*schwärmerischen und nichtswürdigen*

Krimskrams).[9] For Nietzsche it is simply not the case that we ever act from single motive. If we wish to free ourselves from *our* suffering in acts of *Mitleid*, which is what he thinks is taking place, it is also the case, Nietzsche surmises, that with the same act we surrender to an impulse for pleasure, for example, in the thought of praise and gratitude which will come our way if we were to come to someone's aid. The performer of the act can thus take a delight in himself, for example, in the sensation that the action has put an end to an injustice that arouses one's indignation – the release of this indignation can have an invigorating effect. Once again, as is so typical of his middle writings, Nietzsche is asking for psychological probity when it comes to analysing moral matters and what is said to constitute the moral:

> That compassion … should be *of the same ilk* as the suffering in view of which it arises or that compassion possesses an especially keen and penetrating understanding of that suffering, both these claims are contradicted by *experience*, and anyone who has glorified compassion based on just these two aspects *lacked* sufficient experience in precisely this domain of the moral. (D 133)

In and of itself *Mitleid* has as little good character as any other drive: it is only when it is extolled – which happens when we fail to apprehend what is injurious about it and discover in it instead a source of pleasure – that a good conscience attaches itself to it, and only then does one surrender to it readily and not shy away from the impulse (D 134). In conditions, such as existed in Greek culture, when its injurious character is apprehended, it is considered a weakness; it is a 'pathological recurring affect, the danger of which one can remove by temporary, voluntary discharges' (D 134). Nietzsche is not arguing against the idea that physicians of humanity are needed or that humanity does not suffer; rather, his point is that to be a proper physician to humanity one needs to be cautious with regard to the sentiment of compassion; otherwise we will be lamed in all the decisive moments and our knowledge and benevolent hand will be paralysed.

Nietzsche suggests that a culture of compassion could be a very destructive culture; in fact he thinks humankind would perish from it if it became the norm for a day; we might grow sick of it because of feeling so sick about ourselves. Our inability to digest and cope with life's experiences and their severities will induce us to become deeply melancholic. There is a need for us, then, to become much more subtle in our appreciation of this moral affect. *Mitleid* is an affect that, like any other, needs to be brought under control and sifted by reason; otherwise it is as dangerous as any other affect (WP 928).[10]

Nietzsche treats *Mitleid* as a psychological malaise and as a sociological phenomenon of modernity,[11] and the two are intermingled in his account in *Dawn*. For Nietzsche, then, the principal prejudice that holds sway in the Europe of his day is that the sympathetic affects define the essence of the moral, such as actions deemed to be congenial, disinterested, of general utility and so on. He also thinks we are busy building a society of security in which the chief goal is to protect individuals from various hazards of life and so reduce human suffering and conflict. In *Dawn* Nietzsche's focus is not, as is widely supposed, on Christianity as the religion of pity or compassion – he maintains that until the eighteenth century such a virtue was a subsidiary and nonessential aspect of this religion. He then inquires into the source of the feeling that morality consists in disinterested, useful and congenial actions and claims that it is the effect and change of heart wrought upon Europe by Christianity, even though this was neither its intention nor its teaching. Rather, the view that morality means nothing other than disinterested, useful and congenial actions is the residuum of Christian sentiments once the strictly egotistical, foundational belief in the importance of eternal personal salvation, and the dogmas on which this belief rested, receded and there then came into the foreground ancillary beliefs in love and love thy neighbour which harmonized with ecclesiastical charity. There emerges in modernity a cult of love for humanity and the idea of surpassing the Christian ideal became, 'a secret spur of all French freethinkers from Voltaire through to August Comte', for example, the latter's moral formula of '*vivre pour autrui*' (live for others) (D 132).

Nietzsche holds that it is necessary to contest the idea that there is a single moral-making morality since every code of ethics that affirms itself in an exclusive manner 'destroys too much valuable energy and costs humanity much too dearly' (D 164). In place of what he sees as the ruling ethic of sympathy, which he thinks can assume the form of a 'tyrannical encroachment', Nietzsche invites individuals to engage in self-fashioning, cultivating a self that others can look at with pleasure and that still gives vent to the expression, albeit in a subtle and delicate manner, of an altruistic drive:

> *Moral fashion of a commercial society* – Behind the fundamental principle of the contemporary moral fashion: 'moral actions are generated by sympathy (*Sympathie*) for others', I see the work of a collective drive toward timidity masquerading behind an intellectual front: this drive desires … that life be rid of *all the dangers* it once held and that *each and every person* should help toward this end with all one's might: therefore only actions aimed at the common security

and at society's sense of security may be accorded the rating 'good!' – How little pleasure people take in themselves these days, however, when such a tyranny of timidity dictates to them the uppermost moral law (*Sittengesetz*), when, without so much as a protest, they let themselves be commanded to ignore and look beyond themselves and yet have eagle-eyes for *every* distress and *every* suffering existing elsewhere! Are we not, with this prodigious intent to grate off all the rough and sharp edges from life, well on the way to turning humanity into *sand*?... In the meantime, the question itself remains open as to whether one is *more useful* to another by immediately and constantly leaping to his side and *helping* him – which can, in any case, only transpire very superficially, provided the help does not turn into a tyrannical encroachment and transformation – or by *fashioning* out of oneself something the other will behold with pleasure, a lovely, peaceful, self-enclosed garden, for instance, with high walls to protect against the dangers and dust of the roadway, but with a hospitable gate as well. (D 174)

The perspective that Nietzsche adopts here on commercial society – he appears to have encountered the term in Hippolyte Taine[12] – is perhaps a little odd since we typically associate it with an ethic of selfishness and pride. However, as one commentator notes, those who favoured commercial society, such as the French *philosophes*, including thinkers such as Voltaire and Montesquieu, held that by 'establishing bonds among people and making life more comfortable, commerce softens and refines people's manners and promotes humaneness and civility'.[13] In this section Nietzsche is expressing an anxiety that other nineteenth-century social analysts, such as Tocqueville, have, namely, that market-driven atomization and de-individuation can readily lead to a form of communitarian tyranny.[14] We are today creating a society of universal security, but the price being paid for it is, Nietzsche thinks, much too high: 'The maddest thing is that what is being effected is the very opposite of universal security' (D 179). We live within the effect of general opinions about *the* human being, which is a 'bloodless abstraction' and 'fiction' (D 105). Even the modern glorification of work and talk of its blessings can be interpreted as a fear of everything individual. The subjection to hard industriousness from early until late serves as 'the best policeman' since it keeps everyone in bounds and hinders the development of reason, desire and the craving for independence. It uses vast amounts of nervous energy which could be given over to reflection, brooding, dreaming, loving and hating and working through our experiences: 'A society in which there is continuous hard work will have more security: and security is currently worshipped as the supreme divinity' (D 173).

Perhaps Nietzsche's fundamental presupposition in the book is that ours is an age of great uncertainty in which there is emerging individuals who no longer consider themselves to be bound by existing mores and laws and are thus making the first attempts to organize and create for themselves a right. Hitherto such individuals have lived their lives under the jurisdiction of a guilty conscience, being decried as criminals, freethinkers and immoralists (D 164). Although this development will make the coming century a precarious one (it may mean, Nietzsche notes, that a rifle hangs on each and every shoulder), it is one that Nietzsche thinks we should find fitting and good since it at least insures the presence of an oppositional power that will admonish that there is any such thing as a single moral-making morality.

Nietzsche's ethical commitment is clear from aphorism 174 of *Dawn*: a pleasure and care of self that strives for independence and self-sufficiency. One does not isolate oneself from others, but neither does one seek to effect a tyrannical encroachment on them. Instead, one offers a 'hospitable gate' through which others can freely enter and leave, and through self-cultivation one fashions a style of existing that others will behold with pleasure.

The subject in question

It is not a straightforward matter to claim that Nietzsche has an intimate concern with the fate of the subject or self. Today notions of autonomy and sovereign individuality have been placed under suspicion in many quarters of philosophy and in some quarters of Nietzsche-studies.[15] In fact, a suspicion about the subject in Nietzsche dates back to an essay that Gianni Vattimo published in Italian in 1979. Vattimo argued that Nietzsche's critique of morality in *Dawn* is not conducted, 'in the name of the free and responsible subject, for such a subject is likewise a product of neurosis, a thing formed in illness'.[16]

As Arthur Danto has noted, the psychology in *Dawn* is dazzling and precocious. Nietzsche's psychology, he argues, is resolutely anti-Cartesian and has to be inasmuch as his critique of morality entails the view that we do not really know what we are, while Cartesianism is precisely the view that what we essentially are is something immediately present to consciousness, and nothing is true of us psychologically of which we are not directly and noninferentially aware.[17] Here several aphorisms in book two of *Dawn* are especially significant. In aphorism 115 on the 'so-called "ego"' (*Ich*), Nietzsche draws attention to the prejudices of language, noting that they hinder a properly rich and subtle understanding of inner processes and drives. We seem to have words that exist only for the '*superlative* degrees' of these processes and drives: 'Wrath, hate, love, compassion, craving, knowing, joy, pain – these are all names for *extreme* states.' This would not be important were it not for the fact, Nietzsche thinks, that it is the milder middle degrees, as well as the lower ones, which elude us and yet 'collaborate … in the formation of our character and destiny'. In aphorism 116 on the 'unknown world of the "subject"' (*Subject*)', Nietzsche startles us with his assertion that from the most distant times of the past to the present day what has been so difficult for us to comprehend is our ignorance of ourselves: 'The age old delusion that one knows, knows just exactly in every instance *how human action comes about*, lives on.' We superstitiously believe we know what we want, that we are free and can freely assume responsibility for ourselves and hold others responsible for their actions, and so on. He urges us to recognize that actions are never what they appear to be: 'It took so much effort for us to learn that external things are not what they appear to us – now then! It is just the same with the inner world!' In this regard it is necessary to work against both metaphysical and moral 'realism' (D 116). Finally, in aphorism 128 of the book, Nietzsche challenges the Oedipal fantasy that we might have of ourselves in which we exist as our own mother and father. Nietzsche's suggestion is that we are responsible neither for our dreams nor for our waking life and that the idea of freedom of the will 'has human pride and feeling of power for its mother and father' (D 128).

It is perhaps on the basis of a reading of aphorisms like these that Vattimo claims, to repeat, that Nietzsche's critique of morality in *Dawn* is not conducted, 'in the name of the free and responsible subject', since this subject is 'a product of neurosis, a thing formed in illness'.[18] He contends that because there is an inextricable connection between internal or internalized conscience, including the '*individual in* revolt', and social morality, the appeal to freedom in Nietzsche cannot be made in the name of 'the sovereignty of the individual'.[19] He rightly notes that Nietzsche unmasks morality as a set of principles not intended for the utility or the good of the individual on whom they are imposed but for the preservation of society, even to the detriment of individuals; but he also infers that Nietzsche's aim is not to defend the individual against the claims of the group. The reason, he argues, is not because, metaphysically speaking, it is necessary to prefer the claims of determinism over the belief in freedom, 'but simply because there is no subject of such actions. Not: the subject is not free, but simply: the subject is not.'[20] What are we to make of this reading of Nietzsche's position in *Dawn*?

It is true that Nietzsche has done much in the text to deconstruct the fiction of some ontologically given or fixed unified self. However, this does not mean that he has no concern with the ego or self. In aphorism 105, for example, he paints a contrast between one's 'phantom ego' (*Phantom von ego*), which is formed in the heads of those around us and then communicated to us, and makes sure we live 'in a fog of impersonal, half-personal opinions', as well as arbitrary and fictitious evaluations, and one's 'self-established, genuine ego' (*ergründetes ego*), an ego that Nietzsche invites us to juxtapose to the 'common, pallid fiction' of the human being (D 105). It would seem that for Nietzsche this 'self-established ego' is an ethico-aesthetic construction and task, and it includes the freedom to experiment with the 'self'. As he puts it in a note from the end of 1880:

> It is a myth to believe that we will find our authentic self (*eigentliches Selbst*) once we have left out or forgotten this and that. That way we pick ourselves apart in an infinite regression: instead, the task is to *make ourselves*, to *shape* a form out of all the elements! The task is always that of a sculptor! A productive human being! *Not* through knowledge but through practice and an exemplar do we become *ourselves*! Knowledge has, at best, the value of a means! (KSA 9, 7 [213])

Furthermore, while it is true that Nietzsche exposes the extent to which the I or ego is the subject of its drives and affects (it is not the master in its own house we might say, looking ahead to Freud), it is manifestly clear that he is *perturbed* by this fact, that is, troubled by the extent to which the self is little more than a contingency or mere happenstance. In aphorism 119 he explores the drives and notes that no matter how much we struggle for self-knowledge nothing is more incomplete to us than the image of the totality of our drives. It is not only that we cannot call the cruder ones by name, but also more worryingly that their number and strength, their ebb and flow, and most of all the laws of their alimentation remain completely unknown to us:

> This alimentation thus becomes the work of chance: our daily experiences toss willy-nilly to this drive or that drive some prey or other which it seizes greedily, but the whole coming and going of these events exists completely apart from any meaningful connection to the alimentary needs of the sum drives: so that the result will always be two-fold: the starving and stunting of some drives and the overstuffing of others. (D 119)

Our experiences, then, are types of nourishment; the problem is that there is a deficit of knowledge on our part as to the character of our experiences. The result is that we live as contingent beings:

> As a consequence of this contingent alimentation of the parts, the whole, the fully-grown polyp turns out to be a creature no less contingent (*Zufälliges*) than its maturation. (D 119)

The ethical task in Nietzsche, it would seem, is not to allow oneself to be this mere happenstance. We need to experience dissatisfaction with ourselves and assume the risk of experimenting in life, freely taking the journey through our wastelands, quagmires and icy glaciers. The ones who do not take the risk of life will, 'never make the journey around the world (that you yourselves are!), but will remain trapped within yourselves like a knot on the log you were born to, a mere happenstance' (D 343). This is not to deny that the self or subject is not something contingent for Nietzsche: his whole point in *Dawn* is to show the contingencies of our moral formation and deformation and to disclose to the self that it is something other than what it takes itself to be (fixed and stable) and that it may become something more fluid and dynamic, in short, that it may cultivate a 'becoming' of what it is.

To suppose, as Vattimo does, that the subject is by definition something neurotic is to fail to make a distinction between autonomy and heteronomy, a distinction that can be drawn in Nietzschean and not just Kantian terms, and to rule out *tout court* the possibility of an ethics of self-cultivation.[21] For Nietzsche the focus is to be on the cultivation of the drives, and an initial step on the path to self-enlightenment and self-liberation is to know that here we do enjoy a certain liberty. Nietzsche is keen to challenge the doctrine, espoused by Schopenhauer, on the immutability of character:

> One can handle one's drives like a gardener and, though few know it, cultivate the shoots of one's anger, pity, musing, vanity as fruitfully and advantageously as beautiful fruit on espaliers; one can do so with a gardener's good or bad taste and, as it were, in the French or English or Dutch or Chinese style; one can also let nature have her sway and only tend to a little decoration and cleaning-up here and there; finally, one can, without giving them any thought whatsoever, let the plants, in keeping with the natural advantages and disadvantages of their habitat, grow up and fight it out among themselves – indeed, one can take pleasure in such wildness and want to enjoy just this pleasure, even if one has difficulties with it. We are free to do all this: but how many actually know that they are free

to do this? Don't most people *believe in themselves* as completed, *fully-grown facts*? Haven't great philosophers, with their doctrine of the immutability of character, pressed their seal of approval on this prejudice? (D 560)

In *Dawn* Kant, we find, is praised over other moral philosophers, especially Schopenhauer, for esteeming reason over sentiment in ethics and for standing outside the modern movement with its emphasis on defining morality in terms of the sympathetic affects (D 132). The problem, Nietzsche says in *Dawn* section 339, is that Kant demands that duty 'must *always* be something of a burden', never habit and custom, and in this demand 'there is concealed a tiny remnant of ascetic cruelty' (D 339). So, one of Nietzsche's interests in ethics is that duty should cease being a burden and he has the hope that after long practice it can become instead a pleasurable inclination and a need in which the rights of others to whom our duties, and now our inclinations, refer become occasions of pleasant feelings for us. And it is clear that Nietzsche thinks the ethical task of achieving self-mastery, which involves long practice and much daily work, will be made more appealing if it is construed aesthetically: one can take pleasure, even delight, in such an exercise and use the full range of one's senses and reason.

Nietzsche differs from Kant in placing the emphasis on autonomy being a radically individualized task, a duty that he hopes can become a joy. Like Kant, Nietzsche wants us to be astute agents of reason, which involves mastering the affects, working against fanaticism and attaining the modesty of self-control.[22] Unlike Kant, he thinks ethics needs to be directed more pertinently at the particular drives and capacities of individuals, and not presented as an overly rationalistic and universalistic model. For Nietzsche, Kant, we might say, assumes too much: he assumes a moral autonomy that is independent of the actual psychological and existential tasks necessary to carry it out, including the material to be worked on, and the division between heteronomy and autonomy is drawn too radically. Kantian autonomy does not rest on self-love and, in fact, requires the cancellation of the self or ego: the strict command of duty requires self-denial, and this is what Nietzsche means when he identifies in Kant's ethics the remnants of ascetic cruelty.[23]

Ultimately, Nietzsche is offering a modest conception of autonomy centred on the care of self. In *Dawn*, for example, he is keen to deflate the pretensions of the ego to being a self-originating source of potent agency. In section 128 of the text he seeks to indicate that the desire to be our own author has its psychological roots in a narcissistic desire to experience oneself as all-powerful.[24] He wittily draws on the myth of Oedipus to make his point:

> You wish to take responsibility for everything! Only not for your dreams! What miserable frailty, what poverty in the courage of your convictions! Nothing is *more* your own than your dreams! Nothing more *your* work! Content, form, duration, actor, spectator – in these comedies you yourselves are everything! And this is just the place in yourselves you shun and are ashamed of, and even Oedipus, the wise Oedipus, knew how to derive consolation from the idea that we cannot do anything about what it is we dream! I conclude from this: that the vast majority of human beings must be aware that they have abhorrent dreams. Were it otherwise: how greatly this nocturnal poeticizing would have been plundered to bolster human arrogance! – Do I have to add that wise Oedipus was right, that we really aren't responsible for our dreams, but no more for our waking hours either, and that the doctrine of free will has as its mother and father human pride and the human feeling of power? (D 128)

As Michael Ure has noted, Nietzsche is exposing the tragicomedy of existence that results from human pride and the need for the feeling of power (*Machtgefühl*). In the passage just cited, Nietzsche conceives the dreamer on the model of the figure of Oedipus with the dream itself as analogous to a tragicomic work of art. According to Ure, Nietzsche's cheerfully satirical viewpoint is designed to reveal to us the comedy of the Oedipal dreamer. In dreams we disavow what is most our own, and in the case of Oedipus this is the dream of becoming his own father and enjoying the body of his mother. Of course, the twist Nietzsche adds to this story is that one is also not responsible for one's waking state. The critical bite of the moral comes from Nietzsche's attempt to expose the hubris involved in seeking to attribute to ourselves the power of auto-genesis, 'conceiving of ourselves as both mother and father to ourselves, so to speak, we engage in a comic, childish self-inflation designed to satisfy our *Machtgefühl*'.[25] Here the self imagines itself to be completely self-sufficient, free of fate, and conducting the dream of self-authorship. The dangers of leading such an existence are manifold and include what Ure calls a series of 'intersubjective pathologies', such as melancholia and revenge. We see in this and other sections from book two of *Dawn* two important features of Nietzsche's understanding of the self at this time: (1) the psychological claim that the fantasy of auto-genesis is in fact symptomatic of a desire for narcissistic plenitude and (2) the idea that careful self-cultivation is the only therapeutic response that can work against the pathological affects borne of narcissistic loss.[26]

Being with oneself and others

It is widely thought that Nietzsche invokes a notion of subjectivity as self-absorbed, as something whole to itself fully represented and self-contained.[27] In his consideration of the self and other in Nietzsche, Elliot Jurist notes that Nietzsche's concern is with self-gratification – with such things as narcissism, instinctual satisfaction and the will to power – and argues that this concern 'interferes with the way he characterizes the relationship between self and others', and, moreover, that he leaves the issue of our relation to others unresolved: 'Nietzsche himself acknowledges the social constitution of agency; yet he opts not to pursue this and not to concentrate fully on coming to terms with the experience of being-for-another.'[28] Jurist notes the complexity and intricacy, if not the delicacy, of Nietzsche's actual position when he comments on the fact that competing tendencies characterize his attitude towards others. So, on the one hand, Jurist contends, we encounter him seemingly countenancing cruelty and exploitation, and repeatedly stressing the need for solitude. And yet, on the other hand, we see him approaching the study of human relationships 'with a subtlety and a psychological astuteness that should not be overlooked'.[29]

As Ruth Abbey notes, Nietzsche's purpose in attacking the presumptions and prejudices of morality is practical. He wants to discredit and demote values that promote the common interest so as to clear the ground for the creation and resurgence of those that foster an ethics of individual self-care and self-fashioning. This extends to his reappraisal of the value of self-love, in which, as Nietzsche writes, we are to forgive ourselves for our own ego and love ourselves as an act of clemency.[30] Only individuals who experience this love of self are capable of generous and beautiful actions. It becomes necessary, then, for Nietzsche to strip egoism and self-love of their usual adverse connotations, as when he states 'egoism is not evil' (HAH 101)[31] This does not mean for him, of course, that all is vanity or that while all action might derive from egoism all egoism is the same.[32] We need to distinguish between types of egoism and distinguish between crude and immature egoism and egoism that is mature and refined.

I think it prudent to bear in mind a point astutely made by Abbey, namely, that Nietzsche's supposedly scientific analyses of morality have a therapeutic intent, so that when he praises egoism, rather just describing it, he is 'deliberately compensating for the calumny it has suffered and continues to suffer in moral frameworks'.[33] Still, it is important that Nietzsche provide his readers with models of the relation between the self and its others. I think he does this – see especially D 174 and D 449 – and so it is far-fetched to claim, as Jurist does, that Nietzsche is more concerned with narcissism than he is with relatedness.[34] Again, the context of Nietzsche's campaign against morality, as he calls it, is of crucial importance: he is advancing an ethics of self-cultivation as an ethics of resistance and in the context of his worries over the tendencies of commercial society (D 174).

Egoism, for Nietzsche, is at the root of all the human virtues: without this cultivation of the self and pleasure of the assertion of the self, the virtues are meaningless. And, as noted, Nietzsche does not want us to prize all egoisms: while all action may derive from egoism, not all egoism is the same. Indeed, Nietzsche speaks of the unedifying sight of the 'immature, undeveloped crude individual' also understanding crudely its own will and advantage (HAH 95). Nietzsche also regards vanity as a corrupt form of self-affirmation since it signals in fact an absence of self-love and autonomy: the vain person needs the confirmation of others all the time. Moreover, because they are lacking in self-love, the vain person often seeks to demean others: 'One way in which they can feel affirmed is by feeling superior and subordinating others to confirm their falsely inflated value.'[35] Vanity, then, is a corrupt expression of egoism since it takes to the extreme the natural pleasure in self-assertion.

Nietzsche is keen to carry out a revaluation of values, especially the value of the sympathetic affects, including relations one has to oneself and to others. He writes against compassion but not against the sympathetic affects per se, for example benevolence and good will. As a free spirit he is keen to be as enlightened as possible and promote new ways or modes of living, including living together: 'If spouses did not live together, good marriages would be more frequent' (HAH 393). If we live too closely with those we love and care about, we run the risk of losing the very pearls of life (HAH 428) and simply through the deadening effects of repetition and habit. We are creatures of habit, of custom, of vanity and of imitation: various impulses, drives and passions need to be satisfied; but how can we 'perfect' ourselves? How can we learn how to love and hate? (HAH 601) One way forward, Nietzsche thinks, is not to treat ourselves as fixed, stable, 'single individuals' (HAH 618). We need to be attentive and responsive to the different situations of life, and to the multiplicity of selves that each one of us is.

Nietzsche is keen in the texts of the free-spirit period to explore non-Christian sources of ethical thinking and revive interest in the likes of Aristotle, Epictetus

(D 131, 546) and Epicurus (GS 45: they all teach an ethics of self-care). Indeed, Nietzsche regards self-hatred as a great danger to the flourishing of others:

> *Seducing into love.* – Whoever hates himself is a person to fear, for we will be the victim of his rancor and his revenge. Let's see therefore how we can seduce him into loving himself! (D 517)

The same point is echoed in *The Gay Science* when Nietzsche writes that the one thing needful is for a human being to attain satisfaction with themselves since only then is he or she tolerable to look at: 'Whoever is dissatisfied with himself is continually ready for revenge, and we others will be his victims, if only by having to endure his ugly sight. For the sight of what is ugly makes one bad and gloomy' (GS 290).

In *Dawn* 503 Nietzsche makes an interesting distinction: the ancients were profoundly concerned with friendship, whereas we moderns offer to the world idealized sexual love. As he goes on to note, in antiquity the feeling of friendship was considered the highest feeling, 'even higher than the most celebrated pride of the self-sufficient sage' (GS 61). Although Nietzsche is an enemy of *Mitleid*, friendship is one arena where, as Abbey notes, there can be genuine knowledge and sympathy for another and the overcoming of a narrow-centred egoism. Nietzsche will generalize between higher and lower forms of friendship in his writings, but, as Abbey again notes, he is sensitive to particularity: 'Nietzsche never adopts a wholly formulaic approach to this relationship, but recognizes that responsiveness to difference and particularity are among its central characteristics.'[36] Although Nietzsche acknowledges that there can be poor or inadequate friendships – friendships lacking in trust, confidence and genuine concern for the other – he sees it, at its best, as an effort at 'fellow rejoicing' rather than 'fellow suffering' (HAH 499); it is the ability to 'imagine the joy of others and rejoicing at it', which he thinks is a very rare human quality (MOM 62). The ethical work that Nietzsche wants each of us to carry out of ourselves, giving style to our characters for example, does not have to be work undergone and performed in isolation; instead, 'friendship can be a spur to greatness.'[37]

It is not for Nietzsche so much a question of self-knowledge being a precondition for the realization of friendship and realistic friendships; it is rather that honest friends can become a prerequisite of self-knowledge:[38] it is through the observations of others that a more incisive view of ourselves can be attained; friends, then, can pierce our ignorance about the self. Such is Nietzsche's esteem of friendship that in some places he will model marriage on it: 'The best friend will probably acquire the best wife, because a good marriage is founded on the talent for friendship' (HAH 378).[39]

Nietzsche and the care of self

In his middle writings Nietzsche has the inspiration to give up on what he calls the first and last things, the questions of a theologically inspired metaphysics, and devote attention to the closest things. This is not without consequence for how we now live and for how we now practice knowledge. In making this decision Nietzsche is, in fact, reviving the antique conception of ethics as centred on a care of self. Michel Foucault contends that in Greek ethics we find a focus on moral conduct, on relations to oneself and others, rather than a focus on religious problems such as what is our fate after death? What are the gods and do they intervene in life or not? For the Greeks, Foucault argues, these were not significant problems and not directly related to conduct. What they were concerned about was to constitute an ethics that was an aesthetics of existence.[40]

This is remarkably similar to how Nietzsche presents ethics in his middle writings. In modern culture we can detect, Nietzsche writes, a 'feigned disrespect for all the things which human beings in fact take most seriously, *for all the things closest to them*' (WS 5). As Ruth Abbey notes, in devaluing the small, worldly matters Christian and post-Christian sensibility, 'puts people at war with themselves and forbids a close study of which forms of care of the self would be most conducive to individual flourishing'.[41] As Nietzsche notes, most people see the closest things badly and rarely pay heed to them, while '*almost all the physical and psychical frailties* of the individual derive from this lack ... being *unknowledgeable in the smallest and everyday things* and failing to keep an eye on them – this it is that transforms the earth for so many into a "vale of tears"' (WS 6). Nietzsche notes that our greatness does not crumble away all at once but through continual neglect:

> The little vegetation that grows in between everything and understands how to cling everywhere, this is what ruins what is great in us – the quotidian, hourly pitifulness of our environment that goes overlooked, the thousand tiny tendrils of this or that small and small-minded feeling growing out of our neighborhood, our job, the company we keep, the division of our day. If we allow these small weeds to grow unwittingly, then unwittingly they will destroy us! (D 435)

For Foucault self-cultivation takes the form of an 'art of existence' – a *techne tou biou* – and is guided by the principle that one must 'take care of oneself'.[42] Foucault claims that care of self (*epimeleia heautou, cura sui*) is a Socratic notion or one that Socrates consecrates (see also Nietzsche in D 9).[43] However, it only becomes a universal philosophical theme in the Hellenistic period, being promoted by the likes of Epicurus, the Cynics and Stoics such as Seneca. According to Foucault, the Delphic injunction to know one's self was subordinated to self-care. He gives several examples from the literature to vindicate his core thesis, including Epicurus's letter to Menoeceus, a text in which it is stated that it is never too early or too late to occupy oneself with oneself: 'Teachings about everyday life were organized around taking care of oneself in order to help every member of the group with the mutual work of salvation.'[44] For Foucault it is in Epictetus that we find the highest philosophical development of the theme of care of self. For Epictetus the human is destined to care for itself and is where the basic difference between the human and other creatures resides. Moreover, for Epictetus, the care of self 'is a privilege-duty, a gift-obligation that ensures our freedom while forcing us to take ourselves as the object of all our diligence.'[45] He is keen to stress that the conversion to self entails the experience of a pleasure that one takes in oneself:

> This pleasure, for which Seneca usually employs the word *gaudium* or *laetitia*, is a state that is neither accompanied nor followed by any form of disturbance in the body or the mind. It is defined by the fact of not being caused by anything that is independent of ourselves and therefore escapes our control. It arises out of ourselves and within ourselves.[46]

For Foucault the contrast to be made is with *voluptas* that denotes a pleasure whose origin resides outside us and in objects whose presence we cannot be sure of (a pleasure that is precarious in itself). What Foucault is delineating here resonates with the joy of existing that Nietzsche seeks to restore in his middle period as a central concern of a post-metaphysical philosophy and after two centuries of training by morality and religion (see, for example, WS 86).

In all the different schools in antiquity, philosophy is not simply about knowledge but about living a certain kind of life and being a certain type of subject. Knowledge is pursued to the extent that it aids this mode of life and taking care of self. However, this tradition has become obscure to us today and we can account for this obscurity in terms of several developments. Foucault notes that there has been a deep transformation in the moral principles of Western society. We find it difficult to base a morality of austere principles on the precept that we should give ourselves more care than anything else in the world. Rather, we are inclined to see taking care of ourselves as an immorality and as a means of escape from all possible rules. We have inherited the tradition of Christian morality that makes self-renunciation the condition for salvation. Here, 'to know oneself was paradoxically the way to self-renunciation'.[47] Such is our assimilation of this morality of self-denial, to the point where we identify it as the domain of morality in and for itself, that the kind of morality pursued by the ancients strikes us today as an exercise in moral dandyism. We have the paradox of a precept of care of self that signifies for us today either egoism or withdrawal, but which for centuries was a positive principle, serving as the matrix for dedicated moralities. Christianity and the modern world have based the codes of moral strictness on a morality of non-egoism to the point where we forget that such codes originated in an environment marked by the obligation to take care of oneself.

Among the Greeks practices of self-cultivation took the form of a precept, 'to take care of self'. This precept was a principal rule for social and personal conduct and for the art of life. This is not what we ordinarily think when we think of the ancient Greeks: we imagine that they were ruled by the precept, 'Know thyself' (gnothi seauton). Why have we moderns forgotten the original precept of take care of the self and why has it been obscured by the Delphic injunction? In modern philosophy, from Descartes to Husserl, knowledge of the self, or the thinking subject, takes an on an ever-increasing importance and as the first key step in the theory of knowledge. Foucault thinks we moderns have thus inverted what was the hierarchy in the two main principles of antiquity: for the Greeks knowledge was subordinated to ethics (centred on self-care), whereas for us knowledge is what is primary. But even the Delphic principle was not an abstract one concerning life; rather, it was technical advice meaning something like, 'Do not suppose yourself to be a god' or 'Be aware of what you really ask when you come to consult the oracle.'

Two key points are worth making here. First, Foucault insists that taking care of one's self does not simply mean being interested in oneself or having an attachment to or fascination with the self. Rather, 'It describes a sort of work, an activity; it implies attention, knowledge, technique.'[48] Second, regarding the taking care aspect, Foucault stresses that the Greek word – epimeleisthai – designates not simply a mental attitude, a certain form of attention or a way of not forgetting something. He points out that its etymology refers to a series of words such as meletan and melete, and 'meletan', for example, means to practice and train (often coupled with the verb gumnazein). So, the meletai are exercises, such as gymnastic and military ones. Thus, the Greek 'taking care' refers to a form of vigilant, continuous and applied activity more than it does to a mental attitude.

Foucault thinks we may be in a similar situation to the Greek today, 'since most of us no longer believe that ethics is founded in religion'.[49] For him the general Greek problem was not the *tekhne* of the self but that of life, *tekhne tou biou*, or how to live. 'It's quite clear from Socrates to Seneca or Pliny, for instance, that they didn't worry about the afterlife, what happened after death, or whether God exists or not. That was not really a great problem for them; the problem was: Which *tekhne* do I have to use in order to live well as I ought to live?'[50]

This is remarkably similar to how Nietzsche presents the issue of an ethical way of life in the texts of the free-spirit period. Nietzsche, at least in the popular imagination, is taken to be an immoralist in the crude sense identified by Foucault when, on the contrary, he needs to be read as an ethical thinker in the way Foucault thinks we have forgotten ethics. We have developed a bad conscience over an ethics centred on self-care and regard self-renunciation as the basis of morality. We are the inheritors of a secular tradition that sees in external law the basis for morality and this morality is one of asceticism or denial of the self. As Nietzsche astutely points out, if we examine what is often taken to be the summit of the moral in philosophy – the mastery of the affects – we find that there is pleasure to be taken in this mastery. I can impress myself by what I can deny, defer, resist and so on. It is through this mastery that I grow and develop. And yet morality, as we moderns have come to understand it, would have to give this ethical self-mastery a bad conscience. If we take as our criterion of the moral to be self-sacrificing resolution and self-denial, we would have to say, if being honest, that such acts are not performed strictly for the sake of others; my own fulfilment and pride are at work and the other provides the self with an opportunity to relieve itself through self-denial.

Foucault is keen to say that what he is advocating is not the Californian cult of the self and neither is the heroic freedom of Sartrean existentialism. Both have major flaws for him. He likes to give the example of the Stoics as an alternative: 'the experience of the self is not a discovering of a truth hidden inside the self but an attempt to determine what one can and cannot do with one's available freedom'.[51] He makes clear his conception of freedom as ethos in his account of how the Greeks problematized the freedom of the individual as an ethical problem. Here the word 'ethical' denotes a way of being and behaviour. Somebody's ethos is evident in their clothing, appearance, gait and in the calm with which they respond to every event. Thus, a human being possessed of a splendid ethos, which could be admired and put forward as an example, was someone who practised freedom in a certain way. However, extensive work by the self on the self is required for this practice of freedom to take shape in an ethos that can be said to be beautiful, honourable, estimable, memorable and exemplary. It is precisely in these terms that Nietzsche will depict philosophy as a way of life in his writings (see UO II: 5; UO III).

For Foucault the elaboration of one's own life as a personal work of art was at the centre of moral experiences in antiquity (even if it conformed to certain collective canons or practices). In Christianity by contrast, with the religion of the text, the idea of the will of God and the principle of obedience, morality increasingly took on the form of a code of rules. From antiquity to Christianity we pass from a morality that was primarily the search for a personal ethics to a morality as obedience to a system of rules. Foucault holds that for a whole series of reasons the idea of morality as obedience to a code of rules is now disappearing and this absence of morality is to be replaced with the search for an aesthetics of existence.[52]

Here Foucault has been accused of retreating in his late work into an amoral aesthetics, privileging an elitist notion of self-centred stylization, and undermining possibilities of emancipatory politics. Johanna Oksala is a defender of Foucault who argues that Foucault's ethics represent an attempt to seek ways of living and thinking that are transgressive and, like a work of art, are not simply the product of normalizing power. For Oksala one way to contest normalizing power is by shaping one's self and one's lifestyle creatively and the exploration of possibilities for new forms of subjectivity, new fields of experiences, pleasures, modes of living and thinking. She thus argues that the quest for freedom which characterizes Foucault's late work is a question of developing forms of subjectivity that are capable of functioning as resistance to normalizing power. This concern on his part can even enable us to understand better the importance of the ancient practices of the self for Foucault. As he stresses, we cannot find in Stoic ethics the attempt to normalize and there is no attempt to normalize the population. Rather, it was, says Foucault, a matter of personal choice, making the choice to live a beautiful life and to leave to others memories of a beautiful existence.[53] Oksala maintains, then, that Foucault's aesthetics of existence should not be understood as a narcissistic enterprise or as aesthetic in a narrow visual sense of the word as in looking stylish. It is an aesthetics not simply because it calls on us to make ourselves beautiful, but because it calls on us to relate to ourselves in terms of a material or a bios that can be formed and transformed.[54] It is Nietzsche who perhaps best revives this conception of ethics for us moderns.

Neither Nietzsche nor Foucault advocates an ahistorical return to the ancients. In the case of *Dawn* Nietzsche highlights the teaching of Epictetus, for example, as a way of indicating that what we take to be morality today, where it is taken to be coextensive with the sympathetic affects, is not a paradigm of some universal and metahistorical truth. If we look at history we find that there have been different ways of being ethical, and this in itself is sufficient, Nietzsche thinks, to derail the idea that there is a single moral-making morality. Both thinkers seek to work against the construction of moral necessities out of historical contingencies. A key difference from the ancients is that Nietzsche is developing a therapy for the sicknesses of the soul under specifically modern conditions of social control and discipline. Nietzsche's ambition is clear, I think, from the following note, and it centres on the experiment of cultivating what we can call human pluralization and working against the closure of the human:

> My morality [*Moral*] would be to take the general character of man more and more away from him ... to make him to a degree non-understandable to others (and with it an object of experiences, of astonishment, of instruction for them) .... Should not each individual [*Individuum*] be an attempt to achieve a *higher species than man* through its most individual things? (KSA 9, 6 [158]).

Martha Nussbaum claims that in his cult of Stoic strength Nietzsche depicts 'a fearful person, a person who is determined to seal himself off from risk, even at the cost of loss of love and value'.[55] Like the otherworldliness he abhors, the Stoicism he endorses is a form of self-protection, expressing 'a fear of this world and its contingencies'.[56] However, Nietzsche is open to a doctrine of love, but he wants a love that is not free of self-interest and self-enjoyment, and I think it is clear that he is not advocating an ethic of a retreat into the self, one that would be independent of human relations of care and openness to the other (see especially D 449). Nietzsche's campaign against morality, by which he means the 'morality of unselfing' (EH 'D'), possesses a complicated character. His focus on the self and on egoism is of a highly ethical character and in two senses: first, it has a concern with self-cultivation and, second, this cultivation is not without care for others, including the duties and responsibilities that come with such care.

Self-cultivation in Nietzsche denotes a fundamental concern with oneself that aims at a rich and healthy egoism: one has purified oneself of one's opinions and valuations – of what has merely been passed down and unconsciously assimilated – and learns to think and feel for oneself, practising one's own arts of self-preservation and self-enhancement. In *Dawn* the emphasis is on 'knowing one's circumstances' in their widest sense and as a means of knowing one's power: 'One ought to think of oneself as a variable quantity and whose accomplishment can perhaps under favourable circumstances match the highest ever.' Nietzsche argues that one, therefore, needs to reflect on the circumstances and 'spare no diligence' in our contemplation or knowledge of them (D 326). In a note from autumn 1880 he insists that the intellect is the tool of our drives, 'it is *never free*'. What it does is to sharpen itself in the struggle with various drives and thereby refines the activity of each individual drive. But he also insists that the will to power (*der Wille nach Macht*), to the infallibility (*Unfehlbarkeit*) of our person, resides in our greatest justice and integrity (*Redlichkeit*): scepticism just applies to all authority, we do not want to be duped, not even by *our drives*! But what does not *want*? A drive, certainly!' (KSA 9, 6 [130]) So, although we cannot escape the drives in any absolute sense, we can gain a distance from them so that they do not dupe us. And although we share drives with animals, our increase in integrity makes us less dependent on the stimulus of the drives (KSA 9, 6 [234]).

Conclusion

In conclusion, then, what of the point I noted at the beginning of the chapter concerning the seemingly harsh and unattractive character of Nietzsche's conception of ethical practice? Let me end by commenting on just two points. First, an essential test to learn for Nietzsche is the endurance of solitude (D 443). He does not envisage this as a mode of retreat. Rather, solitude has the advantage of providing us with the distant perspective that we need to think well of things: 'On my own I seem to see my friends more clearly and more appealingly than when together with them; and at the time when I loved music most and was most sensitive to it, I loved at a distance from it' (D 485). We need solitude 'so as not to drink out of everyone's cisterns' for among the many we simply do not think as an 'I'. Not only is such solitude of benefit to ourselves, it also improves our relation to others; when we turn angry towards people and fear them we need the desert to become good again (D 491).

Secondly, Nietzsche urges us to get beyond our compassion because he appreciates that free thinking – such as the opening up of new ways of being ethical – will, initially at least, plunge people into despair and grief. For Nietzsche *Mitleid* is the enemy to be focused on because when it rules, and when suffering is seen as the greatest evil, 'people lose the ability to endure hardship and privation as well as the attendant personal strength and resistance'.[57] *Mitleid* 'saps the capacity to inflict suffering as well as to endure it'.[58] For Nietzsche, the achievement of greatness, especially in the unflinching pursuit of knowledge, 'requires the ability to endure, inflict, and witness pain'.[59] As he puts it in *Dawn* 146, and where he presents the idea of a new ploughshare, 'If, with regard to ourselves, we do not heed, in narrow, petty-bourgeois fashion, immediate consequences and sufferings: why should we *have* to do so with our neighbour? ... Why shouldn't some individuals from the current generation be sacrificed for future generations?' (D 146) In making this sacrifice, in which our neighbours and we are included, the aim, he says, is to 'strengthen and elevate the general feeling of human *power* (*Macht*)' and, in this way, seek to effect a positive increase in happiness (D 146). By 'sacrifice' here Nietzsche means sacrifice to the cause of humanity's existential and moral enlightenment. We should note: free spirits try to entice others to see themselves as experiments and as sacrifices; moreover, we should only sacrifice our neighbour to the extent that we are prepared to sacrifice ourselves.

> Supposing we went in for self-sacrifice: what would prohibit us from sacrificing our neighbor as well? – just as state and prince have forever done when they sacrificed one citizen to the other 'in the universal public interest', as they put it. But we too have universal, perhaps more universal interests: why shouldn't some individuals from the current generation be sacrificed for future generations? Such that those individuals' grief, their restlessness, their despair, their blunderings and fearful footsteps be deemed necessary because a new ploughshare is to cleave the ground, rendering it fruitful for all? (D 146)

I think it is clear, both from hints he gives in *Dawn* and says in other texts, that Nietzsche thinks the tasks of free-spirited thinking are ones reserved, and perhaps best reserved, for a few individuals and who will constitute what we might choose to call a moral (or 'immoral') avant-garde.

Philosophical Cheerfulness:
On *The Gay Science*

Introduction

The Gay Science is a highly personal work, one that Nietzsche refers to as 'his most *medial* book', standing as it does at the midpoint of his life and serving as a fulcrum for much of his subsequent thought.[1] Nietzsche reached a crisis point in his life at the end of 1882, but he was indeed soon to turn the muck of his life into gold – in the form of the extraordinary philosophical riches of his next book, *Thus Spoke Zarathustra* (1883–5). This work, which Nietzsche himself regarded as his most important, represents in many ways a dramatic working out of much that has been accomplished in the free-spirit texts, including the announcement of the death of God and the search for a new centre of gravity to existence (eternal recurrence) and a new goal for existence (the *Übermensch*). The text is replete with images of the 'dawn'. *The Gay Science* thus brings to a close an immensely fertile period in Nietzsche's writing, with multiple transformations taking place and new dawns presaged. After *The Gay Science*, as Robert Pippin notes, Nietzsche's themes become even broader, with the conditions relevant to becoming a free spirit more comprehensive, as he turns to write the books most responsible for his reputation, notably, *Zarathustra*, *Beyond Good and Evil* and *On the Genealogy of Morality*.[2] *The Gay Science* displays, like the previous texts of the free-spirit period, Nietzsche the brilliant psychologist at work, mining and undermining humankind's prejudices and fears. Pippin is surely right in suggesting that it is this Nietzsche, and not Heidegger's bombastic designation of him as 'the last metaphysician of the West' (der *letzte Metaphysiker des Abendlandes*) that needs to occupy our attention today,[3] and this makes *The Gay Science* all the more important as a text to read and to study closely. Anyone who probes deeply the middle writings will, I think, concur with Pippin when he contends that

Nietzsche is most fruitfully understood not as a great (German) metaphysician, or as the destroyer or culminator of metaphysics, perhaps not very interested in metaphysics at all, but rather as a thinker who follows in the footsteps of the great French *moralistes*. In his appreciation of *The Gay Science*, Richard Schacht suggests that it is a mystery why it has not received more attention and why it does not figure more centrally in interpretations of Nietzsche's philosophy.[4] In it he thinks we find the essential 'philosophical' Nietzsche. Moreover, he suggests that the cause of understanding Nietzsche would be significantly advanced, if the rest of his corpus was read in relation to it and construed in the light of what he does and writes in it. I think this is right, but what Schacht claims for *The Gay Science* can be claimed for the middle writings as a whole.

In this study my focus is on illuminating Nietzsche's philosophical practice in his middle writings, and in this chapter I turn attention to probing the 'meaning' of his cultivation of philosophical cheerfulness. The bulk of the chapter is devoted to this task. In the final section of the chapter, however, I respond to Robert Pippin's contention that Nietzsche is no longer doing philosophy with the project of 'the gay science', but something else instead, namely 'psychology'.

Introduction to *The Gay Science*

The Gay Science (*Die fröhliche Wissenschaft*) was originally published in four parts, with a prelude in German rhymes in 1882; a fifth part, together with an appendix of songs and a preface, was added and published in 1887. Nietzsche began to compose notes for what would become the book in the summer of 1881, drafting a set of remarkable notes that have yet to be translated into English, many anchored around his experience of the thought of eternal recurrence.[5] Nietzsche's initial plan was for an addition to his previously published book, *Dawn*, and he conceived it as his last book.[6] He wrote to his amanuensis Peter Gast (Heinrich Köselitz) at the end of January 1882 that he had recently completed books 6–8 of *Dawn*, with the two final parts, books 9 and 10, to be reserved for the following winter because, as he put it, 'I have not yet matured enough for the prime ideas which I shall present in these books' (KSB 6, 159).[7] In particular, Nietzsche confides that there is one idea that needs many years to mature and that he needs the strength to express it: a clear reference to the doctrine of eternal recurrence. Approximately two weeks later, however, he reported to Gast that a draft of the new book is well in process. Nietzsche was still resident in Genoa at this time and received a visit from his friend Paul Rée in February of 1882. Upon Rée's departure in March, he made a trip to Messina in Sicily where he wrote more poetry than prose. His return from this trip and journey to Rome towards the end of April 1882 coincided with the beginning of his 'fateful encounter' with Lou Salomé.[8] There now followed a five-month period of intense activity in Nietzsche's personal life, which also involved the editing, proofreading and publication of *The Gay Science*.

Nietzsche clearly saw the book as the final instalment of his free-spirit writings, for he had written on the back cover, 'With this book we arrive at the conclusion of a series of writings by FRIEDRICH NIETZSCHE whose common goal is to erect a new image and ideal of the free spirit.' The title of the book is a rich and fertile one, suggesting the idea of a practice of knowledge, and an intelligence, that is gay, cheerful and joyous. I shall explore the possible meanings of the project, and of these terms, shortly. Like its predecessor *Dawn*, *The Gay Science* covers myriad topics, but it differs in that it contains some of Nietzsche's grandest ideas such as the death of God and the eternal recurrence.

As Pierre Klossowski notes, the gay science is the fruit of 'the greatest imaginable solitude,'[9] and seeks to address those rare and few solitary spirits who have seceded from society. It is clear that Nietzsche is first and foremost writing for himself. As he reveals in a letter to Erwin Rohde of 15 July 1882: '*Mihi ipsi scripsi* [I have written for myself] – and there it stands; and thus everyone should do for himself his best in his own way – that is my morality, the only remaining morality for me' (KSB 6, 226).[10] In large part this is connected to what Nietzsche felt about questions of health, namely, that one must become one's own doctor in which one treats 'soul, mind and body all at once and with the same remedies' (KSB 6, 226–7).[11] It is quite possible, Nietzsche reflects, that others may perish using the same remedies, and this is why, he continues, he exerts so much energy in warning others against him: 'Especially this latest book, which is called *Die fröhliche Wissenschaft*, will scare many people away from me' (KSB 6, 227).[12] In a letter of August 1882 to his former colleague at Basel, the Swiss historian Jacob Burckhardt, Nietzsche confides that *The Gay Science* is a highly personal book, noting that 'everything personal is indeed comic' (KSB 6, 234).[13]

With *The Gay Science* Nietzsche believed he had 'crossed a tropic' (einen *Wendekreis* überschritten):

> Everything that lies before me is new, and it will not be long before I catch sight also of the *terrifying* face of my more distant life task. This long, rich

summer was for me a testing time; I took my leave of it in the best of spirits and proud, for I felt that during this time at least the ugly rift between willing and accomplishment had been bridged. There were hard demands made on my humanity, and I have become equal to the highest demands I have made on myself. This whole interim state between what was and what will be, I call 'in media vita'. (KSB 6, 255)[14]

Of course, Nietzsche did have a powerful need to write and to communicate to and share with others. In a letter of December 1882, he confesses to Heinrich von Stein that he wishes to remove from human existence 'some of its heartbreaking and cruel character' (KSB 6, 288).[15] By the end of 1882, the ill-fated *ménage à trois* with Rée and Salomé was in tatters, and Nietzsche felt deeply bruised by the experience and the betrayals. As he confided to his friend Franz Overbeck on Christmas Day of this remarkable year in his life, he now had the chance to prove to himself what he preached, namely, that all experiences are useful, all days holy and all people divine. Unless he could discover the alchemical trick of turning the muck into gold, he would be lost.[16]

How are we to best characterize Nietzsche's philosophical practice as it matures in the project of 'the gay science'? We know he has a preference for specific types of cheerful thinkers – examples in his writings include Socrates, Montaigne and Emerson – but what exactly is the 'meaning' of *Nietzsche's* cheerfulness? Robin Small has observed a change in tone in *The Gay Science* from the earnest probing of its predecessor, 'an attempt to restore *esprit* to philosophical thought through the use of satirical rhymes, poetic prose and a playfulness, which is no less effective in exposing the errors of conventional beliefs for its light touch'.[17] It is true that Nietzsche has a commitment to philosophical lightness; but is he not also a thinker of great seriousness, one who pronounces the death of God as a 'monstrous event' and who articulates with great solemnity the thought of the eternal recurrence of the same? In short, how are we to negotiate this complex play between lightness and seriousness that seems to characterize Nietzsche's project in *The Gay Science*? A clue is to be found perhaps in *Ecce Homo* when Nietzsche writes that, 'being cheerful (*heiter*) and good-naturedly mocking oneself as well – *ridendo dicere severum* ('through what is laughable say what is sombre'), where *verum dicere* ('saying what is true') would justify any amount of harshness – is humanity itself' (EH 'The Wagner Case', 1; translation slightly modified). In this chapter my aim is to probe the character of Nietzsche's philosophical cheerfulness and to illuminate something of its 'meaning'.

'La gaya scienza'

According to Walter Kaufmann, the title of the book has deliberate polemical overtones, for 'it is meant to be anti-German, anti-professorial, anti-academic,'[18] and it goes well with the idea of the free-minded, good European that Nietzsche has been promoting since the time of *Human, all too Human*. The title also suggests, as Kaufmann remarks, light feet, dancing and laughter, as well as a ridicule of the spirit of gravity. But there is also, as Robert Pippin has pointed out, in Nietzsche's project as a whole a complicated combination of light-heartedness or cheerfulness combined with a sort of heaviness or gravitas. As Pippin observes, such paradoxical formulations commence early in Nietzsche's writings and continue late into them.[19]

The problems Nietzsche pursues in the text are ones that he uncovers and responds to with '*great love*', in which what is cultivated is a personal relationship to these problems: through these problems one can find one's destiny, one's distress and ultimately one's happiness. Indeed, Nietzsche notes that, 'A weakened, thin, extinguished personality that denies itself is no longer fit for anything good – least of all for philosophy. "Selflessness" has no value either in heaven or on earth' (GS 345). Nietzsche, then, will find his philosophical fate or destiny in uncovering these problems and charting their territory perhaps for the first time. As he makes clear in the aphorism that opens up book five of the text (added in 1887), he is in search of new seas and he is keen to navigate them in a spirit of cheerfulness, by which he means a spirit of serenity, even merriment (GS 343).

'La gaya scienza' – Nietzsche added this subtitle to the text for its second edition in 1887 – draws its inspiration from a number of influences. First, there is the example of the troubadours of the Middle Ages, the Provençal poet-knights, who roamed across Europe singing, dancing and practising the art of poetry and who invented courtly love. In *Ecce Homo* Nietzsche reveals that he chose the term 'la gaya scienza' to demonstrate the unity of singer, knight and free spirit that characterized early Provençal culture (EH 'GS'). In *Beyond Good and Evil* he draws attention to the aristocratic or noble origins of '*passionate* love' (die Liebe als *Passion*), referring to the Provençal poet-knights as those 'splendid, inventive people of the "*gai saber*" to whom Europe owes so much – virtually its very self' (BGE 260).

Second, there is the influence of Ralph Waldo Emerson (1803–82), whom Nietzsche first read as a young schoolboy and came to cherish. For the first edition of the frontispiece of the text, he used the following as an epigraph from Emerson: 'To the poet and the sage all things are friendly and hallowed, all experiences profitable, all days holy, and all human beings divine' (see the thirteenth paragraph of Emerson's 'On History'). Emerson even refers to 'professors of the Joyous Science', but it is very doubtful that Nietzsche knew of this reference.[20] In *Twilight of the Idols* Nietzsche writes in praise of Emerson over Thomas Carlyle: of the two thinkers he is the more 'enlightened, more wide-ranging, more multifarious' and 'above all happier'. For Nietzsche, Emerson is a man of taste who lives instinctively on pure ambrosia and leaves 'behind the indigestible in things'. He thus possesses a 'kindly and quick-witted cheerfulness (*gütige und geistreiche Heiterkeit*) which discourages all seriousness' (TI 'Reconnaissance Raids' 13).[21] Nietzsche notes that although Carlyle liked Emerson a great deal he remarked of him that, 'he does not give *us* enough to sink our teeth into'. Nietzsche adds that although this may be said with good reason, it cannot be said at Emerson's expense. Emerson's mind 'is always finding reasons to be content and even grateful' (ibid.). His gratitude is such that Emerson now and then verges on 'the cheerful (*heitere*) transcendence' of the stalwart Roman citizen invoked by Ovid, 'a lover who returns from a tryst where, regrettably, he has not performed very well, but "offering nonetheless a positive report".'[22] Nietzsche cites Ovid, '*Ut desint vires ... tamen est laudanda voluptas*' ('though the potency be lacking, yet the lust is praiseworthy').[23]

Third, there is the influence of the Cynic philosopher, Diogenes of Sinope (ca. 404–423 BC), evident in striking form, for example, in aphorism 125 of the text on the parable of the madman and the death of God. Nietzsche is influenced by the literary style of cynicism that 'mixes humor with earnestness in a serio-comic vein that is marked by caricature, sarcasm, mockery, sharp-witted wordplay, and multi-layered meanings fraught with a moral intensity that presses its message to the limits of obscenity'.[24] As Charles Bambach notes, the text commences with a 'prelude' featuring playful and humorous poems (entitled, 'Joke, Cunning, and Revenge'), which are then followed up in the main body of the text by aphorisms of varying lengths that he sees as playing off the Cynic genre of the *chreia* – 'short philosophical apothegm pregnant with meaning, rife with ambiguity and contradiction, and laced with wit and jest'. The book of aphorisms is then capped by a postlude (the 'Songs of Prince Vogelfrei') featuring a collection of poems that blends 'the Provencal troubadours exuberant balladeering with the Cynic's crude animality, punning on the archaic German term *Vogelfrei* which means "as free as a bird" and yet also an "outlaw" who may be shot on sight'.[25]

The gay science has two key principles: first, to practise life as a means to knowledge; and second, to cultivate knowledge as the most powerful passion. We have seen something of the complex character of the 'passion of knowledge' in Chapter 3. The utilization of the word 'gay' is a reference to the desire to live in defiance of morality, that is, not to accept and conform to existing conventions and customs regarding how one is expected to live and love. We can also note that the love that the gay scientist seeks is a learning kind of love.[26] What takes place in the case of music takes place in the case of life in general: we learn to love all the things we now love, and in the end 'we are rewarded for our good will, our patience, fair-mindedness, and gentleness with what is strange; gradually, it sheds its veil and turns out to be a new and indescribable beauty. That is its *thanks* for our hospitality' (GS 334). Pippin has emphasized the extent to which the gay science is a knowledge of erotics, describing it as 'not so much a knowledge of what love is as how to love and live so well ... in some way that "does justice" to the requirements of love and life'.[27] 'La gaya scienza' is, then, a kind of love poetry, one that is intended to call to mind 'an extremely idealized love and engaged in not for purely aesthetic reasons but for the sake of some conversion, or seduction, and the attachments and commitments it inspires are a "condition of life"'.[28] The book endeavours to bring together, then, the art of poetry and a new conception, playful and cheerful, of disciplined knowledge. In the tradition of courtly love the lover does not seek to transcend the ordinary, empirical world of transient things, but instead practices love as an art capable of valuing mortal objects with no contemplation of transcendence. It is this revaluation of mortal *eros* that appeals to Nietzsche when he draws inspiration from the Provençal troubadours. The gay science aims to 're-channel all the force of *eros*, all its poetic powers of idealization, into those fleeting appearances that the Platonic and Christian tradition had devalued'.[29] The task is to love the empirical world of time and mortality as a world of becoming and to commit oneself to an ungodly reality and eschew the aesthetic or religious desire for 'some Apart, Beyond, Outside, Above' (*Abseits, Jenseits, Ausserhalb, Oberhalb*) (GS Preface 2).

The task of the gay science is to promote the scientific study of moral matters – basically, the conditions of existence of the human animal to date, including the reason, the passion and the superstition involved in them – and to ask whether science can now furnish and fashion goals of existence after it has demonstrated that it can take away goals and annihilate them. Then, Nietzsche writes, 'Experimentation would be in order that would allow every kind of heroism to find satisfaction – centuries of experimentation that may eclipse all the great projects and sacrifices of history to date' (GS 7). In short, can science build its 'cyclopic buildings' into the future and help prepare for the future? Nietzsche is in search of a joyful science in which there is the promise of the future and new possibilities of life and in which different energies of thinking and knowledge will find a new level of integration and synthesis, and this involves artistic energies and the practical wisdom of life joining forces with scientific thinking in an effort to cultivate 'a higher organic system in relation to which scholars, physicians, artists, and legislators – as we know them at present – would have to look like paltry relics of ancient times' (GS 113). Nietzsche, then, does not simply privilege scientific thinking (although he is taking it extremely seriously); rather, his model of progressive knowledge is one that aims to fuse together the energies of art and practical wisdom with scientific thinking.

As I have indicated, the gay science is characterized by a disconcerting combination of seriousness and playfulness.[30] This is evident in Nietzsche's aphorism on the death of God. I want to now examine this aphorism, and then turn my attention to probing more the 'meaning' of Nietzsche's cheerfulness.

The death of God and philosophy

The Gay Science is Nietzsche's first and his most complete attempt to reckon with the death of God and its consequences for Occidental humanity, although the idea has been presaged in *Dawn* (D 96). It is the theme that hovers over the text as a whole, being the explicit beginning of the third and fifth books. With regard to the third book, the death is referred to in the book's opening short aphorism, §108, and it is given a dramatic presentation in aphorism 125. The long aphorism §109 seems to provide vital clues as to what Nietzsche thinks follows on from this death as our specific task; but it is not until the opening aphorism of book five (343), added in 1887, that Nietzsche makes explicit which God is meant and focuses on the question of '*Sinn*': What is the meaning of this event?

The Gay Science 343, which opens book five, is devoted to the topic of Nietzsche's kind of 'cheerfulness' (*Heiterkeit*). It carries the title 'We Fearless Ones' (*Wir Furchtlosen*), which names those who pursue philosophical questions free of moral prejudices and fears. It affords valuable insight into how Nietzsche placed and positioned himself as a philosopher, namely, in the context of the event of God's death and the opportunities and challenges that this event – which signals the collapse of the old metaphysical and moral order – presents for fearless lovers of knowledge. The aphorism speaks of an event that can fairly be considered the greatest of all recent ones and in order to convey its full impact Nietzsche deploys some highly colourful imagery: a setting sun, an eclipsed sun and a world becoming more autumnal. This event will cast a shadow; its actual eventful character will not be perceived and recognized as such by everyone as there are many for whom it will still appear as distant; and much harder to grasp for many is the meaning of this event. It is not only that a religious faith has collapsed; rather, everything that has been built on this faith will now be shaken to the core.

However, Nietzsche says that the free-spirited philosopher can greet the news of God's death with expectation and anticipation, even hope, simply because all the daring of the true lover of knowledge is now permitted once again. Nietzsche seems to be indicating that the philosophers and free spirits have been patiently waiting for this event and are in some deep sense prepared for it. He speaks, for example, of their particular love of knowledge being possible once again. Nietzsche cannot hold back from expressing the sense of liberation that now overwhelms him, and so chooses to draw the aphorism to a close by wondering whether there has ever been such a sea as that which now opens up before us. Yet a note of caution is immediately sounded in the very next aphorism of the text, which is entitled 'How we are still too pious', where he makes it clear that some new and highly demanding tasks now face all free-spirited philosophers and lovers of knowledge. How much 'truth' can we now endure? What new knowledge can we now dare? What can we now 'attempt'? Can we still be lovers of knowledge once the idealization and moralization of the world has been undermined and we confront a universe that is now devoid of meaning and purpose?

Let me seek to clarify the nature of the death of God and illuminate the sense of the cheerfulness Nietzsche appeals to in GS 343. It could be said that the Christian religion is built upon the death of God. It is not simply that Christ, as the Son of God, died on the cross for our sins but that God himself died on it too. Ever since, a Christian-moral culture and civilization has been mourning the death of God and is bound to him in terms of an infinite debt. Nietzsche is not the first philosopher to speak of the death of God. Hegel writes of this death in his *Lectures on the Philosophy of Religion* (1827), referring to a Lutheran hymn of 1641 that contains the phrase 'God himself is dead' (*Gott selbst ist tot*).[31] For Hegel, this expresses an awareness that the distinctively human – the finite, the fragile and the negative – is itself a moment of the divine and within God himself. On the one hand, Hegel says, there is the death of Christ that means principally 'that Christ was the God-man, the God who at the same time had human nature, even unto death. It is the lot of human finitude to die'.[32] On the other hand, a further determination is brought into play, which is that '*God has died, God is dead*' (*Gott ist gestorben, Gott ist tot*), and which is 'the most frightful of all thoughts' (*der fürchterlichste Gedanke*), since it means that 'everything eternal and true *is not*, that negation is found in God' (*daß alles Ewige, alles Wahre nicht ist, die Negation selbst in Gott ist*).[33] Nietzsche's figuration of the death of God is obviously very different from Hegel's, being rooted in a different epochal time and in different philosophical commitments. Gilles Deleuze, for example, says that, in Nietzsche, the death of God is to be understood not as a speculative proposition, but as a dramatic one. The difference is this: the statement contains no essential meaning, no speculative truth in the unfolding and becoming of *Geist*, but is an event or a rupture within which it enjoys multiple meanings or senses since everything depends on the forces that are brought to bear on it.[34]

Nietzsche sees God's death as being bound up with the development of the intellectual conscience: we reach a point when the discipline of truth forbids itself the lie in faith in God. Thus, what really triumphs over the Christian God is Christian morality itself and its concept of truthfulness, which comes to be understood more and more rigorously: 'the father confessor's refinement of the Christian conscience, translated and sublimated into scientific conscience, into intellectual cleanliness' (GS 357). Nietzsche lists what he takes to be now over for us moderns: looking at nature as if it were proof of the goodness and governance of a divine force; interpreting history in honour of a divine reason and a testimony of a moral world order; and interpreting one's experiences as if they were informed and guided by providence and ordained for the salvation of one's soul (GS 285). What stands against all of these things is our modern intellectual conscience: such articles of faith have simply become unbelievable for us.

In Nietzsche the death of God names two things. On the one hand, it names the death of the symbolic God, that is, the death of the particular God of Christianity. Although this God has held European humanity in bondage for two millennia and helped to breed a pathological hatred of the human and the earth, it has also served to protect the human will from theoretical and practical nihilism. On the other hand, it also means that the God of theologians, philosophers and some scientists is also dead, that is, the God that serves as a guarantor that the universe is not devoid of structure, order and purpose (see GS 109).

For Nietzsche, then, humanity has reached a point in history where belief in God has now become unbelievable. Although, as we have seen, Nietzsche is not the first philosopher to speak of the death of God, it is clear that he seeks to give this death a new articulation and meaning. When he speaks of a thing's meaning (*Sinn*), he is speaking of its sense and direction. For him, the death has the status of an event: the humanity that emerges in the wake of it, and that now has to give it a sense and a meaning, and to do so as a task, will be very different to the humanity that preceded it. For Nietzsche, there is a sense in which we have to become equal to this event, hence his emphasis on new tasks and ultimately on a new philosophy conceived as a 'philosophy of the future'. As Richard Schacht has noted, although the pathos of the parable on the crazy man (*der tolle Mensch*) (GS 125) may have been one Nietzsche experienced himself, it is a pathos that he overcame and left behind.[35] Moreover, as Robert Pippin has argued, in the section Nietzsche is suggesting that the madman is pathologically wrong to regard the absence of God as a loss and mistaken to take on the burden of a self-lacerating guilt, and that the village atheists addressed in it are too easily satisfied with a secular materialism, failing to understand 'the erotic aspirations and ideals Nietzsche elsewhere treats as "a condition of life"'.[36] Thus, two forms of pathological reaction are shown to be faulty: a melancholic theatrical guilt and the smug pose of enlightened freethinking.[37]

In a spirited analysis of GS 125, Charles Bambach illuminates the meaning of the madman parable through its relation to Diogenes the Cynic. As he notes, Nietzsche often thought under the influence of the thought of the ancient Cynics, even to the point of declaring that the highest thing one can obtain on earth is 'Cynicism' and offering his final testament, *Ecce Homo*, as an exercise in such Cynicism. The tenets of Cynicism that Nietzsche embraces include the renunciation of worldly goods and possessions for a life stripped bare of its conventional attachments, 'as well as an existence ordered by rigorous discipline and training (*askesis*) that shunned attachments to one's city, native country and land for a life of wandering and exile'.[38] This is a life dedicated to the philosophy of the morning that Nietzsche cultivates in his writings from around 1878 and that is dramatically staged in GS 125 and GS 343, with the promise of new dawns and new seas. The task of the Cynic way of life is to liberate oneself from the shackles of social and moral conventions and that serve as an impediment to our individual flourishing. Bambach expresses it as follows:

'In such a way, by living *kata physin* – "according to nature" – and renouncing the sham existence of culture (*nomos*), the individual might live as richly as a king – or even as nobly as a god.'[39] The aim is to experience 'joy in life itself' and through expressing a complete indifference with reference to all other goods (the *adiaphora*), especially the external goods (riches, honours and even erudition itself). As Bambach notes, the task is to devote oneself to one's self-mastery or autarky, involving one's shameless pursuit of free speech (*parrhesia*) against the suppressions of society.

Nietzsche asks provocatively in the preface to GS: is philosophy really a matter of 'truth' or is there not something else at stake, such as health, power, growth and life? (GS Preface 2) Philosophy is, then, a mode of therapeia, a refined cure for the maladies that afflict European culture and that have afflicted it for centuries. Bambach writes on this: 'Nietzsche affirms the Cynics' notion of philosophy as a lived practice rather than as a scholastic mode of turning out commentary upon commentary.'[40] Nietzsche has been waging a battle against philosophy's descent into scholasticism since the time of his unfashionable observations (1873–6), and it is largely on account of this that he attaches himself in his early period to Schopenhauer as his educator. Part of Nietzsche's adoption of the ancient art of living is his commitment to the virtue of *Redlichkeit*, which questions all conventional modes and expressions of morality, or what it is to actually live a good life.

We can now turn once again to GS 125 and see how Nietzsche puts to work and into play the Cynic mode of shameless comportment, as well as a buffoonery that is 'tinged with the great-hearted virtue that Diogenes calls "humankind's most beautiful thing": *parrhesia*, an unadulterated "freedom of speech" pushed to the limits of blasphemy, obscenity, and subversion.'[41] Bambach rightly sees the scorn that Nietzsche articulates in GS 125 as akin to the Cynic 'watch-dogs', the ones who barked and snapped at the smug citizenry of the ancient polis; so too Nietzsche 'unleashes his satiric scorn and shameless honesty on the complacent burghers' of German bourgeois culture.[42] In the parable of the madman, Nietzsche is consciously echoing Diogenes who lit a lantern in broad daylight and went about the market place seeking 'man', an honest man at that.[43]

It is possible, then, to interpret GS 125 as a 'recuperation of Diogenean parody and satire that comes together as a polemic against the canons of Christian morality' and that dominate Western culture.[44] Whereas, according to Bambach, Diogenes wore the mask of a 'mad Socrates' so as to caricature what he saw as the madness of Plato's philosophy, with its transcendence of the senses, the body and the earth, 'Nietzsche apes the madman in order to expose the madness of *both* Christian morality *and* the Enlightenment atheism that imagines itself free of the metaphysical presuppositions of Christian belief'.[45] The aim is to push this madness to its cynical limits, so as to devalue the otherworldly values of Platonism and then revalue the world of *physis* of nature/the earth. The search for a dead God thus compels the complacent atheists in the marketplace to confront what Nietzsche regards as the whole counterfeiting of transcendence and the above and beyond. Nietzsche regarded academic thinkers as harmless and attacks them as such in *Schopenhauer as Educator.* There he notes that they inspire no terror and unhinge nothing at all. He explicitly refers to Diogenes at this point in the text and he can be seen to be picking up on the legacy of Diogenes once again in GS 125. Nietzsche wants to disturb his readers and to demonstrate that with this 'monstrous' event humanity stands at the threshold of an epochal transfiguration and transvaluation. But part of the meaning of his cheerfulness is that he is ready to face the full consequences of this event and to meet it with amazement and glad tidings, for we face the prospect of genuinely 'new seas'; indeed, never before in the history of Occidental humanity has there been such an 'open sea' (GS 343). What the enlightened atheists gathered in the marketplace fail to comprehend is that the 'idea' of God has been killed. (It is not, then, a question of ascertaining philosophically whether God does or does not exist.) As Bambach rightly notes, the proclamation of God's death is to be understood as referring not simply to the traditional God of Abraham, Isaac and Jacob, 'but rather to Pascal's "God of the philosophers," the God who functioned as the axiological centre of Western values'.[46] With this proclamation, then, philosophy is turned on its head and the typical and standard framing of philosophical questioning is 'assailed with renewed fervor'.[47] As the madman asks of us, must we not become gods ourselves to become worthy of this great event, the event of all events?: 'There has never been a greater deed,' he says, 'and whoever is born after us – for the sake of this deed he will belong to a higher history than all history hitherto' (GS 125).

Gilles Deleuze has written instructively of Nietzsche's atheism as a *serene* atheism. It means that for such a philosophy the death of God is not so much a problem as a condition that one needs to acquire before other more interesting problems emerge, and there is no other modesty. There is an intimate connection here with the kind of serenity that characterizes Nietzsche's explication of the meaning of his cheerfulness at the start of book five of *The Gay Science.* Nietzsche suggests that although there is breakdown, ruin and cataclysm to be expected from the event of the death of the Christian God, he has no desire to be a teacher of gloom concerning this event; rather, there is only a new 'kind of light, happiness, relief, exhilaration, encouragement, dawn' (GS 343).

Deleuze has a specific conception of philosophy, namely, that it exists to defeat sadness or the predominance of the sad passions (*passions tristes*). And yet, this conception of Deleuze's philosophical project neglects the fact that in his book on Nietzsche he conceives the function of philosophy as one of saddening us. How do we reconcile these two commitments? As an art and science of demystification philosophy necessarily has the effect of disillusionment and even disenchantment. I think this is what Deleuze has in mind when he says that the 'use of philosophy is to *sadden*' (*La philosophie sert à attrister*).[48] By 'saddening' in this context Deleuze means to upset and to annoy, in which the philosopher, as Nietzsche says, exists to assume the role of the bad conscience of his age, and in which stupidity is harmed and turned into something shameful. Deleuze sees Nietzsche as part of an Epicurean tradition in which philosophy exists to oppose established powers and values; the thinkers who belong to this tradition forge 'fantastic paths' and make of pluralism a critical art of thinking.[49] Only with the exception of Spinoza has the critical enterprise in Nietzsche been taken so far since Lucretius.[50] It is the powers of religion and the State that seek to instil a fundamental sadness on human beings. If Lucretius exposes the troubles of the soul and those that need them to establish their power and if Spinoza exposes the causes of human sorrow and all those who find their power at the heart of this sorrow, then Nietzsche exposes *ressentiment* and the power of the negative that serves as its principle. Even the murderer of God committed a sad crime owing to the fact that his motivation was sad: he wanted to assume the place of God, the place of transcendence: 'The death of God needs time finally to find its essence and become a joyful event'.[51]

The meaning of Nietzsche's cheerfulness

Let me return to the focus on Nietzsche and now probe the meaning of the cheerfulness that he stages in his writings, notably GS 343. Nietzsche clearly wishes to see the cultivation of a spiritual maturity taking place that will enable us to deal adequately with the new post-metaphysical situation in which we find ourselves and not be overcome by disillusionment and despair. In *Human, all too Human* he had already mentioned the need in a post-metaphysical age for the requisite temperament, namely, a cheerful soul (HAH 34). Indeed, throughout his writings, from first to last, Nietzsche can be found wrestling with the meaning of cheerfulness. In a wide-ranging and incisive contribution to our understanding of this topic, R. Lanier Anderson and Rachel Cristy have argued that Nietzsche's cheerfulness is not of the natural, direct and pre-reflective kind; rather, it is something to be cultivated as a type of second nature.[52] There is some truth to this, and the art of cheerfulness is clearly one that can be cultivated along the lines they suggest. However, it is also necessary to recognize cheerfulness as playing an essential part in Nietzsche's instinctive disposition as a philosopher. I have in mind here the way in which he potently describes his atheism: this, he says, is familiar to him neither as a result nor as an event, but is rather self-evident to him 'from instinct'. He adds, 'I am too curious, too *dubious*, too high-spirited to content myself with a rough-and-ready answer. God is a rough-and-ready answer, an indelicacy against us thinkers – basically even just a rough-and-ready *prohibition* on us: you shall not think!' (EH 'Why I am So Clever', 1). One meaning of Nietzsche's cheerfulness – and there is more than one – is to have an instinctive fearlessness with regard to the questions and difficulties that life throws up for us, and it is such a fearless attitude that informs and guides his atheistic commitment. As a thinker one wants to *search* and to go in search of knowledge; one also wishes to do this in a manner that is calm, serene and even gay.

Nietzsche presents cheerfulness as a philosophical theme in his very first published book, *The Birth of Tragedy* (1872). He mentions the need to secure the proper comprehension of the 'serious and important concept of "Greek cheerfulness"' (BT 7). He is of the view that a misunderstanding of this concept is to be found everywhere today where it is encountered in a state of unendangered comfort. What is missing is any appreciation of the depths of being from which the Greek concept emerged and any sense of the tragic insights that informed and inspired it. In his untimely meditation on *Schopenhauer as Educator*, Nietzsche is keen to show that there are two quite different types of cheerful thinkers. The true thinker always cheers and refreshes, whether he is being serious or humorous, and he does so by expressing his insight not with trembling hands and eyes filled with tears, but with surety and simplicity, with courage and strength and as a victor. What cheers most profoundly, he adds, is that the true thinker enables us to 'behold the victorious god with all the monsters he has combated' (UO III: 2). There is no point in a thinker assuming the guise of a teacher of new insights and new truths unless he has courage, he is able to communicate and knows the costs of what has been conquered. By contrast, the cheerfulness of mediocre writers and brusque thinkers makes us feel miserable. This kind of cheerful thinker, he says, simply does not see the sufferings and monsters he purports to see and combat. The cheerfulness of the shallow thinker needs to be exposed because it tries to convince us that things are easier than they really are (Nietzsche thinks this is the case with the 'cheerfulness' of David Strauss, and whom he had attacked in his first untimely meditation).

The cheerfulness that we can respond to must come from one who has thought most deeply and who loves what is most living. It is perhaps curious that Nietzsche associates deep cheerful thinking with Schopenhauer! Is Schopenhauer not renowned for his deep-rooted pessimism and his view that life is worthless? In *Schopenhauer as Educator* Nietzsche contends, however, that Schopenhauer has a quality in common with Montaigne: both practice 'a genuinely cheering cheerfulness' (*eine wirkliche erheiternde Heiterkeit*). He seems to be suggesting that although a thinker like Schopenhauer deals with nothing less than the 'horrifying' and 'serious' issue of 'the problem of existence', he does so in a way that is calm and serene. A less gifted thinker and writer, Nietzsche surmises, will deal with the same subject but produce in the reader through their work, 'an oppressive and tormenting effect' (UO III: 2). Schopenhauer, then, is a profound thinker who speaks authentically: he neither stammers nor parrots what others say. Schopenhauer's cheerfulness, then, is a kind of victorious serenity, one achieved through a negotiation with, and recognition of, of humanity's deepest and gravest problem, which is 'the problem of existence'. Although, in the course of his intellectual development, Nietzsche will come to change his estimation of Schopenhauer as a thinker, and in significant ways, I think it is clear that he always admires him for dealing with this fundamental problem and with raising the question for us godless moderns of the 'meaning' of existence (see, for example, GS 357). In his untimely meditation Nietzsche makes it clear that he is speaking of the physiological impression that the original encounter with Schopenhauer made on him: 'that magical outpouring of innermost strength from one natural being to another that results from the first, slightest contact' (UO III: 2). The impression consists in an appreciation of Schopenhauer's honesty (*Ehrlichkeit*) – Schopenhauer is honest because he speaks and writes to himself and for himself – his cheerfulness (*Heiterkeit*), and his steadfastness (*Beständigkeit*). I think this latter quality helps to clarify a little what Nietzsche means by 'cheerfulness': it means possessing equanimity in the face of the deepest and gravest problem(s). Of course, Nietzsche acknowledges the limitations of his appreciation of Schopenhauer: he knows him only through his book. The task, though, is 'to peer through the book and imagine the living person whose great testament' we are reading (ibid.); in short, the teaching needs to be incorporated as a way of life.

Nietzsche continues to rely on an appreciation of cheerfulness well into his mature writings. Now, however, the meaning of cheerfulness is identified with a sense of expectation and anticipation: there is to be an amazement at the new seas that are now on the horizon, in short, we moderns have the chance of discovering new possibilities of life. The German word used in section 343 is, once again, *Heiterkeit*, a word that is often used ironically in the sense, for example, of 'that's going to be fun' (*das kann ja heiter werden*), as when one goes out for a walk, sees a big black cloud coming and foresees getting drenched. The walk is taken, even though one knows that risks are involved. The way in which Nietzsche presents his cheerfulness in *The Gay Science* clearly contains something of this sense, indicating a spirit of adventure and fearlessness with regard to the pursuit of knowledge. Nietzsche's cheerfulness has many hidden depths and dimensions to it. In particular, it explains the peculiar sense of distance he himself feels in relation to the monstrous event of the death of the Christian God.

We find echoes of this argument in the preface to the second edition of *The Gay Science*, which Nietzsche composed in the autumn of 1886. Here he speaks as a convalescent for whom the gay science signifies the 'saturnalia of a spirit' who has patiently resisted a terrible, long pressure, without submitting and without hope, but who suddenly finds himself attacked by hope, including the hope for health. He states that a philosopher who has traversed many different kinds of health has gone through an equal number of philosophies and philosophy is nothing other than this 'art of transfiguration' (*Kunst der Transfiguration*) by which the thinker transposes his states into a spiritual form and distance (GS Preface 3). It is certain that our trust in life has gone, and gone forever, simply because life has become a problem for us. Nietzsche counsels us, however, that we should not jump to the conclusion that this problem necessarily makes us gloomy. Love of life is still possible, only it is now like the love of a beloved object that causes doubts in us. Taking delight in the problem of life entails a highly spiritualized thinking that has overcome fear and gloominess. Nietzsche's cheerfulness stems from his experiences of knowledge, including the experience of disillusionment and despair that can result from the practice of the love of knowledge – this is the 'long pressure' that needs to be resisted. Nietzsche's love of knowledge embraces the demands of this love and represents a victory, something that one has won. He will, in fact, frequently speak of the gay science as a reward (GS Preface 7). In *The Gay Science* knowledge is to be conceived in terms of a 'world of dangers and victories in which heroic feelings ... find places to dance and play' (GS 324). He posits as a principle, '*life as a means to knowledge*' (*Das Leben ein Mittel der Erkenntniss*), in which the pursuit of knowledge is not to be conducted in a spirit of duty or as a calamity (*Verhängniss*) or trickery (ibid.). He speaks of the human intellect as 'a clumsy, gloomy, creaking machine' and of how the human being always seems to lose its good spirits when it thinks by becoming too serious (GS 327). He wants to teach the intellect how it does not have to be such a machine and to challenge the prejudice that would hold that where laughter and gaiety inform thinking then this thinking is good for nothing.

Lanier Anderson and Christy write incisively about the happiness regained by Nietzsche through his convalescence and how this might be part of a cultivated cheerfulness. As they note, Nietzsche's happiness does not leave sickness behind, but rather 'incorporates recognition of the pain and loss incurred on the way'.[53] Nietzsche is open to the possibility of a new kind of happiness: 'What makes the happiness novel is that the process of sickness and its redemption not only contributes to its causal origin but is part of its *intentional object*: the convalescent is happy *about* the opportunity for thought ... presented by the problems with which suffering has confronted her'.[54] In this mode Nietzsche's cheerfulness grows out of a frank and fearless recognition of life as a problem; it is not, then, 'the simple and natural affection of the naïve, whose lack of experience attaches them directly to life as an unalloyed good'.[55] Here we have a love of knowledge on Nietzsche's part that enables the convalescent to love life again, 'not *in spite of*, but *because of*, its problematic character'.[56] Although I concur with this appreciation of Nietzsche's cheerfulness, I also wish to maintain that as a thinker Nietzsche has this fearless attitude towards life and existence as part of his instinctive disposition. The thinker is the one who goes in search of knowledge, and conducting this search in a spirit of gaiety and serenity constitutes an essential part of their philosophical practice. Deleuze gets it right, I think, when he argues that philosophy exists for Nietzsche, as it does for Lucretius and Spinoza, to defeat sadness, notably the sadness that induces fear and superstition and that cuts us off from our powers of action.

Nietzsche and philosophy

At the start of this chapter I expressed sympathy with Robert Pippin's position that Nietzsche is better understood when we see him, not as a great German metaphysician, and certainly not as the last metaphysician of the West, but rather as a thinker who follows in the footsteps of the French *moralistes*, including thinkers such as La Rochefoucauld, Montaigne and Pascal. But what are we to make of his further claim that with the gay science Nietzsche has ceased doing philosophy altogether and is now practising psychology? We need to examine his exact position on this important issue more closely.

In the Introduction to his book, Pippin writes that many of Nietzsche's readers, including contemporary philosophers, want to ask Nietzsche questions he himself never directly addresses and to make use of what he does say, 'all in a more conventional philosophical language'. The assumption here is that in spite of his unorthodox style of philosophizing, Nietzsche can ultimately be translated into a conventional philosophical idiom and so shown to be committed to conventional claims in metaphysics, epistemology and say virtue ethics. But Pippin is surely right to insist on the fact that Nietzsche himself constantly raises in his writings the issue of how to read and how not to read the philosophical terminology and framing of his work, as well as pointing to the danger of reading him as a conventional essayist or writer. I think Pippin is also right when he further insists that the important and relevant point is not to simply note Nietzsche's resistance to incorporation into traditional (philosophical) theory, since this point is obvious; rather, we need to reflect on what this resistance means and amounts to, and in terms of reflecting on the issue of just 'what Nietzsche is trying to *do* with his books'.[57] Such a question poses itself to anyone who encounters the strange and graceful texts from the middle period, such as *Dawn* and *The Gay Science*. Put simply, these are not conventional philosophical texts by any stretch of the imagination, and it is far from clear just exactly what Nietzsche thought he was *doing* with them and how he wanted them to be 'read'. But need we go so far as Pippin in his contention that with these writings Nietzsche has given up on philosophical theory? Here Pippin admits to taking his bearing from an argument of Bernard Williams, chiefly, that Nietzsche, like Wittgenstein, was 'trying to say something about what it might mean for philosophy itself to come to an end, for a culture to be "cured" of philosophy'.[58] I have been arguing in this study that Nietzsche is in *search* of philosophy; but might it not be the case that, as Pippin maintains, Nietzsche is no longer doing philosophy?

Much depends here on what we take philosophy to denote as an intellectual practice. As I showed in the chapter on the text *Dawn*, Nietzsche does renounce philosophical theory in a strong way, especially in the sense of it denoting the desire to come up with a solution to the riddle of existence, having a master concept and so on. However, my view is that we need a much richer conception of philosophical practice than we currently have available to us. Two points are worth making.

First, that starting with his middle writings, Nietzsche makes a deliberate decision to break with the tradition of German philosophy, which he found sterile and boring. The art of thinking assumes specific forms in Nietzsche. He does not simply present his readers with disquisitions on philosophical topics but rather dramatizes them through a series of parables, thought experiments, imagined conversations and the like. His aim is always to energize and enliven philosophical style through an admixture of aphoristic and poetic – broadly speaking, 'literary' – forms. When Nietzsche discusses his favourite authors and books in his middle writings it is usually at the expense of German authors and German philosophy. He mentions some of his favourite reading, which includes the likes of Montaigne, La Rochefoucauld, Fontenelle and Chamfort. The works of these authors 'constitute an important link in the great, still continuing chain of the Renaissance' (WS 214). What Nietzsche admires about them is that they are above the changes and vagaries of 'national taste' and also above the 'philosophical colouring' that every modern book radiates as a matter of rule and does so if it wishes to become famous. Moreover, these books 'contain more *real ideas* than all the books of German philosophers put together' (ibid.). German philosophy books are characterized by 'obscurity' and 'exaggeration'. Even Schopenhauer, who has affinities in his style of writing with the French moralists, is said to wander among images of things rather than among the things themselves. With this point in mind we can say that Nietzsche is not so much renouncing philosophy as seeking to reinvent its practice so that it becomes a joyful art of thinking, one that deeply engages the reader and forces them to think and to collaborate in this art of transfiguration.

Second, this suggests to me that what Nietzsche is doing in his middle writings is, in fact, reinventing philosophy as a way of life and seeking to educate himself and his readers in the 'art of life'. Pierre Hadot laments the decline of philosophy from being a total way of life, as it was for the ancients, to becoming an academic specialism with its own technical jargon, and he cites Nietzsche, among other figures such as Schopenhauer and Bergson, as an example of a modern thinker for whom philosophy was indeed a way of life. By this he means 'a mode of existing-in-the-world, which had to be practiced at each instant, and the goal of which was to transform the whole of the individual's life'.[59] Real wisdom,

Hadot further writes, does not merely cause us to know but makes us 'be' in a different way. It seems to me that we lack essential knowledge here: just how does Nietzsche reinvent for us moderns philosophy as a way of life? We need to begin the task of working this out by recognizing that Nietzsche's philosophical practice has much in common with the ancient schools of philosophy, such as the Epicureans and the Stoics. Like Stoicism, Nietzsche is concerned with attaining a 'view from above' and with translating physics into ethics, as in his doctrine of the eternal recurrence, so that it becomes a spiritual exercise designed to test the character of our will (what do we desire to do?) and to gauge the extent of our attachment to life (are we well disposed towards ourselves and towards life?). Just as there is a gymnastics of the body, so we can entertain the idea of exercises of the soul as a form or mode of mental training. Here philosophy is not simply to be conceived as a set of written doctrines but as a set of practices or exercises that seek to transform one's way of life, indeed, one's entire way of being and fundamental orientation in the world.[60] If, as I am contending, Nietzsche is in search of philosophy in his middle writings, it can also be said that he is equally in search of a new mode of life and a new attachment to life, ones that would be appropriate for we godless anti-metaphysicians. To promote this new mode of life he freely draws on ancient practices of thought, including Epicurean and Stoic recipes: 'I view the various moral schools as experimental laboratories in which a considerable number of recipes for the art of living (*Lebensklugheit*) have been thoroughly practiced ... . The results of all their experiments belong to us, as our legitimate property. Thus, we will not hesitate to adopt a Stoic recipe just because we have profited in the past from Epicurean recipes' (KSA 9, 15 [59]).[61]

I think Deleuze is correct to locate in Nietzsche the practice of a rare and powerful unity of life and thought. For Deleuze we are returned in Nietzsche to the pre-Socratic secret that expresses the noble affinity of thought and life: 'life making thought active, thought making life affirmative'.[62] He writes: 'Modes of life inspire ways of thinking, modes of thinking create ways of living. Life *activates* thought, and thought in turn *affirms* life. Of this pre-Socratic unity we no longer have even the slightest idea.'[63] Deleuze contends that the secret of the pre-Socratics was lost at the very beginning of philosophy. Philosophy itself needs to be thought of 'as a force', and as a secret that 'remains to be discovered in the future'.[64] How was the secret forgotten? Here Deleuze refers to the Socratic moment of philosophy when 'metaphysics' is invented and when the philosopher ceases to be a physiologist and a doctor and becomes instead a metaphysician. It is Socrates who invents metaphysics if this is taken to denote the distinction between two worlds, the opposition of essence and appearance, and the distinctions between the true and the false, and between the intelligible and the sensible.

Deleuze has a unique take on Nietzsche's analysis of the moment of philosophy's decline. His concern with the history of philosophy, involving the Socratic moment, the Kantian moment and the dialectical or Hegelian moment is that the philosopher becomes voluntarily and subtly submissive. Although Kant invents a new moment of critique and seems to rediscover the idea of the philosopher as legislator, he never questions the ideal of knowledge: 'he denounces false morality, but he doesn't question the claims of morality or the nature and the origin of its value. He blames us for having confused domains and interests; but the domains remain intact, and the interests of reason, sacred (true knowledge, true morals, true religion)'.[65]

As a result of these developments in philosophy we have come to know only the reactive forms of life and the accusatory forms of thought. From the Socratics to the Hegelians the history of philosophy is the long history of man's submissions; this process of degeneration, Deleuze claims, concerns not only philosophy but becoming in general, including the becoming reactive of man as an agent of life. No wonder, then, that Deleuze goes in search of an alternative tradition of philosophy, a tradition of philosophical outsiders, naturalists for the most part, including Lucretius, Spinoza and Nietzsche. Before Nietzsche, the likes of Lucretius and Spinoza conceive philosophy as the power of affirmation and the practical struggle against mystifications in which the negative is expelled and is no longer the motor of philosophical activity; rather, we find that joy 'emerges as the sole motive for philosophizing'.[66] Although this 'joy' may be a more demanding affair in Nietzsche's case, it is nonetheless the very promise of (his) philosophy. I now wish to explore further the meaning that joy has for Nietzsche, along with a further exploration of his understanding of cheerfulness as a 'reward'.

On Nietzsche's Search for Happiness and Joy

As Richard Bett has noted, Nietzsche likes to give the impression that he is against happiness altogether.[1] A well-known witty aphorism in a late text, *Twilight of the Idols*, is typical in this regard: 'Humanity does not strive for happiness; only the English do that' (TI Maxims and Arrows 12). However, an examination of Nietzsche, especially of the neglected middle-period texts, can show that he is deeply concerned with the fate of happiness and also that he develops rich conceptions of pleasure and joy. In the following I explore various renditions of happiness and joy in Nietzsche's writings, offering a series of perspectives on the topic. I want to begin with an aphorism from *The Gay Science*, number, 45, and simply entitled Epicurus. It is a reflection on the happiness of the afternoon of antiquity; so let me begin there.

The happiness of the afternoon of antiquity[2]

Nietzsche writes that he is proud of the fact that he experiences the character of Epicurus differently from perhaps everybody else: 'Whatever I hear or read of him, I enjoy the happiness of the afternoon of antiquity.' In this aphorism, simply entitled 'Epicurus', Nietzsche writes:

> I see his eyes gaze upon a wide, white sea, across rocks at the shore that are bathed in sunlight, while large and small animals are playing in this light, as secure and calm as the light and his eyes. Such happiness could be invented only by a man who was suffering continually. It is the happiness of eyes that have seen the sea of existence become calm, and now they can never weary of the surface and of the many hues of this tender, shuddering skin of the sea. Never before has voluptuousness (*Wollust*) been so modest. (GS 45)[3]

As Monika Langer has noted in her interpretation of this aphorism, although clearly a paean of sorts to Epicurus, Nietzsche does not elaborate on the origin or nature of his happiness and suffering, but rather tacitly encourages the reader to consider various possibilities. In the end she argues that Nietzsche is reading Epicurus as a figure who while standing securely on firm ground, gazes at the sea and is able to enjoy the possibility of uncertainty it offers. She writes, 'Literally and figuratively he can float on the sea.'⁴ Epicurus is depicted as the antithesis of modernity's shipwrecked man since such is his liberation and serenity that he can 'chart his course or simply set sail and let the wind determine his way'.⁵ Although he might suffer shipwreck and drown or survive, he does not live in fear of dangers and hazards: 'In taking to the sea he might lose his bearings and even his mind.' In contrast to modern man who is keen to leave behind the insecurity of the sea for the safety of dry land, 'Epicurus delights in the ever present possibility of leaving that secure land for the perils of the sea.'⁶

This interpretation misses the essential insight that Nietzsche is developing into Epicurus in the aphorism. Rather than suggesting that the sea calls for further and continued exploration, hiding seductive dangers that Epicurus would not be afraid of, Nietzsche seems to hold to the view that Epicurus is the seasoned traveller of the soul who has no desire to travel anymore and for whom the meaning of the sea has changed. Rather than serving as a means of transportation or something that beckons us towards other shores, the sea has become an object of contemplation in the here and now. It is something to be looked at for its own sake and in a way that discloses its infinite nuances and colours. The scene Nietzsche depicts is one of Epicurean illumination or enlightenment: Epicurus is not estranged from nature and recognizes his kinship with animals and the elements of nature. Rather than deploying his contemplation of the sea to bolster his own ego (thinking of his own safety or taking pride in fearlessness), Epicurus abandons his sense of self altogether so that he can open himself up to the sea of existence. Unlike Christ, Epicurus does not walk on the water but floats serenely on the sea, buoyed up by it and even cradled by it, happy with the gifts life has to offer and existing beyond fear and anxiety, even though he is opening himself up to troubling realities, such as the approach of death and his personal extinction: 'We are born once and cannot be born twice, but we must be no more for all time.'⁷ As Langer rightly notes, the imagery deployed in the aphorism is striking: far from evoking boredom, the serenity of Epicurus signals a kind of ecstatic bliss.⁸

There is much in this aphorism, however, that merits careful exegesis and that, in the end, remains elusive. Why is the sea 'white'?[9] What is the role being played by the animals depicted at the heart of the scene? What does Epicurus suffer from and why does he suffer continually? Let's note that the 'afternoon of antiquity' refers to the specific cultural horizon that characterizes the moment of Epicurus within the history of philosophy: it is not the 'dawn' of the emergence of philosophy with the pre-Socratics, and neither is it the dark period that philosophy is plunged into with the rise of Christian morality. The mention of sunlight is significant since it makes the entire scene clearly visible to anyone who looks upon it; the roll of the waves is obvious to anyone who cares to look and who is not suffering from myopia or a similar affliction, and so it is up to individuals to gaze on the world and attain a standpoint on existence beyond fear and anxiety. We are to learn from animals since they are tethered to the present moment and do not live in anticipation of death and the anxiety that this anticipation generates for human beings. Epicurus might be suffering from physical ailments – we know these were acute at the end of his life – but he is also surely suffering from the anxiety of existence. However, Nietzsche sees the philosophical task as essentially a practical one, namely, that of conquering such anxiety, becoming serene in the process and, like a child playing with a kaleidoscope, appreciating, even being enchanted by, the many shades of colour that characterize existence.

At stake in the Epicurean way of life are those things that threaten human happiness, such as disturbances that arise from our irrational fear of death and the idea that divine decisions impact on the world and on the next life. Therefore, at the heart of Epicurean teaching is freedom from the fear of death and freedom from fear of the gods. An important distinction is made between kinetic pleasure and katastematic pleasure and this works as follows: kinetic pleasure is basic instinctive pleasure produced by action to satisfy a need, such as the ingestion of food or the ejaculation of sperm; this is an unstable kind of pleasure since it is temporary and involves pain – the pleasure of eating will soon be followed by the pain of hunger, etc.; katastematic pleasure is stable in that it endures and involves no pain: it is the pleasure of contentment and serenity, involving the absence of need and desire, and psychic equilibrium. It is superior to the animal pursuits of food and sex and for the Epicureans is to be elevated into the highest goal of life, attaining the state of ataraxia. As Gisela Striker puts it, Epicurus was perhaps the first philosopher who sought to bring this mental state into the framework of a eudaemonist theory and by arguing that it is a special sort of pleasure.[10] It is to be reached by true insight and reasoning. James Porter describes it as the 'basal experience of pleasure' on account of it being the 'criterion of all pleasure'. In this sense, then, it is more than a condition of simple or mere happiness since 'it seems to operate as life's internal formal principle, as that which gives moral sense and shape to a life that is lived.'[11]

In *The Gay Science* 45 Nietzsche makes a specific contribution to our understanding of Epicurean happiness or ataraxia. According to the portrait of Epicurus that he provides, this happiness is hard-won and has a precarious character, being inseparable from suffering: the sea of existence has become calm but, as Bett puts it, 'its continued calmness cannot be guaranteed, and the "shuddering skin of the sea" is a constant reminder of the turmoil that may return.'[12]

Heroic-Idyllic

Another paean to Epicurus from the middle writings can be found in the earlier text, *The Wanderer and His Shadow*. In aphorism 295 Nietzsche depicts an idyllic scene entitled '*Et in Arcadia ego*', involving looking down 'over waves of hills, through fir-trees and spruce trees grave with age, towards a milky green lake' (WS 295). While cattle graze on their own, and gather in groups, the narrator of the aphorism experiences, 'everything at peace in the contentment of evening'. While looking upon the herders in the field, he witnesses mountain slopes and snowfields to the left and, high above him, to the right two gigantic ice-covered peaks that seem to float in a veil of sunlit vapour: 'everything big, still and bright' (ibid.). The beauty of the whole scene induces in him an experience of the sublime, 'a sense of awe and of adoration of the moment of its revelation'; involuntarily, as if completely natural, he inserts 'into this pure, clear world of light', free of desire and expectation, with no looking before or behind, Hellenic heroes, and he compares the feeling to that of Poussin and his pupil (probably Claude Lorrain), at one and the same time heroic and idyllic, noting to himself that some human beings have actually *lived* in accordance with this experience, having 'enduringly *felt* they existed in the world and the world existed in them' (ibid.).[13] Epicurus is singled out for special mention.

The title of this aphorism is borrowed from two paintings of Poussin and was also adopted by Goethe as the motto of his Italian journey (1829). In fact, Poussin's paintings were inspired by Guercino (Giovanni Francesco Barbieri) and his painting of around 1618–22 entitled 'Et in Arcadia ego'. This painting depicts the discovery of death in Arcady, a region of Greece thought to be an earthly paradise: we see two shepherds gazing out of a wood at a skull that has been placed on a masonry plinth, and underneath the skull the inscription 'Et in Arcadia ego' can be read. Such words seem to be intended as a message spoken by death itself, 'I, Death, am also in Arcady'.[14] Poussin's first painting, bearing the same title, dates from 1627 to 1628, and the second painting, with the same title, from 1638 to 1639. In the first painting, which features a skull and two shepherds (but also flanked by a young shepherdess and a river god), the main motif is, once again, the recognition of human mortality. In the second version of the painting, from a decade later, a sarcophagus now lies in the centre of the picture and the scene depicted is much more allegorical. Although still a painting about the discovery of death in Arcadia, the foreground depiction of details such as the skull is omitted and instead we are presented 'with subtle allusions that do not disturb the atmosphere of contemplative but cheerful relaxation'.[15] In the second painting the words 'Et in Arcadia ego' are no longer uttered by death itself but might be the lament of a girl who has died young and who is buried in the sarcophagus: 'I, too, was once in Arcady'. This is how the Abbé Dubos interpreted the painting in the early eighteenth century and this interpretation then exerted an influence on writers and poets such as Schiller and Novalis, where the words are employed as a stock phrase, being adopted in verses that sing longingly of the possibility of a better world and of resignation to the fact of having missed it.[16]

There are several striking things about Nietzsche's turn to, and portrait of, the idyllic. First, we can note the contrast with his earlier critique of the idyll in *The Birth of Tragedy* where it is equated with the superficial and the optimistic (BT 8, 19). Second, in his depiction of the heroic-idyllic scene, the reality of death is completely absent from it. What might be informing Nietzsche's decision to leave death out of the picture is the Epicurean inspiration that the fear of death has been conquered and death is nothing to us.[17] Thus, Nietzsche does not wish the image of the tombstone to cast a shadow over the idyll that he is focusing our attention on: for this reason it is both heroic and idyllic. And third, for Nietzsche, the idyll is not in any inaccessible celestial heavens but belongs in this world and is within our reach, and what takes place after death does not concern us anymore.[18] Nietzsche writes in *Dawn*: 'The after-death no longer concerns us! An unspeakable blessing ... and once again, Epicurus triumphs!' (D 72)

The heroic-idyllic is heroic, then, at least in part, because conquering the fear of death is involved and the human being has the potential to walk on the earth as a god, living a blessed life, and idyllic because Epicurus philosophized, calmly and serenely, and away from the crowd, in a garden. In *Human, all too Human* Nietzsche writes of a refined heroism, 'which disdains to offer itself to the veneration of the great masses ... and goes silently through the world and out of the world' (HH 291). This is deeply Epicurean in inspiration: Epicurus taught that one should die as if one had never lived. There is a modesty of human existence in Epicurean teaching that greatly appeals to Nietzsche in his middle writings.

In each of the different main stages of his intellectual development Nietzsche comes up with a striking conception of philosophy. In his early period he urges philosophy to hold onto to the sublime since it is the sublime, he thinks, that enables us to distinguish between what is great and what is small, and so to appreciate what is rare, extraordinary and stupendous. Here the philosopher is seen as an abnormality and outsider. In the late period, and as is well known, philosophy is defined as legislation and creative positing, and the philosopher is a lawgiver who declares 'thus it shall be!' In the middle period Nietzsche offers a conception of 'heroic-idyllic philosophizing' with the philosopher conceived as a figure of great sobriety and extraordinary serenity. The reality of the 'heroic-idyllic' struck Nietzsche with the force of a revelation. In a note from July to August 1879 he writes, for example:

> The day before yesterday, toward evening, I was completely submerged in Claude Lorrainian delights and finally broke into lengthy, intense crying. That I had still been permitted to experience this! I had not known that the earth could display this and believed that good painters had invented it. The heroic-idyllic is now the discovery of my soul; and everything bucolic of the ancients was all at once unveiled before me and became manifest – up to now, I comprehended nothing of this. (KSA 8, 43 [3])

We can ask though: To what extent does the heroic-idyllic seek a refuge from the city and from public life? One commentator on Poussin argues that the idea of retreat can be interpreted in different ways in relation to his work.[19] One implies an evocation of a Golden Age, with the theme of fertility or of a classical pastoral. Here distance is achieved by setting the subject in the classical world, and so remote from the everyday world. Another is the depiction of figures that symbolize philosophical-cum-spiritual retreat; and then, finally, in the sense of a psychological state of withdrawal, 'there is the idea of an internal retreat from everyday demands in order to achieve "tranquillity of mind".[20] Inspired by both Stoic and Epicurean sources, it is argued that the cult of retreat from public life, and preferably in the country, was one of the standard topoi in the sixteenth and seventeenth centuries. There are classical sources for this inspiration, such as Virgil's second *Georgic* and Horace's second *Epode*, with the advocacy of the retreat being taken in humanist Italy by Petrarch for example. In the country is to be found peace, true freedom and tranquillity. Some writers assume an austere and Stoic vein by advocating a heroic type of retreat from city and country, celebrating renunciation and strenuous endeavour, while other writers of the time adopt a softer, more Epicurean vein by emphasizing the advantages of *otium* (relaxation and enjoyment), and also present in Horace's *Epode*.[21]

But what of Nietzsche's appeal to the heroic-idyllic and search for his own Epicurean garden: Is this too a simple mode of retreat from the city and from the public world? Nietzsche certainly prizes the securing of places of sanctuary so as to foster contemplation and solitude, as well as being in favour of an ethics of *otium*. As Gary Shapiro has noted, as a place of refuge and solitude, the garden provides for Nietzsche congenial conditions for the work of the philosopher as well as a model for the care of the self.[22] However, it is clear that we cannot view Nietzsche's Epicurean commitment to the garden in ahistorical terms as he is clearly responding to the tendencies of commercial society and the creation of a society of universal security (as he observes and interprets these developments), and it is in this quite specific context that we have to see his call to free spirits to isolate themselves so as to cultivate afresh the plant 'man' (see D 174). Although the need to cultivate one's garden may have an echo of Voltaire's *Candide*, as Shapiro points out, this does not have the goal, as Nietzsche has, of fostering new types of humans or *Übermenschen*.

The Epicurean garden appeals to Nietzsche in his middle writings as a place of contemplation and relaxation. He wants a new *vita contemplativa* to be cultivated in the midst of the speed and rapidity of modern life; we need to slow down, to go slowly and to create the time needed to work through our experiences. Even we godless anti-metaphysicians need places for contemplation and in which we can reflect on ourselves and encounter ourselves. However, we are not to do this in the typical spiritual manner of transcendent loftiness, but rather take walks in botanical gardens, the gardens that will replace the churches of old, and look at ourselves 'translated', as Nietzsche memorably puts it, 'into stones and plants' (GS 280). We free spirits have more in common with phenomena of the natural world than we do with the heavenly projections of a religious humanity:

we can be blissfully silent like stones and we have specific conditions of growth like plants, being nourished by the elements of the earth and by the light and heat of the sun. Karl Jaspers notes that one enters the garden of Epicurus in order, overcoming oneself, to abandon it once again, and this neatly captures something of the character of Nietzsche's attachment to Epicurus in the course of his intellectual development.[23]

The happiness of the free spirit

Let me now ask: what kind of happiness does the free spirit seek? In *Human, all too Human* Nietzsche writes of 'the desire for a blissful, serene mobility' as the philosopher's – and artist's – vision of happiness (HH 611). Indeed, a few aphorisms before this one, he notes how human beings construct for themselves 'gardens of happiness' in the midst of the sorrow of the world and upon its volcanic ground. They do this in multiple ways, be it in the manner of someone who observes life and has the eye for wanting knowledge from existence, or of someone who submits and resigns himself to life, or of a person who rejoices in their overcoming of the difficulties of life: in each case of happiness sprouts beside the misfortune (HH 591). The longing for 'blissful' and 'serene' mobility seems to provide the kind of happiness or joy sought by the wandering free spirit prized in the middle-period texts, and anticipates something of the character of the joyful wisdom of the gay science. Of course, Nietzsche does not have a univocal conception of happiness and severely criticizes one form of happiness in particular, which he finds contemptible because it rests on a smug ease and amounts to a religion of comfortableness (see GS 318 and 338). It is against this kind of happiness that Nietzsche advises his readers to build their houses on the slopes of Mt Vesuvius and to live dangerously. In *The Gay Science*, and as we have seen, Nietzsche notes how the happiness of Epicurus is born out of suffering from existence, and yet it is this suffering that makes its precarious attainment something meaningful. Further in this text he notes how the happiness of Homer's soul is a 'melancholy happiness'; it is one that makes you more liable to suffering, simply because there is the fact that one may lose it at any time and in which just a little displeasure and loathing will suffice in the end to make you disgusted with life (GS 302).[24] The idea of loss and mourning is continued in the next aphorism where Nietzsche perceptively writes of the worth and sum of life as meaning more for the person who knows more of life precisely because they have been so often on the verge of losing it, and so they have '*more* of life' than those who have never had this experience. This is a kind of joy and happiness in life that is, in fact, based on experience and as something actually lived. Perhaps the highest kind of personal happiness that Nietzsche prizes is the one described in *The Gay Science* 326. Here Nietzsche attacks preachers of morality, as well as theologians, for painting a too dramatic portrait of the human condition in which the human animal is portrayed in fatally sick terms, and the only cure for its malaise is a radical and final one: the pain and misfortune of existence are painted in a far too exaggerated manner. Instead, Nietzsche favours the capacities that individuals have for overcoming and conquering their pains and misfortunes, pouring sweetness on their bitterness, and finding remedies in their bravery and sublimity: all of this can give rise to new forms of strength. So he writes:

> What fantasies about the 'inner' misery of evil people moral preachers have invented! What *lies* they have told us about the unhappiness of passionate people! 'Lies' is really the proper word here: for they knew very well of the over-rich happiness of this kind of human being, but they kept a deadly silence about it because it refuted their theory according to which all happiness begins only after the annihilation of passion and the silencing of the will. Finally, regarding the prescription of all these physicians of the soul and their praise of a hard, radical cure, it should be permitted to ask: Is our life really painful and burdensome enough to make it advantageous to exchange it for a Stoic way of life and petrifaction? We are *not so badly off* that we have to be as badly off as Stoics. (GS 326)

Nietzsche is not in favour, then, of a radical cure in response to our complex affective conditions of existence – for example, the cure of a Stoic extirpation of the passions – since this results in 'petrifaction'. One needs to have passions in life and a passionate engagement with, and attachment to, it. But what of the passion of knowledge of the free spirit? To where does this lead and what attachment to life does it involve? The happiness of the free spirit appears to be one of an 'eternal liveliness' (WS 350), in which one is open to new experiences and that allow for the emergence of new sources of strength and maturation, and also make one attentive to the complex needs of our bodily and spiritual economy.

In aphorism 309 of *The Gay Science* entitled 'From the Seventh Solitude', Nietzsche writes of the wanderer as being driven by a penchant and passion for the true and that allows no rest and that perpetually seduces him to tarry.

Although the gardens of Armida beckon, he must keep tearing his heart away so to experience *new* bitternesses, and so he goes on since he 'must go on', even if it is with weary and wounded feet and looking back in wrath at the most beautiful things that could not detain him and because they could not detain him.

The deployment in the aphorism of wounded feet may be a reference to Sophocles' play *Philoctetes*. Philoctetes has been bequeathed a bow by Heracles and becomes a master of the weapon and sets forth against Troy with some companions, including Agamemnon. On the way to Troy, however, he and his companions make a stop at an island so as to make a sacrifice to the local deity. As he approaches the shrine, Philoctetes is bitten in the foot by a snake, and as the infection becomes virulent, his groans mean that it becomes impossible to make the sacrifice, as the act would be ruined by these ill-omened sounds. On account of his foul-smelling, suppurating wounded foot, his companions make the decision to desert him since they cannot bear the smell, and they remove him to a nearby island and sail off to Troy without him. Philoctetes then endures years of solitude as a social outcast and wanderer, and is eventually rescued from his plight by Neoptolemus, the son of Achilles, who is sent to the island on which he dwells and as part of a mission to bring him back with his bow so that the Trojans can be finally defeated.[25] The key lesson of the play, or at least one of its key lessons, has been captured well by Edmund Wilson as follows: 'The victim of a malodorous disease which renders him abhorrent to society and periodically degrades him and makes him helpless is also the master of a superhuman art which everybody has to respect and which the normal man feels he needs.'[26]

The tale of Philoctetes serves for Nietzsche, or so I interpret his enigmatic aphorism, to capture an essential aspect of the search of the free spirit and its way of life: an outsider to normal society, enduring long periods of agonizing solitude, and yet committed to the ongoing labour of free-spirited thinking, is the figure that may eventually be of great benefit to others and to society. The task, however, is not to resolve the problem of existence once and for all but to persist in the search for knowledge, and in so doing resist the temptation of tranquil rest offered by the peaceful and enchanted gardens of Armida.

Joy over pleasure

In the preface to *On the Genealogy of Morality*, Nietzsche associates philosophical cheerfulness (*Heiterkeit*) with gay science and he speaks of this cheerfulness as a 'reward': 'a reward for a long, brave, diligent, subterranean seriousness...' (GM Preface 7) The idea that cheerfulness constitutes a cultivated philosophical disposition is of Democritean and Epicurean ancestry; the idea that it may be a 'reward' for intellectual seriousness is of Epicurean inspiration. In *De Rerum Natura* Lucretius, the great disciple of Epicurus, addresses the 'joyless hearts of men' (see the opening of book two of the text), and writes of the joyful character of his intellectual labours as a 'reward', specifically as a 'reward for teaching on these lofty topics' and 'for struggling to loose men's minds from the tight knots of superstition and shedding on dark material the bright beam of my song'.[27]

Nietzsche is strongly wedded to the rewards of joy over the less intense and more comfortable experiences of pleasure. In the preface to the second edition of *The Gay Science*, composed near Genoa in the autumn of 1886, Nietzsche writes importantly on this topic, seeking to highlight his commitment to a joyful enlightenment as his principal intellectual project. He is not seeking to become a 'better' human being, but only a more 'profound' one, and this preference is what informs and guides the kind of inquiry undertaken by the gay or joyful science as an enlightenment endeavour:

> The attraction of everything problematic, the delight in an *x*, however, is so great in such more spiritual, more spiritualized men that this delight flares up again and again like a bright blaze over all the distress of what is problematic, over all the danger of uncertainty, and even over the jealousy of the lover. We know a new happiness. (GS Preface 3)

The joys of experience, as well as the joys of the gay scientist, are born from privation and abysses, including abysses of sickness; here, however, one returns to life 'newborn' and 'with a more delicate taste for joy (*Freude*)' (GS Preface 4). Indeed, Nietzsche writes of 'a second dangerous innocence in joy' in which one is now more childlike 'and yet a hundred times subtler than one has ever been before' (ibid.). One has returned to life from the abysses of existence not with abjectness or with cynical despair, not with jadedness or unwarranted loftiness, but with this 'innocence in joy' that restores one to childhood – one is full of hope and anticipation – and yet one has acquired all the subtleties of age and maturation. There is clearly an element of surprise in the experience of joy, and this is a dimension that Nietzsche captures well in his preface: as sick, one was deprived of hope, but one is now suddenly attacked by the hope of great health. As a convalescent, Nietzsche is surprised by the hopes given to

him in his return to health and to life. In his study of the story of joy, Adam
Potkay notes that in Greek joy (*chara*) is etymologically connected to grace
(*charis*) and as the gift that is freely given. He notes further: 'One may feel
satisfied or relieved by a success one feels one deserves; one rejoices, however,
in what comes as more or less a gift or surprise.'[28] Only in the course of the slow
and painful maturation of his ideas, of his philosophy and of the gay science
does Nietzsche come to experience the 'reward' of his intellectual pursuits, and
this makes the joyful character of his scientific practice all the sweeter and
more delicate.

Nietzsche favours this delicate 'art' of a gay and joyful science over the
intellectual experiences of pleasure that characterize modernity. Indeed, he
tells us in the preface that the 'crude, musty, brown pleasure (*grobe dumpfe
braune Genuss*)' of the 'educated' (*Gebildeten*) strikes him as repulsive, while
the sublime of the 'romantic uproar' – 'elevated, inflated, exaggerated' – hurts
his senses, including his sense of hearing (the reference is surely to Wagner's
music). Writing as a convalescent – since he has returned from sickness and
its abysses – he finds himself in need of an 'art' that is 'mocking, light, fleeting,
divinely untroubled' (ibid.). The will to truth that pursues truth at any price is
to be viewed as a piece of youthful madness and as bad taste: gay scientists are
'too experienced, too serious, too merry, too burned, too *profound*' to have belief
in a simple-minded love of truth. Moreover, 'Today we consider it a matter of
decency not to wish to see everything naked, or to be present at everything, or to
understand and "know" everything' (ibid.).

Nietzsche's fundamental teaching in the preface to the second edition of
The Gay Science is that without sickness and great pain we cannot be genuine
questioners of existence. If we are to become such questioners, we need to be
shaken out of our familiar and complacent attitude towards life and out of a secure
being in the world. However, this questioning out of the abysses of existence and
the depths of experience is not to be motivated by despair or disappointment but
rather by the rewards of joy, including the joy of anticipation, expectation and
amazement: in short, there are now 'new seas' to navigate and explore.

Conclusion

At various points in this work I have claimed that an Epicurean enlightenment
informs Nietzsche's practice of philosophy in his middle writings. In conclusion

I wish to offer some further reflections on Nietzsche's Epicurean commitments in these writings.

We might see, as Schopenhauer did, the Epicurean quest for *ataraxia* as akin to the Buddhist attainment of Nirvana.[29] This is how one commentator has seen the Epicurean philosophy, entailing the attainment of the highest enjoyment in the removal of all vivid sensations, including pain, desire and activity.[30] However, the garden of Epicurus is not an idyll that seeks escape from being or that refuses to acknowledge the terrible character of existence. As another commentator on Nietzsche's reception of Epicurus has put it, Epicurus's denial of immortality, 'affirms the most terrible character of existence as one of the first principles of the good life'.[31] It is even suggested that we find in Epicurus a conception of human existence and the world that is more finite and hence more terrible than Nietzsche's (Epicurus lives without the consolation – if that is what it is – of eternal recurrence). Moreover, Epicurus's remaining true to the earth 'was not pathologically conditioned by his desire to put an end to suffering and pain'; rather, it is the case that his 'insight into the unity of truth and appearances arose out of a profound recognition of human finitude'.[32] In Epicurean *ataraxia* we encounter 'the calm of strength and nothing of the calm of weakness'.[33] Far from being the repose of the deepest sleep, such *ataraxia* is 'an awakening of the active forces of life, an affirmation of the world as an aesthetic outpouring'.[34] This is to say that for the Epicurean, *ataraxia* 'is a direct experience of the intrinsic pleasure of life itself, of the active forces of a life form freed from the reactive force of desire'. We now directly participate in the blessed life of the gods, 'dwelling in the divine state of forbearance from reaction'.[35]

In the middle writings Epicurus is deployed, at least in part, as a way of breaking with fanatical enthusiasms and intoxications, including quite possibly Nietzsche's own early Dionysian ones. The serene teaching of Epicurus provides Nietzsche with one way of shedding his previous skin, that of *The Birth of Tragedy*, and now conducting the patient labour of self-analysis and self-cultivation as a therapy of body and soul. For the middle period Nietzsche Epicurus is the philosopher who affirms the moment, having neither resentment towards the past nor fear of the future.[36] Moreover, he teaches us the value of self-sufficiency, and his cultivation of a refined egoism greatly appeals to Nietzsche. Nietzsche finds in Epicurus a victory over pessimism in which death becomes the last celebration of a life that is constantly embellished.[37] This last of the Greek philosophers teaches the joy of living in the midst of a world in decay and where all moral doctrines preach suffering. As Richard Roos puts it, 'The example of Epicurus teaches that a life filled with pain and renunciation prepares one to savour the little joys of the everyday better. Relinquishing Dionysian intoxication, Nietzsche becomes a student of this master of moderate pleasures and careful dosages.'[38] Like Epicurus, then, Nietzsche seeks to live and philosophize 'away from the masses, without masters or gods, idyllically and heroically'.[39] Here we encounter that refined heroism that accepts death without fear and chooses not to even speak about it. Roos asks what I think is the decisive question concerning this appropriation of Epicurus: Can this teaching fill the void left by the loss of faith, the abandonment of Schopenhauer and the renunciation of Dionysian music? His answer to the question is incisive: 'He clings to Epicurus and his consolations with a vigour proportional to the violence of the Christian temptation.'[40]

As James Porter observes, there is not one Epicurus in Nietzsche's thinking; Epicurus sometimes assumes the role of a figure of thought, and on other occasions is a literary device, 'capable of taking on different colors according to the requirements of the moment'.[41] In Nietzsche's late writings, such as *The Anti-Christ*, Epicurus is depicted as a decadent, indeed, a 'typical' decadent (AC 30),[42] and in one note Nietzsche informs his readers that he has presented such terrible images of knowledge to humanity that any Epicurean delight is out of the question and only Dionysian joy is sufficient: he has been the first to discover the tragic (KSA 11, 25 [95]; WP 1029). This characterization informs the basic contrast that Nietzsche provides in *The Gay Science* 370 between the human being who is richest in the fullness of life ('the Dionysian god and human being') and the one who suffers most and is poorest in life; the former can afford the sight of the terrible and questionable as well as the terrible deed and luxury of destruction and negation; the latter, however, needs first and foremost goodness in thought and deed. Nietzsche contends that those who are poorest in life are the ones who need mildness and peacefulness, as well as logic, or the 'conceptual understandability of existence' since this gives calm and confidence, providing a 'warm narrowness that keeps away fear and encloses one in optimistic horizons' (GS 370). It is insight into this type, Nietzsche confides, that enabled him to gradually learn to understand Epicurus, 'the opposite of a Dionysian pessimist; also the "Christian" who is actually only a kind of Epicurean' (ibid.).

In his late writings, then, Epicurus has become an ambivalent figure for Nietzsche, and we are presented with an essential contrast between 'Epicurean delight' and 'Dionysian joy'. What has changed in his thinking? To begin with, we can note that Nietzsche's later thinking directs its critique at forms of philosophy that espouse contemplation as the goal of intellectual activity. Consider in this regard a note from 1885 to 1886, which runs:

> As a great educator, one would have to scourge such a race of 'blessed people' mercilessly into unhappiness. The danger of dwarfing, of relaxation is present at once: – against Spinozistic or Epicurean happiness and against all relaxation in contemplative states. (KSA 12, 1 [123]; WP 911)

Nietzsche, then, is suspicious of all attempts to attain philosophical beatitude through contemplative states since he thinks they represent a nihilistic flight from existence into a pure realm of being free of pain and free of appreciating the rich ambiguity of existence. The 'tragic' is for him essentially what allows for a greater attachment to life and signifies the affirmation of life beyond good and evil: it wants and affirms the total economy of life. Several notes from the final period of his output make this clear, as do several key aphorisms from the published corpus (e.g. GS 370). Nietzsche seeks what he calls a 'pessimism of strength' in which one has a penchant for the 'terrible and questionable' because of what one is (terrible and questionable): 'the *Dionysian* in will, spirit, taste' (KSA 13, 11 [228]; WP 1020). This is, Nietzsche confides, an 'experimental philosophy' in which the possibilities of the most fundamental nihilism are anticipated, but in which there is no halting at a negation of existence but rather a crossing over to a 'Dionysian affirmation of the world as it is', an affirmation that wants 'the eternal circulation', 'the same logic and illogic of entanglements'. To stand in a Dionysian relationship to existence is to practise *amor fati*, in which the difficult, cruel, painful, even detestable aspects of existence cannot be thought away (KSA 13, 16 [32]; WP 1041). For Nietzsche to attain real height, one has to grasp that everything that actually happens does so as it ought to happen, and this means that every kind of imperfection, and the suffering it gives rise to, are part of the highest desirability (KSA 13, 11 [30]; WP 1004). For Nietzsche the highest joy in existence, which for him is Dionysian, is to be had on the basis of this kind of affirmation of life.

There are weaknesses in Nietzsche's later appreciation of Epicurus. It is odd that he should accuse Epicurus of nihilism and of pursuing nothingness when it is clear that much of the latter's thinking was directed at what one might call an 'incipient nihilism of his time', as when in the letter to Menoeceus he takes to task the wisdom that declares it is good not to be born and once born to then pass through the gates of death as quickly as possible. Does Epicurus not invite us to recognize the mortality of the soul and the inevitability of total loss, in which, to quote Howard Caygill, the 'desired result is not utter dereliction and the ruin of life, but an openness to life's gifts and pleasures'?[43] As A. J. H. Knight astutely notes, Nietzsche's later comparison of Epicureanism with Christianity is misguided and unfair. Epicurean philosophy is not one founded on 'fear and timid optimism; it is rather one which tells men that they must *not* be afraid of God, Punishment, "Afterworld"'.[44] In the middle writings Epicurus is prized as one of those rare souls who remain true to the earth by demythologizing nature, and accept human mortality and human non-exceptionalism. In heroic-idyllic philosophizing we feel, as Nietzsche so eloquently puts it, that we exist in the world and that the world exists in us; in such a condition our estrangement from life is overcome. The lessons of this Epicurean-inspired appreciation of life, so characteristic of the middle writings and their search for philosophical sobriety, and which are partly existential and partly ecological, remain invaluable.

Notes

Introduction

1 Recent studies of these texts include Jonathan R. Cohen, *Science, Culture, and Free Spirits. A Study of Nietzsche's Human, all too Human* (Prometheus Books, 2009); Paul Franco, *Nietzsche's Enlightenment. The Free Spirit Trilogy of the Middle Period* (Chicago: University of Chicago Press, 2011), Monika M. Langer, *Nietzsche's Gay Science. Dancing Coherence* (Basingstoke: Palgrave Macmillan, 2010). See also Michael Ure, Nietzsche's *The Gay Science. An Introduction* (Cambridge: Cambridge University Press, forthcoming). In addition, there is the pioneering study of Nietzsche's middle period texts by Ruth Abbey, *Nietzsche's Middle Period* (Oxford: Oxford University Press, 2000).

2 Ruth Abbey, *Nietzsche's Middle Period* (Oxford University Press, 2000), xii.

3 Ibid.

4 Ibid., xiv.

5 Paolo D'Iorio, *Nietzsche's Journey to Sorrento. Genesis of the Philosophy of the Free Spirit*, trans. Sylvia Mae Gorelick (Chicago and London: University of Chicago Press, 2016), 49.

6 See letter to Franz Overbeck dated 7 April 1884, in Christopher Middleton (ed.), *Selected Letters of Friedrich Nietzsche*, trans. and ed. Middleton (Indianapolis: Hackett, 1996), 223.

7 See Michel Foucault, *Politics, Philosophy, Culture. Interviews and Other Writings 1977-1984*, ed. Lawrence D. Kritzman, trans. Alan Sheridan and others (London: Routledge 1988), 33.

8 This is not true of Vattimo whose project of weak thinking has its source, in part, in aspects of Nietzsche's middle period thinking. He has written instructive and provocative essays on some of the texts from the middle period. See especially G. Vattimo, *Dialogue with Nietzsche*, trans. William McCuaig (New: Columbia University Press, 2006).

9 On the one hand, Heidegger contends that Nietzsche finds himself as a thinker in the years between 1880 and 1883 – but this period covers core texts, such as *Dawn,*

that he never subjects to analysis and about which he has nothing to say (with the exception of some remarks about, and analysis of, *The Gay Science*). On the other hand, he maintains that, 'Nietzsche's philosophy proper ... did not assume a final form and was not published in any book, neither in the decade between 1879 and 1889 nor during the years preceding. What Nietzsche himself published during his creative life was always foreground'. M. Heidegger, *Nietzsche. Volume One. The Will to Power as Art*, trans. David Farrell Krell (London: Routledge and Kegan Paul, 1981), 8-9.

10 John Cottingham, *Philosophy and the Good Life: Reason and the Passions in Greek, Cartesian, and Psychoanalytic Ethics* (Cambridge: Cambridge University Press, 1998), 12.

11 Ibid., 13.

12 Karl Jaspers, *The Great Philosophers, volume III* (New York: Harcourt Brace & Company, 1993), 111.

13 Karl Jaspers, *Nietzsche. An Introduction to the Understanding of His Philosophical Activity,* trans. Charles F. Wallraff and Frederick J. Schmitz (Chicago: Henry Regnery, 1965), 3.

14 Here I paraphrase Nietzsche himself and as presented in Jaspers, *Nietzsche*, 386 (no source given for the citation).

15 Jaspers, *Nietzsche*, 389.

16 Peter Sloterdijk (*Nietzsche Apostle*, Los Angeles: Semiotext (e), 2013, 8) has raised the question whether we ought to stop from producing commentaries on Nietzsche and instead read and re-read him. My view is that we need commentaries that encourage this practice of reading.

17 Jaspers, *Nietzsche*, 4.

18 Lawrence Hatab, 'Laughter in Nietzsche's Thought: A Philosophical Tragi-Comedy', *International Studies in Philosophy,* 20: 2 (Summer 1988), 77–8, and as cited in Kathleen Higgins, *Comic Relief: Nietzsche's* Gay Science (Oxford: Oxford University Press, 1999), 72.

19 P. Franco, *Nietzsche's Enlightenment*, p. xiv.

20 Pierre Hadot, *Philosophy as a Way of Life*, trans. Michael Chase (Oxford: Basil Blackwell, 1995), 87.

21 Epicurus, 'Vatican Sayings', no. 45 in *The Essential Epicurus*, trans. Eugene O' Connor (Amherst and New York: Prometheus Books, 1993).

22 Voula Tsouna, 'Epicurean Therapeutic Strategies', in *The Cambridge Companion to Epicureanism* ed. James Warren (Cambridge: Cambridge University Press, 2009), 249–66, 257–8.

23 R. Safranski, *Nietzsche. A Philosophical Biography*, trans. Shelley Frisch (New York and London: W. W. Norton & Company, 2002), 210.

24 Richard Schacht, 'How to Naturalize Cheerfully: Nietzsche's *Fröhliche Wissenschaft*', in *Making Sense of Nietzsche*, Richard Schacht (Urbana: University of Illinois Press, 1995), 187–206, 187.

25 Schacht, 'How to Naturalize Cheerfully', 187.

26 *Selected Letters of Friedrich Nietzsche*, trans. and ed. Christopher Middleton (Indianapolis: Hackett, 1996), 177.

27 Pierre Klossowski, 'On Some Fundamental Themes of Nietzsche's *Gaya Scienza*', in *Such a Deathly Desire*, ed. Pierre Klossowski, trans. Russell Ford (New York: SUNY Press, 2007), 16.

28 See Horst Hutter, *Shaping the Future: Nietzsche's New Regime of the Soul and its Ascetic Practices* (Lanham, MD: Lexington Books, 2006), 4.

29 Hutter, *Shaping the Future*, 5.

30 See Havelock Ellis, *Affirmations* (London: Walter Scott, Ltd, 1898), 35.

31 Paul Franco, *Nietzsche's Enlightenment*, 227.

Chapter 1

1 See William H. Schaberg, *The Nietzsche Canon. A Publication History and Bibliography* (Chicago: University of Chicago Press, 1995), 56.

2 Ibid., 58–9.

3 Letter to Mathilde Maier, dated 15 July 1878. See Christopher Middleton, *Selected Letters of Friedrich Nietzsche*, trans. and ed. Middleton (Indianapolis: Hackett, 1996), 167.

4 Gary Handwerk, Afterword to F. Nietzsche, *Human, all too Human* (1), trans. G. Handwerk (Stanford: Stanford University Press, 1995), 376.

5 Marion Faber, *Human, all too Human*, trans. Marion Faber (Lincoln: University of Nebraska Press, 1984), xxi.

6 Ibid.

7 Ibid., 377.

8 Ibid.

9 Ibid., 378.

10 Ibid.

11 Ibid.

12 Ibid.

13 Richard Schacht, Introduction to *Human, all too Human*, trans. R. J. Hollingdale (Cambridge: Cambridge University Press, 1996), vii.

14 Ibid.

15 Ibid., xi.

16 Ibid., xx.

17 Ibid., xv.

18 For insight into man's need for metaphysics, see Schopenhauer, *The World as Will and Representation*, trans. E. F. J. Payne (New York: Dover Press, 1966), volume two, chapter XVII. For Schopenhauer, man alone is 'an *animal metaphysicum*' (160). Furthermore, although wonder is at the beginnings of philosophical speculation, philosophical astonishment is qualified by recognition of wickedness, evil and death as constituting essential features of the world: 'Not merely that the world exists, but still more that it is such a miserable and melancholy world, is the *punctum pruriens* (tormenting problem) of metaphysics' (172).

19 In his early period Nietzsche holds to the view that philosophy is the selective knowledge-drive in which the aim is to place knowledge in the service of the best life, even if this means 'One must even *desire illusion*' (KSA 7, 19 [35]).

20 Mazzino Montinari, *Reading Nietzsche*, trans. Greg Whitlock (Urbana: University of Illinois Press, 2003), 60.

21 Helmut Heit, 'Nietzsche's Genealogy of Early Greek Philosophy', in *Nietzsche as a Scholar of Antiquity*, ed. Anthony K. Jensen and Helmut Heit (London: Bloomsbury Press, 2013), pp. 217–33, 228.

22 For Nietzsche the earliest philosophers are magnificent superhuman types who come up with intuitions into existence that fill us with awe. Our confrontation with the Heraclitean insight into eternal becoming, for example, has something that is both terrifying and uncanny: 'The strongest comparison is to the sensation whereby someone in the middle of the ocean or during an earthquake, observes all things in motion'. Nietzsche then notes that it requires an 'astonishing power to transmit the effects of the sublime (*des Erhabenen*) and joyful awe to those confronting it' (KGW IV.2: p. 272). Heraclitus comes up with a sublime image (*erhabenes Gleichniss*) to do just this: 'Only in the play of the child (or that of the artist) does there exist a Becoming and Passing Away without any moralistic calculations' (ibid., 278).

23 See Michael Ure, 'Nietzsche's "View from Above"', in *Nietzsche's Therapeutic Teaching*, ed. Horst Hutter and Eli Friedland (London and New York: Bloomsbury Press, 2013), 117-141, 123. Passion and enthusiasm return to Nietzsche in his late writings, but it is also a question of having reverence for oneself and keeping one's enthusiasm in bounds. See AC Foreword.

24 J. Habermas, *Knowledge and Human Interests* (Oxford: Polity Press, 1987), 295.

25 Ure, 'Nietzsche's "View from Above"', 117.

26 Ibid.

27 Ibid., 118.

28 Ibid.

29 Nietzsche's portrait of Christ is a complex one in his middle writings, made up of critical insights and specific affirmations of his teaching and example such as the need to refrain from judgement and to be just (MOM 33). Nietzsche is indeed not only the anti-Christian but also positions himself contra Christ and in a fundamental sense. It is as the practitioner of 'the warmest heart' that Nietzsche opposes Christ and it is as a champion of greatness in culture that he must oppose him. Although Nietzsche describes Christ as 'the noblest human being' in HAH (HAH 475) as a thinker who affirms the agonistic dimension of human existence, he must oppose Christ where Christ is conceived as having 'the warmest of hearts' (HAH 235). By aligning himself with the poor in spirit, Christ promoted 'human stupidity' and so 'delayed the engendering of the greatest intellect' (ibid.). What is needed, Nietzsche maintains, is an image of 'the perfect sage' who will 'just as necessarily obstruct the engendering of a Christ' (ibid.). The engendering of genius requires that life retain something of its violent character in which 'savage powers and energies' are repeatedly called forth. What Nietzsche calls 'the warm, sympathetic heart' is one that yearns for the elimination of life's violent and savage character. Nietzsche locates a contradiction here: Is this heart not itself motivated by a passion of life that takes its 'fire' and its 'heat' from life's violent and savage character? Surely, he asks, this would mean that the warmest heart would endeavour to eliminate its own foundation and in the process destroy itself. Is this not, then, a philosophy of life that is devoid of intelligence? Nietzsche, then, sees a fundamental conflict between philosophy and sentiment, or between the sage and the religiously motivated person. Perhaps Nietzsche's most challenging thought in HAH is that the highest intelligence and the warmest heart cannot coexist in the same person. Thus, 'The sage who pronounces judgement on life also sets himself above goodness and regards it as only one thing to be appraised in taking account of life as a whole' (ibid.). Thus, the sage works to mount a resistance, resisting the 'excessive desires for unintelligent goodness' (ibid.). The sage does not believe in utopia conceived as the realization on earth of a 'perfect state', such as inspires the dream of socialism. For Nietzsche this will only lead to an enfeebled humanity and one that will perish of its own contradictions.

30 In a letter to Paul Rée of 1879, Nietzsche refers to his project as 'my Epicurean garden' (KSB 5, 460), while earlier in the same year he writes to his amanuensis Peter Gast, '*Where* are we going to renew the garden of Epicurus?' (KSB 5, 399)

31 Pierre Hadot, *Philosophy as a Way of Life*, trans. Michael Chase (Oxford: Basil Blackwell, 1995), 87.

32 In a note from the autumn of 1880, Nietzsche maintains that the metaphysical need is not the source of religion, as might be supposed, but rather the after-effect of its decline: the 'need' is a result and not an origin (Nietzsche, *KSA* 9, 6 [290]). See also GS 151 where Nietzsche makes it clear that he is arguing contra Schopenhauer on

this point. For Schopenhauer on the 'metaphysical need', see *The World as Will and Representation*, volume two: chapter 17.

33 Pierre Hadot, *Philosophy as a Way of Life*, trans. Michael Chase (Oxford: Blackwell, 1995), 265–6.

34 Catherine Wilson, *Epicureanism at the Origins of Modernity* (Oxford: Oxford University Press, 2008), 7. See also Epicurus in Brad Inwood and L. P. Gerson, *The Epicurus Reader* (Indianapolis: Hackett, 1994), 29: 'For there is nothing fearful in life for one who has grasped that there is nothing fearful in the absence of life. … The wise man neither rejects life nor fears death'. As James Porter notes: 'In Epicureanism *love of life is love of a mortal life* and not a love of life as abstracted from death, much less of immortal life', 'Epicurean Attachments: Life, Pleasure, Beauty, Friendship, and Piety', *Cronache Ercolanesi*, 33 (2003), 205–27, 212.

35 Karl Marx, 'Difference Between the Democritean and Epicurean Philosophy of Nature', in *Collected Works: Volume One 1835-43*, (London: Lawrence & Wishart, 1975), 73.

36 Jean-Marie Guyau, *La Morale D'Epicure* (Paris: Librairie Gemer Baillière, 1878), 280.

37 Norman Wentworth De Witt, *Epicurus and His Philosophy* (Minneapolis: University of Minnesota Press, 1954), 3.

38 Neven Leddy and Avi S. Lifschitz (eds), *Epicurus in the Enlightenment* (Oxford: Voltaire Foundation, 2009), 4.

39 The other three pairs are: Goethe and Spinoza, Plato and Rousseau, and Pascal and Schopenhauer. On Montaigne's relation to Epicurean doctrine, see Howard Jones, *The Epicurean Tradition* (London and New York: Routledge, 1992), 159–62.

40 Epicurus, 'Letter to Herodotus', in *The Epicurus Reader*, ed. Brad Inwood and L. P. Gerson (Indianapolis: Hackett, 1994), 5.

41 Voula Tsouna, 'Epicurean Therapeutic Strategies', in *The Cambridge Companion to Epicureanism*, ed. James Warren (Cambridge: Cambridge University Press, 2009), 249–66, 257.

42 Michel Foucault, *The Hermeneutics of the Subject. Lectures at the Collège de France 1981-1982*, trans. Graham Burchell (Basingstoke: Palgrave Macmillan, 2005), 238. Epicurus writes: 'The study of nature does not make men practice boastful speech or display a learning highly coveted by the rabble; rather, it makes men modest and self-sufficient, taking pride in the good that lies in themselves, not in their estate', *The Essential Epicurus*, trans. O'Connor, 1993, 81. On the need to avoid public opinion and accolades of the crowd, see also *Vatican Sayings* 29 (79).

43 Foucault, *The Hermeneutics of the Subject*, 240.

44 Ibid.

45 For further insight into how Foucault deploys the contrast between savoir and connaissance, see Foucault, *Lectures on the Will to Know. Lectures at the Collège de*

France 1970-1971 (Basingstoke: Palgrave Macmillan, 2013), including the opening lecture of 9 December 1970, and the translator's note.

46 Ibid., 241. See Epicurus, *Vatican Sayings* 27 (*Essential Epicurus*, 79): 'In other occupations, reward comes with difficulty after their completion, but in philosophy delight coincides with knowledge. For enjoyment does not come after learning, but learning and enjoyment come together'.

47 Ibid.

48 B. Inwood and L. P. Gerson (eds.), *The Epicurus Reader* (Indianapolis: Hackett, 1994), 6. We might think such conceptions make Epicurus a straightforward empiricist who adheres to the doctrine of the infallibility of sensation, but this would be an error. On Epicurus and empiricism, see the instructive comments by de Witt, 1954, 26, 135–42. For a more recent consideration of the topic, see Elizabeth Asmis, 'Epicurean empiricism', in *The Cambridge Companion to Epicureanism*, ed. James Warren (Cambridge: Cambridge University Press, 2009), 84–105.

49 See J. Donald Hughes, *Pan's Travail: Environmental Problems of the Ancient Greeks and Romans* (Baltimore: John Hopkins University Press, 1994).

50 Inwood and Gerson, *The Epicurus Reader*, 6.

51 Ibid., 7.

52 Epicurus, 'Letter to Pythocles' cited in Diogenes Laertius, *Lives of Eminent Philosophers*, trans. R. D. Hicks (Loeb Classical Library, 1931), X: 87, 615.

53 Inwood and Gerson, *The Epicurus Reader*, 30.

54 Howard Jones, *The Epicurean Tradition* (London: Routledge, 1989), 152.

55 Inwood and Gerson, *The Epicurus Reader*, 29.

56 Ibid.

57 Ibid.

58 See, for example, Peter Saint-Andre, *Letters on Happiness: An Epicurean Dialogue* (Colorado: Monadnock Valley Press, 2013), 38. See also Benjamin Farrington, *The Faith of Epicurus* (London: Weidenfeld & Nicolson, 1967), 132. According to one commentator, the point of departure for Epicurus was not hedonism at all. See Malte Hossenfelder, 'Epicurus – hedonist malgré lui', in *The Norms of Nature: Studies in Hellenistic Ethics*, ed. Malcolm Schofield and Gisela Striker (Cambridge: Cambridge University Press, 1986), 245–65, 245.

59 Julian Young, *Friedrich Nietzsche. A Philosophical Biography* (Cambridge: Cambridge University Press, 2010), 279.

60 Young describes the asceticism advocated by Epicurus as a 'eudaemonic asceticism', which is clearly very different to ascetic practices of world denial and self-denial (2010, 279). On these points one can also appeal to earlier readers of Epicurus, such as Kant for whom Epicurus has been misunderstood as a philosopher of pleasure: 'We still have a letter from him [the letter to Menoeceus], in which he invites someone to dine, but promises to receive him with nothing else but a cheerful heart

and a dish of polenta'. I. Kant. *Lectures on Ethics*, trans. Peter Heath (Cambridge: Cambridge University Press, 1997), 46. See also 384–7. Kant also distinguishes between 'a brutish Epicureanism' and 'the true Epicureanism' (66).

61 Richard Roos, 'Nietzsche et Épicure: l'idylle héroique', in *Lectures de Nietzsche*, ed. Jean-François Balaudé and Patrick Wotling (Paris: Librairie Générale Française, 2000), 283–350, 298.

62 Friedrich Albert Lange, *The History of Materialism* (London: Kegan Paul, 1925), First Book, 102.

63 Ibid.

64 Roos, 'Nietzsche et Épicure', 299.

65 Ibid., 309.

66 Ibid., 300.

67 For insight into the importance of Montaigne, see Jessica Berry, 'The Pyrrhonian Revival in Montaigne and Nietzsche', *Journal of the History of Ideas*, 65: 3 (2004), 497–514.

68 Horst Hutter, *Shaping the Future: Nietzsche's New Regime of the Soul and its Ascetic Practices* (Lanham, MD: Lexington Books, 2006), 5.

Chapter 2

1 An exception is Bernard Reginster, 'What is a Free Spirit? Nietzsche on Fanaticism', *Archiv f. Geschichte d. Philosophie* (2003), 51–85, 85. His focus is, however, different to mine, though it is a most useful contribution to the barely existent literature on Nietzsche and fanaticism.

2 For recognition of the importance of the 'whole heritage' of the Enlightenment for Nietzsche, see Walter Kaufmann, *Nietzsche. Philosopher, Psychologist, Antichrist* (Princeton: Princeton University Press, 1974, fourth edition), 350 and 361.

3 Nicholas Martin, '*Aufklärung und Kein Ende*: The Place of Enlightenment in Friedrich Nietzsche's Thought', *German Life and Letters*, 61: 1 (2008), 79–97, 79.

4 J. Habermas, *The Philosophical Discourse of Modernity*, trans. Frederick Lawrence (Cambridge: Polity Press, 1987), 105.

5 Martin, 'The Place of Enlightenment in Friedrich Nietzsche's Thought', 80.

6 Ibid.

7 Kant famously defines enlightenment as a human being's emergence from their self-incurred immaturity or the courage to use their own understanding without the guidance of another. See I. Kant, 'An Answer to the question: "What is Enlightenment?"' (1784) in Kant, *Political Writings*, ed. Hans Reiss (Cambridge: Cambridge University Press, 1991), 54. For Kant it is religious immaturity that is 'the most pernicious and dishonourable variety of all' (59). 'Laziness and cowardice',

Kant writes, 'are the reasons why such a large proportion of men, even when nature has long emancipated them from alien guidance ... nevertheless gladly remain immature for life'. Compare the opening to Nietzsche's *Schopenhauer as Educator*. For insight into Kant and enlightenment, see Katerina Deligiorgi, *Kant and the Culture of Enlightenment* (New York: SUNY Press, 2005).

8 For insight into Voltaire's role as a thinker of the Enlightenment, see Jonathan I. Israel, *Enlightenment Contested* (Oxford: Oxford University Press, 2006), 751–62. Nietzsche extols the virtues of Voltaire's play on fanaticism, *Mahomet*, in HAH 221. See also Voltaire's work of 1763, *Treatise on Toleration*. For insight into Rousseau's reception of Voltaire's play, *Mahomet,* see Christopher Kelly, 'Pious Cruelty: Rousseau on Voltaire's *Mahomet*', in *Rousseau and l'Infâme: Religion, Toleration, and Fanaticism in the Age of Enlightenment,* ed. Ourida Mostefai and John T. Scott (Amsterdam and New York: Rodopi, 2009), 175–87.

9 Ourida Mostefai and John T. Scott (eds), Editors' preface, *Rousseau and l'Infâme: Religion, Toleration, and Fanaticism in the Age of Enlightenment* (Amsterdam and New York: Rodopi, 2009), 9–19, 9.

10 Ibid., 10. As Mostefai and Scott point out, Rousseau sought to stake out an uneasy position between the theologians and the philosophers, and he did so by engaging with the *philosophes*, including Voltaire, 'in which he both appropriated and rejected their own approach to religion, toleration, and fanaticism' (ibid., 12).

11 Martin, 'The Place of Enlightenment in Friedrich Nietzsche's Thought', 94.

12 Nietzsche holds that Europe remains behind Indian culture in terms of the progress it needs to make with respect to religious matters since it has not yet attained the 'free-minded naiveté' of the Brahmins. The priests of India demonstrated 'pleasure in thinking' in which observances – prayers, ceremonies, sacrifices and hymns – are celebrated as the givers of all good things. One step further, he adds, and one also throws aside the gods – 'which is what Europe will also have to do one day' (D 96). Europe remains distant, he muses, from the level of culture attained in the appearance of the Buddha, the teacher of self-redemption. Nietzsche anticipates an age when all the observances and customs of the old moralities and religions have come to an end. In a reversal of the Christian meaning of the expression '*In hoc signo vinces* [In this sign (cross) you will be the victor]', which heads *Dawn* 96, Nietzsche is suggesting that the conquest will take place under the sign that the redemptive God is dead. Buddha is a significant teacher because his religion is one of self-redemption, and this is a valuable step along the way of ultimate redemption from religion and from God. Instead of speculating on what will then emerge into existence, he calls for a new community of non-believers to make their sign and communicate with one another: 'There exist today among the different nations of Europe perhaps ten to twenty million people who no longer "believe in God" – is it too much to ask that they *give a sign* to one another?' He imagines these people

constituting a new power in Europe, between nations, classes, rulers and subjects, and between the unpeaceable and the most peaceable.

13 Jean-Jacques Rousseau, *Emile, or on Education*, trans. and ed. Christopher Kelly and Allan Bloom (Hanover and London: Dartmouth College Press, 2010), 479.

14 Hume cited in Mostefai and Scott, Editors' preface, *Rousseau and l'Infâme*, 14.

15 It should be noted that elsewhere in *Dawn* Nietzsche appeals to the progressive cultural forces at work in Indian history, such as the free-minded naivete of the Brahmins and the redemptive teaching of the Buddha (see D 96).

16 Mazzino Montinari, 'Enlightenment and Revolution: Nietzsche and the Later Goethe', in *Reading Nietzsche*, trans. Greg Whitlock (Urbana and Chicago: University of Illinois Press, 2003), 50–7, 51.

17 The note is not translated in Montinari's essay and was prepared for me by Duncan Large.

18 Ibid., 52.

19 I borrow this schema of enlightenment in Nietzsche's thought from Montinari, 'Enlightenment and Revolution', 52. See also Martin, 'The Place of Enlightenment in Nietzsche's Thought', 89–90.

20 'The Place of Enlightenment in Nietzsche's Thought', 89.

21 Ibid., 94.

22 Graeme Garrard, 'Nietzsche For and Against the Enlightenment', *The Review of Politics* 70 (2008), 595–608, 601.

23 Ibid.

24 In an article on fanaticism and philosophy John Passmore has written that '... philosophical, as distinct from psychological or historical, works which announce that they are directed against fanaticism are exceedingly rare', John Passmore, 'Fanaticism, Toleration, and Philosophy', *Journal of Political Philosophy* 11: 2 (2003), 211–22. One might reasonably contend that Nietzsche's *Dawn* is one such work.

25 See Michael Ure, 'Nietzsche's Free Spirit Trilogy and Stoic Therapy', *Journal of Nietzsche Studies*, 38 (2009), 60–85, 63.

26 A. Toscano, *Fanaticism: The Uses of an Idea* (London: Verso, 2010), 120–1.

27 Nietzsche does not come to this insight into Kant and fanaticism until the 1886 preface to *Dawn;* he also criticizes him for making a sacrifice to the 'Moloch of abstraction' in *The Anti-Christ* (AC 11). In *Dawn* itself he actually praises Kant for standing outside the modern movement of ethics with its emphasis on the sympathetic affects (D 132). The problem with Kant's ethics is that it can only show duty to be always a burden and never how it can become habit and custom, and in this there is a 'tiny remnant of ascetic cruelty' (D 339).

28 Although Nietzsche holds Rousseau to be responsible for being the Revolution's intellectual inspiration and for setting the Enlightenment on 'its fanatical (*fanatische*) head' and with 'perfidious enthusiasm (*Begeisterung*)' (WS 221),

one commentator observes that Rousseau was in fact terrified at the prospect of revolution, Christopher Brooke, *Philosophic Pride: Stoicism and Political Thought from Lipsius to Rousseau* (Princeton: Princeton University Press, 2012), 207. His intention was not to foment revolt and he was of the view that in our postlapsarian state insurrections could only intensify the enslavement they are so keen to remedy, Thomas M. Kavanagh, *Enlightened Pleasures: Eighteenth-Century France and the New Epicureanism* (New Haven: Yale University Press, 2010, 127).

29 See Kant, *Political Writings*, 57: 'One age cannot enter into an alliance on oath to put the next age in a position where it would be impossible to extend and correct its knowledge … or to make any progress whatsoever in enlightenment'.

30 Compare Kant, *Political Writings*, 55: 'A revolution may well put an end to an autocratic despotism and to rapacious or power-seeking oppression, but it will never produce a true reform in ways of thinking. Instead new prejudices, like the ones replaced, will serve as a leash to control the great unthinking mass'.

31 For insight, see Anthony J. La Vopa, 'The Philosopher and the *Schwärmer*: On the Career of a German Epithet from Luther to Kant', in *Enthusiasm and Enlightenment in Europe, 1650-1850*, ed. Lawrence E. Klein and Anthony J. La Vopa (San Marino, CA: Huntington Library, 1998), 85–117, 90–1, 103–4.

32 Passmore, 'Fanaticism, Toleration, and Philosophy', 212.

33 For example, see David Hume, *Selected Essays*, ed. Stephen Copley and Andrew Edgar (Oxford: Oxford University Press, 1998), 38–43. For Kant on 'genuine enthusiasm', see the essay, 'An Old Question Raised Again: Is the Human Race constantly Progressing?' in I. Kant, *On History*, trans. Robert E. Anchor, ed. Lewis White Beck (Indianapolis: Bobbs-Merrill), 137–54.

34 Kant, *Critique of Judgment*, trans. W. S. Pluhar (Indianapolis: Hackett, 1989), 135. As Toscano rightly points out, for Kant fanaticism is immanent to human rationality: 'Vigilance against unreason is no longer simply a matter of proper political arrangements or social therapies, of establishing secularism or policing madness: it is intrinsic to reason's own operations and capacities, requiring reason's immanent, legitimate uses to be separated from its transcendent or illegitimate ones', Toscano, *Fanaticism*, 121.

35 Kant, *Political Writings*, 181.

36 Ibid., 188.

Chapter 3

1 Marco Brusotti, 'Erkenntnis als Passion: Nietzsches Denkweg zwischen *Morgenröthe* und der *Fröhlichen Wissenschaft*', *Nietzsche-Studien*, 26 (1997), 199–225, 199. For

insight into the passion of knowledge in Nietzsche, see also Mazzino Montinari, 'Nietzsche's Philosophy as the "Passion for Knowledge,"' in *Reading Nietzsche*, trans. Greg Whitlock (Urbana: University of Illinois Press, 2003), 57–69.

2 Paul Franco, *Nietzsche's Enlightenment: The Free-Spirit Trilogy of the Middle Period* (Chicago, University of Chicago Press, 2011), 61.

3 Ibid., 91.

4 M. Foucault, *The Use of Pleasure: The History of Sexuality volume 2*, trans. Robert Hurley (Harmondsworth: Penguin, 1985), 8.

5 Curtis Cate, *Friedrich Nietzsche* (London: Hutchinson, 2002), 298.

6 See KSA 9, p. 408: '*Die Pflugschar:* Gedanken über die moralischen Vorurtheile'. Nietzsche also had this title for his aborted fifth untimely meditation and it was also the working title for *Human, all too Human*. See also UO III: 3 on Schopenhauer's 'plowshare' that will 'cut into the soul of modern humanity'. For further insight into the image of the ploughshare and Nietzsche's adoption of it, see Duncan Large, 'Nietzsche's "Helmbrecht," or: How to Philosophise with a Ploughshare', *Journal of Nietzsche Studies* 13 (Spring 1997), 3–23.

7 Nietzsche first visited Genoa in October 1876 as a stopover on the way to Nice. He resided in Genoa and its environs for three successive winters in 1880–1, 1881–2, and 1882–3 in Rapallo in the Gulf of Genoa. On Nietzsche's fondness for the maritime city that also gave him access to the mountains, see Duncan Large, 'Nietzsche and the Figure of Columbus', *Nietzsche-Studien*, 24 (1995), 162–83.

8 Duncan Large, 'Nietzsche and the Figure of Columbus', *Nietzsche-Studien*, 24 (1995), 162–83, 174.

9 My thanks to Daniel Conway for insight into this appreciation of the text.

10 D. Large, 'Nietzsche and the Figure of Columbus', *Nietzsche-Studien*, 24 (1995), 162–83, 163.

11 See the letter dated mid-July 1881: 'So read the book, if you will pardon my saying so, from an angle I would *counsel* other readers *against*, from an entirely personal point of view (sisters also have privileges, after all). Seek out everything that you guess is *what* might be most useful for your brother and what he might need most, *what* he wants and does not want. In particular you should read the fifth book, where much is written between the lines. *Where all* my efforts lead cannot be said in a word – and if I had that word, I would not utter it' (KGB III: 1, 108).

12 Arthur C. Danto, *Nietzsche as Philosopher*, expanded edition (New York: Columbia University Press, 2005), 246. For a different appreciation, see Franco, *Nietzsche's Enlightenment*, 61.

13 Danto, *Nietzsche as Philosopher*, 247.

14 Ibid., 249.

15 Catherine Wilson, *Epicureanism at the Origins of Modernity* (Oxford: Oxford University Press, 2008), 7. See Epicurus in Brad Inwood and L. P. Gerson, *The*

Epicurus Reader (Indianapolis: Hackett, 1994), 29: 'For there is nothing fearful in life for one who has grasped that there is nothing fearful in the absence of life. ... The wise man neither rejects life nor fears death'.

16 In a note from the autumn of 1880, Nietzsche maintains that the metaphysical need is not the source of religion, as might be supposed, but rather the after-effect of its decline: the 'need' is a result and not an origin. Nietzsche, *KSA* 9, 6 [290]. See also GS 151 where Nietzsche makes it clear that he is arguing contra Schopenhauer on this point.

17 The texts of the middle period find Nietzsche seeking to emancipate himself from Wagner and his youthful captivation by his music. In HH 153 he states that the free spirit's intellectual probity is put to the test in moments when it listens to something like Beethoven's Ninth Symphony which makes him feel that he is hovering above the earth in a dome of stars and with the dream of immortality in his heart: 'If he becomes aware of being in this condition he feels a profound stab in the heart and sighs for the man who will lead him back to his lost love, whether she be called religion or metaphysics'.

18 In D 202 Nietzsche encourages us to do with away with the concepts of 'sin' and 'punishment': 'May these banished monsters henceforth live somewhere other than among human beings, if they want to go on living at all and do not perish of disgust with themselves!' In D 208 entitled 'Question of Conscience' he states what he wishes to see changed: 'We want to cease making causes into sinners and consequences into executioners'. In D 53 he notes that it is the most conscientious who suffer so dreadfully from the fears of Hell: 'Thus life has been made gloomy precisely for those who had need of cheerfulness and pleasant pictures'.

19 On Epicurus on fear and chance, see Pierre Hadot, *Philosophy as a Way of Life: Spiritual Exercises from Socrates to Foucault*, trans. Michael Chase (Oxford: Blackwell, 1995), 87, 223, and 252.

20 *Selected Letters of Friedrich Nietzsche*, trans. and ed. Christopher Middleton (Indianapolis: Hackett, 1996): 177.

21 Edwin Curley, *Behind the Geometrical Method: A Reading of Spinoza's* Ethics (Princeton: Princeton University Press, 1988), 128–9. For a recent instructive study that goes beyond Curley's scepticism, see Stuart Pethick, *Affectivity and Philosophy after Spinoza and Nietzsche: Making Knowledge the Most Powerful Affect* (Basingstoke: Palgrave Macmillan, 2015).

22 Franco, *Nietzsche's Enlightenment*, 97.

23 Ibid.

24 Robert Hull, 'Skepticism, Enigma and Integrity: Horizons of Affirmation in Nietzsche's Philosophy', *Man and World* (1990), 23, 375–91, 382.

25 Yirmiahu Yovel, *Spinoza and Other Heretics: The Adventures of Immanence* (Princeton: Princeton University Press, 1989): 106.

26 The link between the sublime and terror is, of course, the one made by Edmund
    Burke, *A Philosophical Enquiry into the Origin of our Ideas of the Sublime and
    Beautiful* (Oxford: Oxford University Press, 1998), part 1, section VII and part II,
    section II. Compare Immanuel Kant, *Critique of Judgment*, trans. Werner S. Pluhar
    (Indianapolis: Hackett, 1987), section 28.

27 Book five of *GS*, which Nietzsche added to the text's second edition in 1887, is
    entitled 'We Fearless Ones'.

28 See also D 435 on perishing as a *'sublime ruin'* [erhabene Trümmer] and not as a
    'molehill'.

29 On Schopenhauer compare Wittgenstein: 'Schopenhauer is quite a *crude* mind,
    one might say. I.e. though he has refinement, this suddenly becomes exhausted at
    a certain level and the he is as crude as the crudest. Where real depth starts, his
    comes to an end. One could say of Schopenhauer: he never searches his conscience',
    Ludwig Wittgenstein, *Culture and Value*, trans. Peter Winch (Chicago: University
    of Chicago Press, 1980), 36e. For a rich analysis of Rousseau and his motto *vitam
    impendere vero*, see Christopher Kelly, *Rousseau as Author: Consecrating One's Like
    to the Truth* (Chicago: University of Chicago Press, 2003).

30 See also Z I: 8: 'The liberated in spirit must yet purify himself. Much prison
    and mustiness is in him yet: his eye must yet become pure'. Ironically perhaps,
    Schopenhauer's own insight into Goethe seems to anticipate Nietzsche: 'Such a life,
    therefore, exalts the man and sets him above fate and its fluctuations. It consists in
    constant thinking, learning, experimenting, and practising, and gradually becomes
    the chief existence to which the personal is subordinated as the mere means to an
    end. An example of the independent and separate nature of this intellectual life is
    furnished by Goethe', Schopenhauer, *Parerga and Paralipomena*, volume two, 75.

31 Nietzsche's conception of the genius surely has affinities with Schopenhauer who
    defines genius as 'the highest degree of the *objectivity* of knowledge' (this knowledge
    is a synthesis of perception and imagination and found in a rare state and abnormal
    individuals), Arthur Schopenhauer, *The World as Will and Representation*: volume
    two, 292; see also chapter XXXI.

32 In GS 83 Nietzsche refers to the 'wings of the butterfly that is called moment'
    (*Augenblick*).

33 Since the fourteenth century Catholic churches sounded a bell at morning, noon
    and evening as reminder to recite Ave Maria, the prayer which celebrates the
    annunciation of the both of Christ to Mary by the angel Gabriel. Note by translator
    of *Dawn*, Brittain Smith.

34 See also Z II 'The Dance Song': 'Into your eye I looked of late, O Life! And into the
    unfathomable I seemed them to be sinking. But you pulled me out with a golden
    fishing-rod; mockingly you laughed when I called you unfathomable. "So runs

the talk of all fishes," you said; "What *they* do not fathom is unfathomable. But changeable am I only and wild in all things, a woman and not a virtuous one."

35 See D 117 entitled 'In prison', which ends: 'We sit within our net, we spiders, and whatever we may catch in it, we catch nothing at all except that which allows itself to be caught precisely in *our* net'. See also, from book five of the text, GS 374 on 'our new "infinite"'.

36 The dawn philosophy is a philosophy of the morning and, as such, it has its suspicions about thoughts that come to us in the evening. Several aphorisms in the book address this point. In aphorism 539, for example, Nietzsche draws attention to how our seeing of the world is coloured by different emotions and moods and different hours of the day: 'Doesn't your morning shine upon things differently from your evening?' (D 539) Aphorism 542 begins with Nietzsche declaring that, 'It is not wise to let evening judge the day: for all too often weariness then becomes the judge of energy, success, and good will' (D 542). Nietzsche may have been inspired in these reflections by Schopenhauer: 'For the morning is the youth of the day; everything is bright, fresh, and easy; we feel strong and have at our complete disposal all our faculties. ... Evening, on the other hand, is the day's old age; at such a time we are dull, garrulous, and frivolous. ... For night imparts to everything its black colour', Arthur Schopenhauer, *Parerga and Paralipomena* (in two volumes), trans. E. F. J. Payne, Oxford, 1974: volume one, 434–5.

37 In his middle writings Nietzsche is concerned with exposing a range of errors, which include belief in freedom of the will as a 'primary error' made by the organic, belief in unconditioned substances and identical things (HH 18), and the fabrication of 'unities' (HAH 19). In GS 115 Nietzsche notes that man has been educated by his errors and he lists four notable ones: that he sees himself incompletely; he endows himself with fictitious attributes; he places himself in a false order of rank in relation to animals and nature; and he invents new tables of goods which he accepts them as eternal and unconditional. In WS 9-11 Nietzsche clarifies the conception of freedom of the will he has in mind when he criticizes it, namely, one that supposes an atomism in the domain of acting and willing which is the supposition that every action is isolate and indivisible (WS 11).

38 Lars Svendsen, *A Philosophy of Fear*, trans. John Irons (London, 2008), 91. Svendsen's book sets itself a laudable aim: to 'break down the climate of fear that surrounds us today' and that has colonized our life-world (8). The fear at work here is what he calls 'low-intensity fear' (75).

39 In a note of 1872–3, Nietzsche writes, 'Fright (*Das Erschrecken*) is the best part of humanity' (KSA 7, 19 [80]). The context in which he states this is a consideration of the conditions under which we venerate what is rare and great, including what we imagine them to be and including the miraculous. Nietzsche's preoccupation with greatness in the *Untimelies* has to be understood in the context of his attack on a

self-satisfied and philistine bourgeois culture. The context of his reflections on the fate of fear and reverence in *Dawn* is quite different; they are part of the philosophy of the free spirit and European wanderer.

40 Svendsen, *A Philosophy of Fear*, 73.

41 This is not to deny that there is not at work in Nietzsche a will to the terrifying and questionable character of existence since this is one of the distinguishing features of the strong type as he conceives it (KSA 12, 10 [168], 555–7, WP 852). The point to be stressed, however, is that Nietzsche always appeals to 'courage' as the best destroyer and to a courageous humanity, not a fearful one. BT can also be read as being beyond a philosophy of fear: 'We are forced to gaze into the terrors (*die Schrecken*) of individual existence – and yet we are not to freeze in fear (*und sollen doch nicht erstarren*)' (BT 17). *The Birth of Tragedy*, trans. Ronald Speirs (Cambridge: Cambridge University Press, 1999) (translation modified). See also a revealing note from 1887: 'Everywhere that a culture *posits evil*, it gives expression to a relationship of *fear*, thus a *weakness*' (KSA 12, 9 [138], 413, WP 1025).

42 Although the concept of nihilism does not appear in Nietzsche's published writings until 1886 with *BGE*, he is thinking about nihilism in his notebooks of 1880 which contain notes on the nihilists, including the Russian nihilists. See KSA 9, 4 [103], 4 [108], 125 and 127.

43 Robert B. Pippin, *Nietzsche, Psychology, & First Philosophy* (Chicago: University of Chicago Press, 2010), 38.

Chapter 4

1 See Deleuze, *Spinoza: Practical Philosophy*, trans. Robert Hurley (San Francisco: City Lights Books, 1988), chapter two; Michel Foucault, *Ethics: The Essential Works 1*, ed. Paul Rabinow (London: Penguin, 1997). For Deleuze whereas 'ethics' refers to a typology of 'immanent modes of existence', 'morality' refers existence to otherworldly, spiritual or transcendent values and is the judgement of God or the system of judgement. Thus the transcendent opposition of the values good and evil is replaced by the qualitative difference of the modes of existence that we can call good and bad. As Nietzsche points out, to think beyond good and evil does not mean thinking 'beyond good and bad'. Nietzsche. GM I: 17.

2 See Paul Rée, *Basic Writings*, trans. and ed. Robin Small (Urbana and Chicago: University of Illinois Press, 2003), 87 and 89–99.

3 David E. Cartwright, 'Kant, Schopenhauer, and Nietzsche on the Morality of Pity', *Journal of the History of Ideas*, XLV: 1 (1984), 83–98, 96.

4 Ibid., 96–7.

5 Ibid., 98.

6 See especially Nietzsche, *Dawn*, sections 132–8. It is perhaps important to bear
   in mind that in taking to task *Mitleid* in the ways that he does in these sections of
   Dawn Nietzsche is working with Schopenhauer's conception of it where it involves
   the complete identification with the suffering of another. See A. Schopenhauer, *On
   the Basis of Morality*, trans. E. F. J. Payne (Providence: Berghahn Books, 1995), 144.

7 Martha C. Nussbaum, 'Pity and Mercy: Nietzsche's Stoicism', in *Nietzsche,
   Genealogy, Morality*, ed. Richard Schacht (Berkeley: University of California Press,
   1994), 139–67, 140. Nussbaum claims that in his cult of Stoic strength Nietzsche
   depicts 'a fearful person, a person who is determined to seal himself off from risk,
   even at the cost of loss of love and value' (1994, 160). Like the otherworldliness he
   abhors, the Stoicism he endorses is a form of self-protection, expressing 'a fear of
   this world and its contingencies' (ibid.). This picture of Nietzsche does not tally
   with the stress we find placed in *Dawn* on the need for the individual that wishes to
   become sovereign to take risks and to experiment. We will grow, Nietzsche stresses,
   only by experiencing dissatisfaction with ourselves and assuming the risk of
   experimenting in life, freely taking the journey through our wastelands, quagmires
   and icy glaciers. The ones who do not take the risk of life, he says, will never make
   the journey around the world that they themselves are, but will remain trapped
   within themselves like a knot on the log they were born to, a mere happenstance
   (D 343). The figure that Nussbaum esteems over Nietzsche is Rousseau, who is
   prized for his 'eloquent writings on pity' (1994, 140) and whose thinking lies at
   the basis of 'democratic-socialist thinking' (1994, 159). For an intelligent response
   to some of Nussbaum's concerns over Nietzsche on *Mitleid*, see von Gudrun von
   Tevenar, 'Nietzsche's Objections to Pity and Compassion', in *Nietzsche and Ethics*,
   ed. von Tevenar (Bern: Peter Lang, 2007), 263–81. For criticisms of Rousseau on
   pity, see Richard Boyd, 'Pity's Pathologies Portrayed: Rousseau and the Limits
   of Democratic Compassion', *Political Theory*, 32: 4 (2004), 519–46, and Michael
   Ure, 'The Irony of Pity: Nietzsche contra Schopenhauer and Rousseau', *Journal
   of Nietzsche Studies*, 32 (2006), 68–92. For Nussbaum's criticism of Nietzsche's
   Stoicism, see also Nussbaum, *Upheavals of Thought: The Intelligence of Emotions*
   (Cambridge: Cambridge University Press, 2001), 362 and 384.

8 See R. O. Elveton, 'Nietzsche's Stoicism: The Depths are Inside', in *Nietzsche and
   Antiquity: His Reaction and Response to the Classical Tradition*, ed. Paul Bishop
   (New York: Camden House, 2004), 192–203, 193.

9 Schopenhauer notes that when one person connects with another through
   compassion what they have done, in effect, is to have pierced the veil of Maya, that
   is, they have broken the spell of individuation and now can see that 'all is One'. This
   is why Schopenhauer says that virtue is 'practical mysticism' that springs from the
   same knowledge that constitutes the essence of all mysticism. For Schopenhauer,

metaphysics is virtue translated into action and proceeds from the immediate and intuitive knowledge of the identity of all beings. See Schopenhauer, *The World as Will and Representation* (in two volumes), trans. E. F. J. Payne (New York: Dover, 1969), volume one, 373.

10 In this note Nietzsche writes that 'greatness of character' consists in *possessing* the affects to the highest degree but also having them under control.

11 Ure, 'The Irony of Pity', 81.

12 See H. A. Taine, *History of English Literature: volume four*, trans. H. Van Laun (London: Chatto & Windus, 1906), 191. Taine writes here of 'aristocratical and commercial society'. My thanks to Andreas Sommer for this reference.

13 Dennis C. Rasmussen, *The Problems and Promise of Commercial Society: Adam Smith's Response to Rousseau* (University Park, PA: Penn State University Press, 2008), 18.

14 See Ure, 'The Irony of Pity', 82.

15 For a sceptical treatment of the sovereign individual, which contests the claim that it represents Nietzsche's ideal, see Christa Davis Acampora, 'On Sovereignty and Overhumanity: Why It Matters How We Read Nietzsche's *Genealogy* II: 2', in *Nietzsche's On the Genealogy of Morals: Critical Essays,* ed. Christa Davis Acampora (Lanham and Oxford: Rowman & Littlefield, 2006), 147–63.

16 G. Vattimo, *Dialogue with Nietzsche*, trans. William McCuaig (New York: Columbia University Press, 2006), 164.

17 Arthur C. Danto, *Nietzsche as Philosopher* (New York: Columbia University Press, expanded edition, 2005), 249.

18 Vattimo, *Dialogue with Nietzsche*, 164.

19 Ibid., 162–3.

20 Ibid., 161.

21 For further insight into Nietzsche's relation to the Kantian conception of autonomy, see Carl B. Sachs, 'Nietzsche's *Daybreak*: Toward a Naturalized Theory of Autonomy', *Epoché* 13: 1 (2008), 81–100.

22 See Kant (*Groundwork,* 61): 'Moderation in affections and passions, self-control, and sober reflection are not only good in many respects: they may even seem to constitute part of the inner *worth* of a person'.

23 Kant writes: 'Out of love for humanity I am willing to allow that most of our actions may accord with duty; but if we look more closely at our scheming and striving, we everywhere come across the dear self, which is always turning up; and it is on this that the purpose of our actions is based – not on the strict commands of duty, which often require self-denial' (Kant, *Groundwork,* 75).

24 See M. Ure, *Nietzsche's Therapy: Self-Cultivation in the Middle Works* (Lanham, MD: Lexington Books, 2008), 46.

25 Ibid., 46.

26 On these points, see Ure, *Nietzsche's Therapy*, 47.

27 For a critical treatment of this commonplace, see Alison Ainley, "'Ideal Selfishness": Nietzsche's Metaphor of Maternity', in *Exceedingly Nietzsche: Aspects of Contemporary Nietzsche-Interpretation*, ed. David Farrell Krell and David Wood (London: Routledge, 1988), 116–31, 124.

28 Elliot L. Jurist, *Beyond Hegel and Nietzsche. Philosophy, Culture, and Agency* (Cambridge, MA: MIT Press, 2000), 258.

29 Jurist, *Beyond Hegel and Nietzsche*, 246.

30 Ruth Abbey, *Nietzsche's Middle Period* (Oxford: Oxford University Press), 35.

31 Cited in Abbey, *Nietzsche's Middle Period*, 36.

32 Abbey, *Nietzsche's Middle Period*, 36.

33 Ibid., 38.

34 Jurist, *Beyond Hegel and Nietzsche*, 261.

35 Abbey, Nietzsche's Middle Period, 40.

36 Ibid., 73.

37 Ibid., 81. See also Walter Kaufmann, *Nietzsche. Philosopher, Psychologist, Antichrist* (Princeton: Princeton University Press, 1974, fourth edition), 365: 'Self-perfection is perhaps best sought not in seclusion, nor through exclusive preoccupation with oneself, but in community with others. This is exactly what Nietzsche himself proposed'.

38 Ibid., 77.

39 It may well be that aspects of Nietzsche's thinking on friendship were inspired by Emerson's essay on the topic. For Emerson the friend affords valuable opportunities for me to learn about myself and for me to become the one that I am: 'A friend therefore is a sort of paradox in nature. I who alone am, I who see nothing in nature whose existence I can affirm with equal evidence to my own, behold now the semblances of my being, in all its height, variety, and curiosity, reiterated in foreign form; so that a friend may well be reckoned the masterpiece of nature' (Emerson, *Essential Writings* (New York: The Modern Library, 2000, 208). Emerson anticipates Nietzsche in wanting the friend-relation not to be one based on complacency, as when he writes: 'Let him be to thee forever a beautiful enemy, untameable, devoutly revered, and not a trivial conveniency to be soon outgrown and cast aside'. For further insight into Nietzsche on friendship, see Willow Verkerk, 'Nietzsche's Goal of Friendship', *Journal of Nietzsche Studies*, 45: 3 (2014), 279–92.

40 Michel Foucault, 'On The Genealogy of Ethics: An Overview of work in progress', in Foucault, *Ethics: The essential works 1*, ed. Paul Rabinow, trans. Robert Hurley et al. (Harmondsworth: Penguin 1997), 255.

41 Ruth Abbey, *Nietzsche's Middle Period* (Oxford: Oxford University Press, 2000), 99.

42 Michel Foucault, *The Care of the Self: The History of Sexuality 3*, trans. Robert Hurley (Harmondsworth: Penguin. 1986), 43.

43 Ibid., 44.

44 M. Foucault, 'Technologies of the Self', in *Technologies of the Self: A Seminar with Michel Foucault,* ed. Luther H. Martin et al. (London: Tavistock, 1988), 16–50, 21.

45 Foucault, *The Care of the Self,* 47.

46 Ibid., 66.

47 Foucault, 'Technologies of the Self', 22.

48 M. Foucault, Foucault, *Ethics: The Essential Works 1,* ed. Paul Rabinow (Middlesex: Penguin, 1997), 269.

49 Foucault, *Ethics,* 255.

50 Ibid., 260.

51 Ibid., 276.

52 M. Foucault, 'An Aesthetics of Existence', in Michel Foucault: *Politics, Philosophy, Culture: Interviews and Writings 1977-84,* trans. Alan Sheridan et al. (London: Routledge, 1990), 49.

53 Foucault, *Ethics,* 254.

54 Joanna Oksala *Foucault on Freedom* (Cambridge: Cambridge University Press 2005), 169.

55 Nussbaum, 'Pity and Mercy: Nietzsche's Stoicism', 140.

56 Ibid.

57 Abbey, *Nietzsche's Middle Period,* 61.

58 Ibid. See also John Richardson, *Nietzsche's New Darwinism* (Oxford: Oxford University Press, 2004), 176–80.

59 Abbey, *Nietzsche's Middle Period,* 61.

Chapter 5

1 David B. Allison, 'The Gay Science', in *Reading the New Nietzsche* (Lanham, MD and Oxford: Rowman & Littlefield, 2001), 71.

2 Robert B. Pippin, *Nietzsche, Psychology, and First Philosophy* (Chicago and London: University of Chicago Press, 2010), 33, n. 18.

3 Pippin, *Nietzsche, Psychology, and First Philosophy,* 9; see Heidegger, *Nietzsche,* trans. David Farrell Krell, 2 (vols 3 and 4), 8; *Nietzsche,* 1, 480.

4 R. Schacht, 'How to Philosophize Cheerfully Nietzsche's *Fröhliche Wissenschaft*', in *Making Sense of Nietzsche,* ed. R. Schacht (Urbana: University of Illinois Press, 1995), 189.

5 For a selection of these notes translated into English, see Keith Ansell-Pearson and Duncan Large, *The Nietzsche Reader* (Malden, MA: Blackwell, 2006), 238–41.

6   See Walter Kaufmann, 'Translator's Introduction' to *The Gay Science*, trans. Walter
    Kaufmann (New York: Random House, 1974), 3–26, 19.

7   Cited in William H. Schaberg, *The Nietzsche Canon. A Publication History and
    Bibliography* (Chicago: University of Chicago Press, 1995), 83; see also Kaufmann,
    'Translator's Introduction', *The Gay Science*, 18.

8   See Schaberg, *The Nietzsche Canon*, 84. For insight into Nietzsche's relationship
    to Salomé, see the biographies by Curtis Cate, *Friedrich Nietzsche* (London:
    Hutchinson, 2002), 320–43, and Julian Young, *Nietzsche: An Intellectual Biography*
    (Cambridge: Cambridge University Press, 2010), 339–57.

9   Pierre Klossowski, 'On Some Fundamental Themes of Nietzsche's *Gaya Scienza*', in
    Such a Deathly Desire, ed. Pierre Klossowski, trans. Russell Ford (New York: SUNY
    Press, 2007), 16.

10 Nietzsche, *Selected Letters*, ed. and trans. C. Middleton (Indianapolis: Hackett,
    1996), 187.

11 Nietzsche, *Selected Letters*, 187.

12 Ibid.

13 Ibid., 190.

14 Letter to Franz Overbeck, September 1882, in *Selected Letters*, 193.

15 Nietzsche, *Selected Letters*, 197.

16 Ibid., 199.

17 Robin Small, *Nietzsche and Rée: A Star Friendship* (Oxford: Oxford University Press,
    2005), xix.

18 Kaufmann, 'Translator's Introduction', in *The Gay Science*, 7.

19 Pippin, *Nietzsche, Psychology, and First Philosophy*, 36.

20 See Ralph Waldo Emerson, *The Early Lectures. Volume III 1838*-1842, ed. Robert E.
    Spiller and Wallace E. Williams (Cambridge, MA: Harvard University Press, 1972),
    368. See also Pippin, who refers to Thomas Carlyle's contrast between a 'gay science'
    and the 'dismal sciences' as a possible influence (*Nietzsche, Psychology, and First
    Philosophy*, 34).

21 In an early draft to *Ecce Homo* Nietzsche describes his development and reading,
    and he praises Emerson as a writer who has been 'a good friend' and cheered him up
    in dark times. He is said to possess 'so much skepsis, so many "possibilities"' (KSA
    14, 476–7). For insight into Nietzsche's reading of Emerson over the course of his
    intellectual life, see Thomas H. Brobjer, *Nietzsche and the 'English': The Influence of
    British and American Thinking on his Philosophy* (New York: Humanity Books, 2008),
    155–67. During his travels in England in the early 1830s Emerson met Carlyle and
    initiated a lasting friendship with him. See Russell B. Goodman, *American Philosophy
    before Pragmatism* (Oxford: Oxford University Press, 2015), 163. See also the discussion
    of Nietzsche on Emerson and Carlyle in Kenneth Marc Harris, *Carlyle and Emerson:
    Their Long Debate* (Cambridge, MA: Harvard University Press, 1978), 165–71.

22 See David Farrell Krell, 'Emerson – Nietzsche's Voluptuary?', *Comparative and Continental Philosophy*, 7: 1 (2015), 8–17, 15.

23 As Duncan Large notes in his translator's notes, Ovid has 'voluntas' (will) for 'voluptas' (lust). See Nietzsche, *Twilight of the Idols*, trans. Duncan Large (Oxford: Oxford University Press, 1998), 102.

24 Charles Bambach, 'Nietzsche's Madman Parable: A Cynical Reading', *American Catholic Philosophical Quarterly*, 84: 2 (2010), 441–57, 443.

25 Ibid., 445. For insight into Nietzsche as a neo-Cynic see also William Desmond, *Cynics* (Stocksfield: Acumen, 2008), 136, 150, 192 and especially 231–4.

26 See GS 334, entitled 'One must learn to love'.

27 Pippin, *Nietzsche, Psychology, and First Philosophy*, 35.

28 Ibid., 41.

29 Michael Ure, *Nietzsche's* The Gay Science*: An Introduction* (Cambridge: Cambridge University Press, forthcoming).

30 For a fascinating exchange on the nature of Nietzsche's philosophical practice in these terms, see Katia Hay and Herman Siemens, 'On Seriousness and Laughter: A Dialogue Concerning Nietzsche's *Gay Science*', *Pli. The Warwick Journal of Philosophy*, 25 (2014), 77–91.

31 G. W. F. Hegel, *Werke in 20 Bänden*, ed. Eva Moldenhauer and Karl Markus Michel, 20 vols (Frankfurt am Main: Suhrkamp, 1986), 17: 297.

32 Hegel, *Werke*, 17: 289; *The Hegel Reader*, ed. Stephen Houlgate (Oxford: Basil Blackwell, 1998), 497–8.

33 Hegel, *Werke*, 17: 291; *The Hegel Reader*, ed. Houlgate, 497–8.

34 Gilles Deleuze, *Nietzsche and Philosophy*, trans. Hugh Tomlinson (London: Continuum Press, 1983), 152–6.

35 Richard Schacht, 'How to Philosophize Cheerfully Nietzsche's *Fröhliche Wissenschaft*', in *Making Sense of Nietzsche,* ed. Richard Schacht (Urbana: University of Illinois Press, 1995), 187–206. Compare Nietzsche on nihilism, where he presents himself as 'the first perfect nihilist of Europe who, however, has even now lived through the whole of nihilism, to the end, leaving it behind, outside himself' (*der erste vollkommene Nihilist Europas, der aber den Nihilismus selbst schon in sich zu Ende gelebt hat, – der ihn hinter sich, unter sich, außer sich hat*; WP Preface §3; KSA 13, 11[411], 190).

36 Pippin, *Nietzsche, Psychology, and First Philosophy*, 51. As Stephen Mulhall points out, Nietzsche's madman is addressing two audiences with his search for God and announcement of his death: the atheists in the marketplace and the theists who call him to account in the churches he visits at the denouement to the aphorism. For his reading of this, and his claim that the idea of the death of God is 'absolutely integral' to Christianity (which, as we have seen, is at work in Hegel), see his essay, 'The Madman and the Masters: Nietzsche', in Mulhall, *Philosophical*

Myths of the Fall (Princeton: Princeton University Press, 2005), 16–46, especially 20 and 29–32.

37 Pippin, *Nietzsche, Psychology, and First Philosophy*, 54.

38 Bambach, 'Nietzsche's Madman Parable', 442.

39 Ibid.

40 Ibid., 443.

41 Ibid., 444. Foucault draws out well that the word *parrhesia* refers to a relationship between the speaker and what he says, in which the speaker makes it clear that what he says is his own opinion. He further writes: 'The fact that a speaker says something dangerous – different from what the majority believes – is a strong indication that he is a *parrhesiastes*' – these insights capture well aspects of Nietzsche's philosophical practice. See Michel Foucault, *Fearless Speech*, ed. Joseph Pearson (Los Angeles: Semiotexte, 2001), 15.

42 Ibid.

43 For Diogenes see *Diogenes the Cynic: Sayings and Anecdotes with other Popular Moralists*, trans. Robin Hard (Oxford: Oxford University Press, 2012), 19.

44 Bambach, 'Nietzsche's Madman Parable', 450.

45 Ibid.

46 Ibid., 455.

47 Ibid.

48 Gilles Deleuze, *Nietzsche and Philosophy*, trans. Hugh Tomlinson (London: Athlone Press, 1983), 106.

49 Ibid., 106–7.

50 Ibid., 190.

51 Ibid.

52 See R. Lanier Anderson and Rachel Cristy, 'What Is "The Meaning of Our Cheerfulness"? Philosophy as a Way of Life in Nietzsche and Montaigne', *European Journal of Philosophy* (2017), 1–36 (DOI: 10, 111/ejop 12235).

53 R. Lanier Anderson and Rachel Cristy, 'What Is "The Meaning of Our Cheerfulness"?', 8.

54 Ibid.

55 Ibid.

56 Ibid.

57 Pippin, *Nietzsche, Psychology, and First Philosophy*, xv.

58 Ibid., xiv.

59 Pierre Hadot, *Philosophy as a Way of Life*, trans. Michael Chase (Oxford: Blackwell, 1995), 265.

60 For further insight see John Sellars, *The Art of Living. The Stoics on the Nature and Function of Philosophy* (London: Bristol Classical Press, an imprint of Bloomsbury Academic, 2011), 111.

61 Cited in Pierre Hadot, *What is Ancient Philosophy?*, trans. Michael Chase
    (Cambridge, MA: Harvard University Press, 2002), 277.
62 Deleuze, *Nietzsche and Philosophy*, 101.
63 G. Deleuze, 'Nietzsche', in *Pure Immanence. Essays on A Life*, trans. Anne Boyman
    (New York: Zone Books, 2005), 66.
64 Ibid., 68.
65 Ibid., 70.
66 Ibid., 84.

Chapter 6

1 Richard Bett, 'Nietzsche, the Greeks, and Happiness (with special reference to
   Aristotle and Epicurus)', *Philosophical Topics*, 33: 2 (2005), 45–70, 45.
2 My appreciation of this aphorism from *The Gay Science* was greatly enriched by
   the graduate seminar that I taught on Nietzsche at Warwick University in the
   spring term of 2013, and especially the contributions of Robert Kron and Jeffrey
   Pickernell. Thanks also for inspiration to Beatrice Han-Pile and Rainer Hanshe.
3 For insight into the 'distinctly Genoese' character of the Epicurean bliss that
   Nietzsche is writing about in this aphorism, see Martina Kolb, Martina Kolb's
   study, *Nietzsche, Freud, Benn, and the Azure Spell of Liguria* (Toronto: University
   of Toronto Press, 2013), 113. She sees Nietzsche 'gay science' as 'an admixture of
   Greek serenity combined with various psycho-poetic Provençalisms' (ibid.). She
   further writes that it is in Genoa, Liguria, 'that Nietzsche finds self-sufficiency, self-
   liberation, self-love ...' (114).
4 Monika M. Langer, *Nietzsche's Gay Science: Dancing Coherence* (Basingstoke:
   Palgrave Macmillan, 2010), 67.
5 Ibid.
6 Ibid.
7 Epicurus, 'Vatican Sayings', number 14.
8 Langer, *Nietzsche's Gay Science*, 67.
9 For interesting speculation on this, see Kolb, *Nietzsche, Freud, Benn, and the Azure
   Spell of Liguria*, 116.
10 G. Striker, '*Ataraxia*: Happiness as Tranquillity', in *Essays on Hellenistic Epistemology
   and Ethics* (Cambridge: Cambridge University Press, 1996), 183–96, 185.
11 James I. Porter, 'Epicurean Attachments: Life, Pleasure, Beauty, Friendship, and
   Piety', *Cronache Ercolanesi*, 33 (2003), 205–27, 218.
12 Bett, 'Nietzsche, the Greeks, and Happiness', 63.
13 One might even see in this contemplation of nature, where all is peace and
   calm and where we have moved beyond 'desire and expectation', something of

Schopenhauer's ideas on art, including the release from the subjectivity of the will. Schopenhauer, in fact, depicted such a state in Epicurean terms: 'Then all at once the peace, always sought but always escaping us on that first path of willing, comes to us of its own accord, and all is well with us. It is the painless state, prized by Epicurus as the highest good and as the state of the gods; for that moment we are delivered from the miserable pressure of the will'. Schopenhauer, *The World as Will and Representation*, volume one, section 38, 196. See also Schopenhauer on the 'aesthetic delight' to be had from the experience of light: 'Light is most pleasant and delightful; it has become the symbol of all that is good and salutary', 199.

14 Henry Keazor, *Poussin* (Köln: Taschen, 2007), 57. See also Erwin Panofsky, '*Et in Arcadia Ego*: Poussin and the Elegiac Tradition', *Meaning in the Visual Arts* (Middlesex: Penguin, 1987), 340–67.

15 Ibid., 58.

16 Ibid. Schopenhauer refers to Schiller's belief that 'we are all born in Arcadia' in chapter five of his 'Aphorisms on the Wisdom of Life' (1974) in *Parerga and Paralipomena*, trans. E. F. J. Payne (Oxford: Clarendon Press, 1974), volume one, 408. Schopenhauer interprets this as the view that we come into the world with claims to happiness and pleasure; he insists though that 'fate' soon enters the picture of life and seizes us harshly and roughly, teaching us that nothing belongs to us but everything to it. In short, our yearning after happiness and pleasure is a fanciful if noble ideal that we have to learn to modify and moderate: 'We then recognize that the best the world has to offer is a painless, quiet, and tolerable existence to which we restrict our claims in order to be the more certain of making them good. For the surest way not to become very unhappy is for us not to expect to be very happy' (ibid.).

17 Bett, 'Nietzsche, the Greeks, and Happiness', 65.

18 Richard Roos, 'Nietzsche et Épicure: l'idylle héroïque', in *Lectures de Nietzsche*, ed. Jean-François Balaudé and Patrick Wotling (Paris: Librairie GénéralFrançaise, 2000), 283–350, 322.

19 Claire Pace, '"Peace and Tranquillity of Mind": The Theme of Retreat and Poussin's Landscapes', in *Poussin and Nature. Arcadian Visions,* ed. Pierre Rosenberg and Keith Christiansen (New Haven: Yale University Press, 2008), 73–91, 86–7.

20 Ibid., 87.

21 Ibid., 83.

22 Gary Shapiro, 'Earth's Garden-Happiness: Nietzsche's Geoaesthetics of the Anthropocene', *Nietzsche-Studien*, 42 (2013), 67–84, 83.

23 Karl Jaspers, *The Great Philosophers, volume III* (New York: Harcourt Brace & Company, 1993), 111.

24 On melancholy, see also GS 291 and 337.

25 For Nietzsche's familiarity and identification with the fate of Philoctetes, see his letter to Heinrich von Stein from Sils-Maria and dated 18 September 1884, in Middleton, *Selected Letters of Friedrich Nietzsche*, 231.

26 See Edmund Wilson, *The Wound and the Bow; Seven Studies in Literature* (New York: Oxford University Press, 1947), 294.

27 Lucretius, *On the Nature of the Universe*, trans. R. E. Latham, revised by John Godwin (Middlesex: Penguin, 1994), book four, lines 6–9.

28 Adam Potkay, *The Story of Joy: From the Bible to Romanticism* (Cambridge: Cambridge University Press, 2007), 12.

29 For further insight into Nietzsche's 'Epicurus' as mediated by Schopenhauer, see Fritz Bornmann, 'Nietzsches Epikur', *Nietzsche-Studien*, 13 (1984), 177–89; and Andrea Christian Bertino, 'Nietzsche und die hellenistische Philosophie: Der Übermensch und der Weise', *Nietzsche-Studien*, 36 (2007), 95–131. See also Roos, 'Nietzsche et Épicure: l'idylle héroïque', 293. Roos also notes the influence of Montaigne and Jacob Burckhardt on Nietzsche's appreciation of Epicurus.

30 See A. H. J. Knight, 'Nietzsche and Epicurean Philosophy', *Philosophy*, 8 (1933), 431–45, 439.

31 Joseph P. Vincenzo, 'Nietzsche and Epicurus', *Man and World*, 27 (1994), 383–97, 387.

32 Ibid., 390.

33 Ibid., 391.

34 Ibid., 392.

35 Ibid.

36 Howard Caygill, 'The Consolation of Philosophy; or neither Dionysus nor the Crucified', *Journal of Nietzsche Studies*, 7 (1994), 131–51, 144.

37 Roos, 'Nietzsche et Épicure: l'idylle héroïque', 283–350, 299.

38 Ibid., 309.

39 Ibid., 303.

40 Ibid., 333.

41 Ibid.

42 For insight into this characterization of Epicurus that we encounter in the late Nietzsche, see Philippe Choulet, '"L'Épicure" de Nietzsche: Une Figure de la Décadence', *Revue Philosophique de la France et de l'Étranger*, 3 (1998), 311–30. On decadence, see George E. McCarthy, *Dialectics and Decadence: Echoes of Antiquity in Marx and Nietzsche* (London: Rowman & Littlefield, 1994), and Daniel W. Conway, *Nietzsche's Dangerous Game. Philosophy in the Twilight of the Idols* (Cambridge: Cambridge University Press, 1997), especially chapter two.

43 Caygill, 'The Consolation of Philosophy', 143.

44 A. J. H. Knight, 'Nietzsche and Epicurean Philosophy', *Philosophy*, 8 (1933), 431–45, 435.

Index